D0340595

The Feminine

The Feminine

in Jungian Psychology
and in Christian Theology

Ann Belford Ulanov

Northwestern University Press

Evanston   1971

FOURTH PRINTING, 1978

Ann Belford Ulanov is an associate professor of psychiatry and
religion at Union Theological Seminary and a psychotherapist
in private practice.

Permission to quote from the following works has been granted
by the publishers:

The Collected Works of C. G. Jung, Bollingen Series XX, trans.
R. F. C. Hull: Vol. VII, Two Essays on Analytical Psychology,
copyright © 1953 by Bollingen Foundation, Inc.; Vol. VIII, The
Structure and Dynamics of the Psyche, copyright © 1960 by
Bollingen Foundation, Inc.; Vol. IX, Part I, The Archetypes and
the Collective Unconscious, copyright © 1959 by Bollingen Foun-
dation, Inc.; Vol. IX, Part II, Aion, copyright © 1959 by Bollingen
Foundation, Inc.; Vol. X, Civilization in Transition, copyright ©
1964, by Bollingen Foundation, Inc.; Vol. XI, Psychology and
Religion, copyright © 1968 by Bollingen Foundation, Inc.; Vol.
XIII, Alchemical Studies, copyright © 1967, by Bollingen Foun-
dation, Inc.; Vol. XIV, Mysterium Coniunctionis, copyright ©
1963, by Bollingen Foundation, Inc., reprinted by permission of
Princeton University Press. Vladimir Solovyev, The Meaning of
Love, trans. Jane Marshall, copyright © 1945, Geoffrey Bles, Ltd.
Suzanne Lilar, Aspects of Love, trans. Jonathan Griffin, copyright
© 1965, Thames and Hudson. Erich Neumann, "The Psycho-
logical Stages of Feminine Development," Spring (1959), The
Analytical Psychology Club of New York. Edward F. Edinger,
"An Outline of Analytical Psychology," Quadrant, I (Spring,
1968), The C. J. Jung Foundation for Analytical Psychology.

For Barry

Contents

Preface   ix

PART I: JUNG AND THE PSYCHE

CHAPTER ONE
Point of View   3

CHAPTER TWO
Jung's Approach to the Psyche   16

CHAPTER THREE
The Structure of the Psyche   26

PART II: RELIGION AND THE PSYCHE

CHAPTER FOUR
The Religious Function of the Psyche   85

CHAPTER FIVE
The Symbol and Theology   96

CHAPTER SIX
Analytical Psychology and Religion   111

CHAPTER SEVEN
Remythologizing Life 128

PART III: THE PSYCHOLOGY OF THE FEMININE

CHAPTER EIGHT
Descriptions of the Feminine 139

CHAPTER NINE
Feminine Consciousness, Feminine Spirit 168

CHAPTER TEN
Archetypes of the Feminine 193

CHAPTER ELEVEN
Stages of Anima Development 212

CHAPTER TWELVE
Stages of Animus Development 241

PART IV: THE FEMININE AND CHRISTIAN THEOLOGY

CHAPTER THIRTEEN
The Feminine, the Religious Function, and the
Doctrine of Man 289

CHAPTER FOURTEEN
The Feminine and the Doctrines of God and Christ 314

CHAPTER FIFTEEN
The Feminine and the Doctrine of Spirit 324

Appendix 335

Index 343

Preface

THE TITLE of this book, *The Feminine in Jungian Psychology and in Christian Theology*, although long, was originally even longer. I had wanted to indicate precisely what I would be investigating—the implications for Christian theology of Jung's special insights into the feminine. Jung's initial work on the feminine and the continuation of that study by some of his followers led me to the purpose of this book: to gather together in one volume what Jung and Jungians have discovered about the feminine and to explore the opportunities that the Jungian approach has given us to see the place of the feminine in Christian theology.

Jung focuses on the human person and sees as central to it its mixture of masculine and feminine elements. In a time when so much is being said about women in our society, their needs and rights and roles, it is especially significant that Jung asserts the existence of the feminine as a leading element, not only in women but in men as well. The com-

bination of the perspectives and emphases of depth psychology and Christian theology will, I hope, make us more deeply
aware of sexual expression in aspects of life where for too
long it has gone unrewarded and unrespected, or where
sometimes it has not even been allowed to emerge at all.
From these combined perspectives we can see sexuality as
much more than a physical expression and perhaps understand some of the multiple meanings of the physical exchanges that are part of any depth experience of another
person, of our own unconscious life, or of the divine.

In his understanding of human sexuality Jung drew from
Christian tradition, and from those ancient traditions which
Christianity itself relied upon, materials that insist upon the
unconscious as matrix, as feminine container, as anima, as a
central resource of the feminine spirit. Our understanding of
the person is severely limited without a similarly clear grasp
of the feminine in all its dimensions. Wholeness of the human
depends on understanding its masculine and feminine elements; if we lack understanding of one of these elements
we cannot have a true sense of the other, let alone mature
into a whole masculine or feminine person. Because the
feminine has been particularly neglected, recovery of its
place in human sexuality must surely bring with it a sense
of the role of the feminine in human consciousness, in the
development of the human spirit, and in relation to religious
life. To seek to understand as much of this as possible, I
have followed a carefully planned sequence of presentation
and analysis, beginning with Jung's approach to the psyche
and his formulation of the religious function of the psyche,
and following with a discussion of what can be gathered
concerning the nature of the feminine. Out of this I have
drawn conclusions that seem to me to be inescapable for
what we call religious experience.

The connections between theology and depth psychology
are implicit throughout the book and refer back to the
meditative world where Jung found them and where others
like myself have found them also. For my knowledge of this

world I am indebted to the theological and psychological schools that have trained me. I want to acknowledge with special thanks those who have been so good to me at Union Theological Seminary, at The American Foundation of Religion and Psychiatry, and at The New York Institute of the C. G. Jung Foundation for Analytical Psychology. Among those many people I want particularly to acknowledge my old friend and teacher, the late Paul Tillich, my teacher and present colleague, Daniel Day Williams, and my colleague and close associate in psychological work, Anneliese Aumüller. My husband's energy, humor, and patience have been of inestimable value; my dedication of the book to him is some small suggestion of how much his vital presence has meant in the making of this work.

ANN BELFORD ULANOV

PART I

Jung and the Psyche

To ask the right question is already half the solution of a problem.

C. G. Jung

Indeed, I do not forget that my voice is but one voice, my experience a mere drop in the sea, my knowledge no greater than the visual field in a microscope, my mind's eye a mirror that reflects a corner of the world, and my ideas—a subjective confession.

C. G. Jung

CHAPTER ONE
Point of View

Q UESTIONS are doorways. A question gives us access to material by conducting dimly felt intuitions into articulate inquiry. Systematic articulations of thought are differentiated from each other more by the way questions are asked than by the way answers are given. The way issues are conceived shapes their resolution.

A point of view thus becomes a point of departure. Familiar material looked at in a new way suggests new insights. To look at the feminine from both a psychological and a theological point of view is to produce a conjunction that may yield fresh insight into the feminine as a category of being. Because Jung focuses on the feminine in an original way and in a way that consistently respects the unique qualities of the feminine, I have chosen him to represent the psychological point of view. Our point of departure, then, is to ask what implications Jung's understanding of the feminine has for Christian theology?

Even to ask such a question assumes the joining of the concerns of theology and depth psychology. Both disciplines support that compassionate interest in human interiority for which the twentieth century is justly noted. The very upsurge of the depth-psychology movement is based on the discovery that the psyche—mind and soul—can be an object of study. People spend time and money week after week to make tangible such intangible realities as dreams or the subtleties of feelings. They hunt down memories which hold the missing piece of a present misery and attend carefully to the intricacies of love and the effects of its absence. In all of these procedures, they seek conscious perception of, as well as the heartfelt relation to, their own depths. People spend time and money to learn to participate with skill as well as care in the lives of other human beings, to listen and enter into those lives without exploitation in order to elicit healing and love. To the age-old religious meditations on the procedures of love, which heals by making whole, psychology brings the technical achievements of twentieth-century science—the batteries of tests, the shock treatments, the empirical studies of the learning process, chemotherapy, group therapy, child therapy, marriage counseling, and psychoanalyses of all durations and techniques.

Depth psychology uses many means to examine love, some of which deny that that is their subject matter at all. Love is examined in persons, in peak experiences, in object relations, and in inner relations; it is explored in the experiences of inferiority and superiority, transference and countertransference, sexuality and aggression; it is looked for in society, in morality and culture, in myths, dreams, and fantasy.

Theology and depth psychology have each developed a vocabulary of concepts, root metaphors, and modal constructions, a mosaic of facts with which to style their particular points of view and reference. Each meets the other in drawing upon the common treasury of love, and thus love's interest is compounded.

THEOLOGY AND DEPTH PSYCHOLOGY

THE POINT OF VIEW of each discipline is the point of differentiation between them, and though each speaks out of, about,
and to love's reality, each speaks in different ways. Theology's task has been to interpret the contents of Christian
faith to the ever-changing human situation. Depth psychology has been concerned with investigating the psyche and
forming hypotheses about its structure and functioning—for
therapeutic purposes as well as for a greater understanding
of the nature of man. In the twentieth century, depth psychology has become an important part of the situation to
which theology must speak. In his daily work the analyst is
confronted with people unashamedly asking theological questions such as, "If there is a God, why has this misery happened to me?" "What makes me unable to reach out to love
when it's given to me?" "Is this event part of a greater plan
in life?" "What is the point of living?"

In fulfilling their tasks both disciplines work with symbols.
Theology focuses on our experience of being limited and
finite and yet related to that which is limitless and infinite.
Living on this boundary line prompts questions of what life
is about, what it means, why it is, and how we are related to
the meaning and power of being. These questions arise
especially in moments of personal anxiety when we feel the
gap between what we could be and what we actually are,
when we seek lucidity and find ambiguity, or when we claim
integrity only to have to settle for compromise and bargain-
ing.

We ask questions about life collectively too, in what Paul
Tillich calls our "human situation." We are concerned with
not only the states in which we live with the particular conditioning factors of history, but also with our interpretation
of those states as expressed in artistic, scientific, ethical, po-

litical, and religious terms.[1] Theology thus speaks to actual events and to the interpretation of those events expressed in the symbol systems of our culture. The answer theology brings to the central questions about the meaning of life is the "new being" manifest in Jesus Christ and formulated in the symbols of Christianity. These symbols are continually reinterpreted in the language of the human situation. Hence, theology works out of symbols to symbols, articulating and structuring the timeless truth of Christ to the particular temporal human situation.

The changing interpretations of the atonement offered by theologians are examples of this procedure. To people in slavery the event was symbolized as ransom. For those accustomed to Jewish sacrificial rites, it was the perfect sacrifice. For minds conditioned by Roman jurisprudence, atonement was to be interpreted as justification. To the twentieth century, which sees itself as broken and estranged, atonement means healing, reunion, wholeness.

That depth psychology works with symbols is obvious to even the casual reader, who can choose anything from Ronald Fairbairn's symbolic model of the ego with its object relations, to Freud's mechanistic-causal model of id-ego-superego with its interchanges of energy and satisfaction, to the vast reaches of Jung's archetypal dramas. Images are everywhere and are dealt with everywhere—in dreams, fantasies, transference, complexes, images of oneself, of others, and of God. Moreover, depth psychology as a whole is now part of the human situation to which theology must address its interpretation of Christ. Depth psychology itself is a symbolic system expressing interpretations of human existence.

Although the tasks and procedures of the two disciplines touch each other, there are discernible differences as well. Theology deals with the "meaning of being," as Tillich calls

1. See Paul Tillich, *Systematic Theology*, 3 vols. (Chicago: University of Chicago Press, 1951–63), I, 3–4.

it, and the theologian does so with an attitude of passionate commitment to the contents of the Christian faith. Depth psychology deals with psychic material and the experience of meaning and meaninglessness; it does so with an empirical attitude. Theology focuses on the specific revelation in Jesus Christ as the source of meaning as it is mediated through Church and Scripture. Depth psychology focuses on the reality of the psyche as it is mediated in conscious and unconscious material. Theology's concern is soteriological; it relates the categories of being to the quest for "the new being." Depth psychology is phenomenological; it observes and classifies psychic phenomena in relation to the psychotherapeutic task of healing psychic disturbances. Theology seeks the saving truth of Christ; depth psychology seeks the practical truth of "what works," whether Christian or not: "Das was wirkt, ist wirklich." [2]

The question of the relation of depth psychology and theology must include the perception that there is no basis for conflict or mutual negation because there is no precise common ground; their respective points of view shape their methods, attitudes, tasks, materials, and images of truth differently. In Tillich's view, theological statements about man's nature are expressions of his self-understanding in relation to what concerns him ultimately; they are in a different category from psychoanalytic statements which are the product of empirical investigation. [3] Psychology does not share theology's interest in correlating its statements with the contents of Christian faith, and thus psychoanalytic hypotheses neither confirm nor refute theological statements. Similarly, theology can neither confirm nor refute psychoanalytic hypotheses because it does not have the clinical data at its disposal. Shaped by their respective points of view and meeting in their concerns with the reality of persons and of

2. Jung, "Über das Unbewusste," as quoted in Raymond Hostie, S. J., *Religion and the Psychology of Jung*, trans. G. R. Lamb (New York: Sheed & Ward, 1957), p. 15.
3. Paul Tillich, "Psychiatry and Theology," unpublished paper, n.d.

love, the relation between theology and psychology is best described as mutual support and criticism.

Theologians can support psychologists by probing the ontological assumptions and the implicit doctrine of man in a psychological system and can encourage psychologists to consider such wider ramifications of their empirical work. Theologians can correlate the psychologists' empirical picture of man with the contents of Christian faith. This keeps lively and relevant the interchange between the timeless truths contained in Christian symbols and the fluctuating human situation. Psychological investigation can furnish empirical data to flesh out theological categories which otherwise are often empty abstractions. Psychologists can press the theologians to shape the message of Christianity in more concrete language.

The empirical description, for example, of vast energies and mental contents which are unconscious and not at the ego's disposal, but in which the ego is embedded, anchors Tillich's description of man living on the boundary line of the finite and infinite. The exploration of compelling unconscious motives concretizes the theological doctrine of "bondage of the will" which asserts that all our actions are perforated by ambiguity and a mixture of good and evil intentions. Studies of the shattering effects of parents' unresolved problems on their children give fresh poignancy to the saying, "The sins of the forefathers are visited upon the children." Empirical descriptions of states of "omnipotence," "inflation," "oral fixation," "projection," etc., make palpable our ancient sins of pride, anger, greed, envy, etc.

The psychoanalytic use of nonverbal channels of healing supports the value theology sees in sacraments and symbols. The process of analysis itself reflects the religious belief that acceptance precedes transformation, and that being nailed to the cross-purposes in one's being precedes their reconciliation.

Theology criticizes psychology by opposing the "psychologizing away" of the mysterious contents of revelatory experience as mere unconscious products, as if that meant that they were self-originated or sublimated distortions of some psychic function. Conversely, psychology stands against the too quick tendency of theology to catalogue psychic material in traditional religious terms, preferring to let symbols of unconscious contents reveal their meanings in their own tempo. Theology distinguishes between neurotic and existential aspects of human experience, such as guilt or anxiety, refusing to let the pathological swallow up the inevitable tensions of human life. Psychology points out the conditioning influence of the sociological and familial milieu upon the religious symbols which emerge, thus opposing the dangerous coercion and rigidity attendant on the insistence that a specific theological position is the only possible one. Depth psychology, as part of the human situation in Western culture to which theology addresses its interpretations of Christian symbols, formulates certain problem areas in the Christian tradition and thus implicitly suggests its re-examination from new points of view. This happens whether or not the specific school of depth psychology is overtly concerned with religion, because all psychology in the West must deal with human beings who speak the language and see the images and are shaped by the symbols of two thousand years of Judeo-Christian tradition and culture. Whether or not the particular patient agrees or disagrees with that tradition, is liberated or crushed by it, his psyche, his history, and his implicit assumptions about life are all colored by Christian preconceptions with which he must come to terms. Hence psychology, which studies persons in depth, has a unique perspective on the psychological experience of these traditions as well as on what is neglected by them.

The force of this interpretation is borne out by many clinical examples. In contemporary theology there is concern with secularism, which is a recent version of the Church-in-relation-to-the-world problem. Secularism is belief in reliance on human powers without recognition of, or relation to, any guiding influence outside the control of the human ego. For the patient in the therapist's office, secularism has failed. Recourse to reason, will power, and good intentions has proved inadequate to resolve the problem which brings the patient to analysis. Contact with the autonomous power of the psyche only strengthens this sense of inadequacy. The experience is not unlike the radical change effected by the Copernican revolution: the individual discovers that his psychic universe does not revolve around his own conscious ego position but rather is merely one of several planets orbiting around a greater center, a center which is as essential to life as the sun is to the earth. If the analysis goes well, the patient recovers and renews his sense of life, revolving around a deeper center which he relates to as to God. Dreams which flatly contradict conscious conceptions often initiate this revolution. For instance, one of my patients, a man who enjoyed mocking religious "superstitions," dreamt of a man dressed up in a clown costume, with a paper cone on his nose, who was hanging by his neck from a rope. A dream voice stated: "This is what happens to him who mocks religion." [4]

A major trend in recent theology is the death-of-God movement, which is a contemporary version of the transcendent-immanent dispute in discussions of the doctrine of God. For many patients the idea of God as a transcendent being living in a special dimension is dead, as is the image of God as the merely natural unfolding of immanent capacities. There is a struggle in the direction of a deeply felt personal relation to God, not as someone out there, nor as something identifiable with human powers, but as a deep center within the soul, intimately touching every aspect of daily life in the flesh of concrete events. There is a yearning to experience at first hand what religions preach: to respond to God's call as Abraham did, to live as faithfully in touch with God's will as Jesus did.

In contradistinction to the present emphasis of the churches

4. All references to patients and their material, unless otherwise noted, are taken from my practice as a psychotherapist.

on community, social action, and civil rights, depth psychology focuses on the individuals who make up a community, not only as individuals but in their relations with others, past and present. The psyche in dreams and symptoms seems to say repeatedly that the individual must develop the authority of his own soul. One must not adopt collective standards at the expense of personal identity. A young woman who suffered from anxiety and a fear that she "was not really a person" had the following dream that indicated a main source of her trouble: "I was with my friends and seemed to have no clothes of my own. I went to the ladies' room and there found lots of dresses, scarves, and shoes belonging to the group. I tried to squeeze my feet into various pairs of shoes but none of them fit. I felt I was going to be sick." Instead of trying to find her own standpoint—her own shoes—she was trying to squeeze herself into the standpoints of others.

Individual neurosis almost always reflects the splits within our culture, splits which seem to suggest that Christianity suffers from an insufficient valuation of the ego and of sexuality. An example is a woman who was a devout Christian and was determined to put into practice her deep belief in the Scripture text, "Not I but Christ liveth in me." She suffered from severe anxiety attacks, which always seemed to occur when she suppressed a strong personal preference in order to deny herself for Christ's sake, or when she put her neighbor's interest before her own. Her urge to assert herself struck at the heart of her Christian ideals. Her analysis not only dealt with her symptoms but also led to a major reinterpretation of her faith. Though extreme, this example is not untypical. Many persons seeking analysis see questionable values in competitiveness, self-assertion, and ambition. Sexuality, whether defiantly endorsed or covertly suppressed, presents an equal problem. It is astonishing how often patients assume that sexuality is not good in itself, even as a means of articulating love, but rather must be baptized by responsibility, or commitment, or concern. It is in such areas as these that depth psychology must deal with Christian traditions and often must suggest a reinterpretation of them.

THE QUESTION OF THE FEMININE

THIS WRITER'S INTEREST in Jung centers on his concern with the psychic aspects of religion and his articulation of the feminine as a category of being. Depth psychology as a whole not only offers new examinations of the range of human life but also opens up a new dimension of reality: the psyche. Depth psychology witnesses to this fact—that the psyche is an objective reality to be studied—and evolves methods for dealing with this new content. Jung, in particular, stresses the objectivity of the psyche, suggesting that we relate to it as if it bespeaks a dynamic structure and intentionality which is independent of, but not unrelated to, the conscious ego. Unashamedly, he confesses his wonder and astonishment at the sight of this new continent of human experience. He brings to the rigors of scientific method an appreciation of mystery as revealed in one's own depths.

Jung sees as operative in the psyche a "religious function" which is a drive for meaningful relation of the personal self to the transpersonal source of the power and meaning of being. This drive manifests itself in the production of images which make perceptible the symbolic meaning of experience —in particular, images of God which articulate ultimate meaning and act as a totalizing and unifying center in the psychic universe. The drive to religion seems to urge the full development of the individual personality, because the symbols produced are characterized by their central function: to reconcile the opposing tendencies of the psyche, such as conscious-unconscious, inner-outer, reason-instinct, finite-infinite, intellect-imagination, empirical-mysterious, active-passive, etc. The exterior manifestation of this drive is the production of religious systems, dogmas, and theologies.

The interior manifestation is the movement toward a wholeness which does not abrogate the opposites but fulfills them in relation to each other. Hence, for Jung the psyche is structured in polarities. Their tension generates the energy of life. Their full expression in relation to each other—not dominating, detaching from, or submitting to each other—produces integrity.

The polarity which encompasses in its symbolism all the psychic polarities is the masculine-feminine. Of these two poles, the feminine has been most neglected in psychoanalytic literature. It is usually treated as a tangent of the masculine and confined to its literal sexuality, which is then seen as deficient because it lacks the masculine organs. Jung, in contrast, explores the feminine as a distinct category of being and a mode of perception inherent in all men, all women, and all culture. The feminine has been poorly understood, whether overvalued or undervalued; and though Jung is often contradictory and abstruse about an already abstruse subject, he has initiated a new and fundamentally important point of view: a study of the symbolic meaning of the feminine and its role in psychic functioning.

The symbolic meaning of the feminine touches three important areas for Christian theology. The first is that the feminine is one pole of the primary polarity which symbolizes all the polarities out of which psychic wholeness is constructed. Jung concretizes this in his hypothesis of the contrasexual element which is an integral part of the individual psyche—the anima in the male and the animus in the female. The sexual polarity is not only experienced in outer relationship with parent, friend, or spouse but is also counterpointed in one's experience of oneself. This polarity has important implications for the Christian doctrine of man and introduces a new point of view in regard to sexuality. Just as we are indebted to Freud for his study of the instinctive side of sexuality, Jung deserves our thanks for investigating its symbolic meaning. The sexual polarity, inner and outer, which symbolizes all the dynamic opposites of the psyche, is the primary modality of achieving wholeness. Sexuality in its symbolic dimension has a spiritual function: it is the means and signification of reunion with oneself, one's neighbor, and God as the source of one's life. The anima and animus are the gateways to the self, and only their fullest development— that is, the fullest expression of the inner sexual polarity—can effect wholeness.

The second area is that in which the feminine, symbolizing a quality of consciousness and spirit, is seen as a necessary mode of perception in the reception of religious symbols. Without that mode, meaning may somehow be understood, but it will have no transforming effect. The psyche has a religious function, an unavoidable urge to meaning, in which the feminine mode of perception is especially important because it is particularly suited to apprehension of nonrational reality. In Jung's view, the psyche requires direct relation to something beyond its personal center, and if this need is not met by a legitimate religion it will have to be satisfied by an illegitimate one, such as the private religion of psychosis or the world of neurotic symptoms, or the political "isms," such as communism, capitalism, anarchism, etc. Finally, then, the feminine as a mode of perception and relation to ultimate meaning has important implications for the Christian doctrine of Spirit.

The third area is to be found in the question Jung raises about Christianity's evaluation of the feminine. If it is true that the feminine is part of the central polarity of being, and if it is also true that the feminine as a symbolic concept articulates the qualities of consciousness and spirit necessary in response to religious mystery, then why, one must ask, has the feminine so little symbolic representation in Christian dogma? Or, one may ask, where does the feminine element appear in the pageantry of Christian symbolism, and how can it be made more explicit? These questions have important implications for the Christian doctrines of God and Christ.

PROCEDURE

THESE QUESTIONS must be explored if one believes that Jung's psychology of the feminine has fundamental importance for Christian theology. In order to find words for and make clear the obscure and mysterious areas of the feminine, let alone the psyche's religious instinct, it is necessary to explicate Jung's particular symbolic approach to the psyche. It is equally necessary to examine in detail Jung's empirical investigation of the religious function of the psyche and his conviction that the drive to wholeness is conjugated in polarities. One must consider Jung's description of the feminine as a symbolic concept representing definite modes of being and apperception, and one must also consider how Jung's initial insights have been elaborated on by his followers. Finally, one must examine the implications for theology of the feminine as the neglected pole in the polarity of being which is intrinsic to wholeness, and also as the symbol of the nonrational perception that is necessary to religious experience. These explications, explorations, considerations, and examinations make up the body of the book that follows.

CHAPTER TWO

Jung's Approach to the Psyche

T HE FOLLOWING FAIRY TALE is a fitting introduction to Jung's analytical psychology, I think, because it is likely that he wrote it himself, as a description of his work and of how it has been misunderstood.

There once was a queer old man who lived in a cave, where he had sought refuge from the noise of the villages. He was reputed to be a sorcerer, and therefore he had disciples who hoped to learn the art of sorcery from him. But he himself was not thinking of any such thing. He was only seeking to know what it was he did not know, but which, he felt certain, was always happening. After meditating for a very long time on that which is beyond meditation, he saw no other way of escape from his predicament than to take a piece of red chalk and draw all kinds of diagrams on the walls of his cave, in order to find out what that which he did not know might look like. After many attempts he hit on the circle. "That's right," he felt, "and now for the quadrangle inside it!"—which made it better

still. His disciples were curious; but all they could make out
was that the old man was up to something, and they would
have given anything to know what he was doing. But when
they asked him: "What are you doing there?" he made no
reply. Then they discovered the diagrams on the wall and
said: "That's it!"—and they all imitated the diagrams. But
in doing so they turned the whole process upside down,
without noticing it: they anticipated the result in the hope
of making the process repeat itself which had led to that
result. This is how it happened then and how it still happens
today.[1]

Jung's work has been criticized for being too mystical, too
complicated, too philosophical. He has been called a gnostic,
an agnostic, a materialist, and even a schizophrenic. His
work has been exalted as the new truth or the new religion,
instead of being seen as a new way to relate to truth or
religious phenomena. The fairy tale reveals the errors, as
Jung understood them, of both his critics and his admirers,
who seized upon the result without grasping the initiating
point of view and thus turned everything upside down. The
tale also illustrates Jung's style of communication. Rarely
did he systematize his work into abstract schemes; he pre-
ferred the storytelling approach in order to engage the whole
person and not just the intellect of his reader.

The Empirical Approach

Jung's approach to the psyche holds the key to his entire
theory; it can be described as empirical and symbolic.[2] "Empirical" refers to the object studied as well as to the method

---

1. Jung, "Concerning Rebirth," *The Archetypes and the Collective
Unconscious* (*Collected Works*, Vol. IX, Part I, 1959), pp. 129–30.
   Note: *The Collected Works of C. G. Jung*, translated by R. F. C.
Hull, are published by the Bollingen Foundation (Bollingen Series XX)
in the United States of America by Princeton University Press and in
England by Routledge & Kegan Paul. The *Collected Works* will
hereafter be referred to as "*CW*."
2. See Jung, "Psychology and Religion," *Psychology and Religion:
West and East* (*CW*, XI, 1958), pp. 5–6.

of study. The object studied is the psyche; Jung hypothesizes that it is *sui generis,* an objective datum accessible to observation and description as it is manifested in dreams, visions, fantasies, behavioral and affective patterns, symbols, and symptoms. The psyche is not identifiable either with the body or with consciousness alone. Although he acknowledges the intimate and influential connection between psyche and soma, the materialistic hypothesis that all reality is physical or an epiphenomenon of the physical dares too much: "The only thing that can be established with certainty, in the present state of our knowledge, is our ignorance of the nature of the psyche." [3] The equation of the psyche with our common subjective experience of it—as consciousness or a conscious sense of identity, or as a sense of self formed by cultural influences—dares too little. It reduces the whole of the psyche simply to what we are aware of.

Jung observes the striking parallel between individual psychic material and the universal motifs found in religions and mythologies of all ages and cultures. On the basis of this observation, Jung hypothesizes that the psyche is an autonomously existing reality which operates upon us according to its own laws and patterns. The psyche exists prior to and independently of consciousness, which emerges from it.[4] Paradoxically, the psyche is an objective reality which we are accustomed to think of as existing within us or as being a function of our subjective consciousness ("my experience," "my dream," as if I created it), but which, in fact, acts in relation to us as an "other," even as another person. It is in this way that images of the feminine assume such psychological and theological importance—through associations with otherness or the "other." In a culture that has been fashioned primarily along the lines of masculine values, so that consciousness itself is often characterized in masculine

3. Jung, "Concerning the Archetypes, With Special Reference to the Anima Concept," *Archetypes and the Collective Unconscious,* p. 58.
4. See Jung, "Conscious, Unconscious, and Individuation," *Archetypes and the Collective Unconscious,* pp. 280–81.

terms, this sense of otherness frequently comes in images associated with the feminine, such as female figures who tempt one against one's will, or who are helpful sisters, or who are wise women full of secrets. Although masculine images fulfill this same purpose for women, the lack of ease of women with each other, their bewilderment about their own feminine reality, and their eagerness to trace their discomfort to centuries of male domination—all suggest that even for females, images of the feminine hold a much needed contact with contents and perspectives that they want to make part of themselves.

Jung was the first to concentrate on this autonomous *a priori* objective dimension of the psyche. He accepts Freud's hypostatization of the ego and of the unconscious as repressed infantile life and calls this the "personal unconscious." In addition he draws attention to the more fundamental dimension, common to all people, which is not the result of repression but is prior to the emergence of any subjective conscious life. Jung calls this the "collective unconscious" or the "objective psyche." To account for the interaction of the ego and the objective psyche, he postulates a higher instance, the self, that synthesizes these two elements. The self as the total personality is the object of analytical psychology.

Just as Jung rejects the notion of the psyche as a mere tangent to the soma, or as reducible to consciousness, he also distinguishes the psyche from questions of metaphysical or ontological status, as a legitimate focus of research in itself. His approach to religious images and beliefs is to investigate their effect and function in the total economy of the psyche. He does not inquire whether metaphysical claims are "true." He simply determines that they exist psychologically—that they are uttered by a psyche and have effects on that psyche.[5]

Jung's approach is empirical, but paradoxically he uses a

5. See Jung, "The Transcendent Function," *The Structure and Dynamics of the Psyche* (*CW*, VIII, 1960), p. 91; and "On the Nature of the Psyche," *Structure and Dynamics of the Psyche, passim.*

nonexperimental method to study the psyche. Clear-cut experiments with controllable results are impossible with the psyche because the psychological investigator cannot abstract himself from his own psychic experience in his study of psychic phenomena. His observations and his judgments about the psyche all come from personal experience, his own or his patients'. Furthermore, his object of study is the psyche as a whole, the self. This alone invalidates the traditional experimental approach, because experiments necessarily impose specific conditions and exclude what in the eyes of the experimenter is irrelevant or disturbing. The purpose of Jung's investigation is to grasp what the psyche says and shows about itself, its structure, and its dynamics, not to find out what he as the experimenter wants to know.

Jung's empirical method proceeds by careful observation and description of psychic facts, and by correlation of one fact with another, to establish hypotheses about the nature and structure of the psyche as a whole. The advantage of such hypotheses is that they give the fullest and simplest explanation of all facts under review as well as providing a basis for further research. These hypotheses must frequently be rejected or replaced because of the nature of the work: "Work in this field is pioneer work. I have often made mistakes and had many times to forget what I had learned. But I know . . . that as surely as light comes out of darkness, so truth is born of error . . . and have therefore neither feared my mistakes nor seriously regretted them." [6]

THE SYMBOLIC APPROACH

JUNG'S SYMBOLIC APPROACH to the psyche is his special contribution to depth psychology. It is dictated by the empirical fact that unconscious processes are not directly accessible to our senses. They cannot be seen, touched, heard, or tasted,

6. Jung, *Two Essays on Analytical Psychology* (CW, VII, 1953), p. 118.

nor adequately described by the rational categories of causality, time, space, and physical substance that structure our conscious processes. A new approach commensurate with the intangible quality of the psyche is needed. The psyche speaks in symbols. If we are to understand it, we must learn its language and enter into symbolic modes of communication.

By symbol, Jung means a nonrational, figurative constellation that points beyond itself to unknown or unknowable objective reality and makes that reality perceptible to us. Hence, the symbol has a mediating function; it makes accessible to our consciousness something that is inaccessible to our direct sensory experience and to our reason. The symbol cannot be produced at will, however, nor can it be automatically translated into some known problem or drive as, for example, with Freud or Adler, where so often the symbol is translated into sexual or power drives. For Jung, the symbol must be met in terms of its own details and qualities. It is the expression of the little known or the unknown fact that cannot be translated into familiar elements or more clearly represented.[7]

Because the psyche speaks in symbols and because symbols communicate through analogies, Jung, too, uses the indirect approach of analogies to mediate the intangible and intuitive quality of the psyche.[8] His method of analogy describes the material in terms of an "as if" or "as though"; it is an attempt to say not that the psyche is such and such but rather that it is "as though" this or that aspect of the psyche behaved in such and such a way, "as if" such and such an intention were implied. Furthermore, the symbol is approached "as if" what it depicted had meaning for the whole psyche. This is the best possible way to describe something that is indescribable in itself. The analogy based on a symbolic image makes a bridge from what is known to what is unknown.

7. See Jung, *Psychological Types,* trans. H. Godwin Baynes (London: Kegan Paul, Trench, Trübner & Co., 1946), p. 601.
8. See Jung, "Transcendent Function," *passim.*

A person, for example, dreams that he is held up by a masked gunman. The masked gunman and the action of being held up are symbolic. The dreamer knows what these things are. But he does not really know that something in his own psychic processes is behaving "as if" it were a masked gunman, holding him up on his way in life and robbing him of major resources. The symbols convey to him the quality, the intention, and the effect of this psychic datum on his whole personality. By making an analogy on the basis of something known (the figure of the gunman), knowledge of something unknown (the attitude in him which behaves like a gunman) is mediated. The attitude in him that behaves as though it were a gunman can only be approached and grasped through the symbol; it is not a physical thing, nor is it an abstract concept, nor is it subject to his conscious control. Rather, it appears in an image that arises spontaneously and is independent of his conscious control. The symbolic approach takes the image seriously, "as if" the psyche purposefully selected a particular symbol to convey a particular message which could not otherwise be conveyed with the same accuracy, flavor, or emphasis. In order to locate the gunman attitude precisely, further investigation of the symbol by the process of association is needed. Even if this man associates the gunman with his own sexual drive, what obstructs him is not his sexuality *per se* but the fact that he and his sexuality seem to be relating to each other as robber and victim.

Symptoms are treated differently with the symbolic approach. Jung adds his synthetic-constructive method to the Freudian causal-reductive method that interprets symptoms as the product and expression of past developmental conflicts. From that point of view, symptoms are seen as deviations from normalcy that need to be corrected.[9]

Jung's synthetic-constructive method of interpretation

9. See Jung, "General Aspects of Dream Psychology," *Structure and Dynamics of the Psyche, passim; Two Essays on Analytical Psychology*, pp. 83–89; and *Psychological Types*, pp. 538, 606.

asks what meaning, message, or direction for the future a symptom tries to convey, what neglected psychic attitude it calls to our attention to indicate that we have become too one-sided. Instead of judging symptoms solely by collective standards of normalcy, the synthetic method also sees them symbolically as descriptions of unrealized facts that indicate in which direction to look for one's individual solution to a conflict. To the standard of normalcy, Jung adds the goal of individuation—to become fully one's own self. Symptoms may represent weak attempts, even if unsuccessful, to struggle for a new life synthesis.[10]

As an example of this method, let us consider a young woman's daydream about spiders coming to find her, a fantasy that occurred when she was working under considerable pressure. Reductively interpreted, this symptom is seen as a result of the negative influence of her mother's possessiveness and resentment toward the daughter's independent work. The spider, then, represents the threat of regression even to the point of an incestuous desire to give up independence and return to the mother's womb, as represented by the furry legs of the insect and the peril of being caught in its web. Constructively seen, the detail of the spider looking for her especially when she was working hard might have additional meaning. The woman associated with the spider the skill of building, out of itself, an ordered, delicate web where "everything had its place." Not only could this ordering capacity be of enormous help to her in work that demanded she keep countless details within her grasp, but it might also allow her to find the necessary place for her feelings about her mother. Instead of being trapped by the delicate-looking but unyielding strands of her mother's love, she saw in the spider's industry and ability to construct a complex web an attitude that could help her in time of great pressure. It was "as if" this attitude sought her out.

10. See Jung, "Transcendent Function," pp. 72–74; and "Conscious, Unconscious and Individuation," p. 275.

Jung uses symbolic concepts to describe the structure of the psyche in order to meet the psyche on its own ground. Instead of trying to translate unconscious processes into rational, abstract structures, he uses personifications (e.g., "shadow," "anima") and encourages active encounter with these concrete entities. Instead of seeing the psyche's symbolic language as inferior and pathological, he tries to learn that language and understand its message. Instead of viewing the unconscious as a subsidiary of consciousness, he acknowledges the unconscious as an objective fact which relates to consciousness "as though" it were an autonomous personality. If the unconscious is pushed, it pushes back; if it is shut out, it bangs on the door; if one enters into conversation with it, it will respond; if one fails to look for its purposes, one may be forced to do so by neurosis. Instead of translating all psychic processes into the rational ego's space-time, into the logic of cause and effect, Jung encourages the ego's adoption of nonrational symbolic modes of apprehension, by dream analysis, active use of the imagination, and even painting and sculpture, in order to capture what the unconscious is saying. Of a woman who drew herself as imprisoned by rocks, Jung writes: "She had overlooked the fact that the initial situation, her imprisonment in the rock, was already irrational and symbolic and could not be solved in a rational way. It had to be done by an equally irrational process." [11] Even though her reason wanted to determine how her picture should be, Jung continues, her "eyes held fast to their vision and finally forced the picture to come out as it actually did and not in accordance with rationalistic expectations." [12]

The symbolic nature of Jung's concepts is dictated by empirical materials: "The fact that the unconscious spontaneously personifies certain affectively toned contents in dreams is the reason why I have taken over these personifications in

11. Jung, "A Study in the Process of Individuation," *Archetypes and the Collective Unconscious*, p. 302.
12. *Ibid.*

my terminology and formulated them as names." [13] Jung's terms are conceptual insofar as they abstract from empirical data, collect them into ideas, and designate with general names the essential character of the data. The concepts are symbolic insofar as they are images that mediate to consciousness the nature, emotional quality, and effect of this psychic datum in the total personality: "The names are of little use by themselves. Shadow, animus, and anima are relatively colorless terms for conditions which in real life sometimes mean not only dramatic, but tragic, even hopeless, complications of destiny." [14]

13. *Ibid.*, p. 285.
14. Jung, "Shadow, Animus and Anima," trans. William H. Kennedy (property of The Kristine Mann Library, The Analytical Psychology Club of New York, p. 1).

CHAPTER THREE

The Structure
of the Psyche

THE PSYCHE consists of energy, consciousness, the personal unconscious, and the collective unconscious or the objective psyche.[1] Libido is Jung's term for the psychic energy which directs and motivates the personality; it "is the dynamism of the life process as manifested in the psychic sphere."[2] To give attention to, to value, to be interested in something are all expressions of libido. The more value an object is felt to have, the more libido has been invested in it. Libido can be apprehended in a definite form only through images: hence the symbolic approach is necessitated.

1. See Jung, "The Structure of the Psyche," *The Structure and Dynamics of the Psyche* (*CW*, VIII, 1960), p. 151.
2. Edward F. Edinger, "An Outline of Analytical Psychology," *Quadrant*, I (Spring, 1968), 9. See also Jung, "On Psychic Energy," *Structure and Dynamics of the Psyche*, pp. 29-30.

Psychic Polarities

Libido is connected with two laws. The first is the law of conservation of energy: "Libido can be transformed or displaced, but not destroyed." [3] If the quantity of libido given to one person or interest decreases, it will increase in relation to something else. The second is the law of opposites. [4] Jung understands the psyche to be a self-regulating system structured in polarities, such as consciousness-unconsciousness, reason-instinct, love-hate, etc. The polar tension between the opposites is the source of the psyche's energy as well as the matrix for its functioning and its growth into wholeness. If one pole of a polarity is excessively emphasized, the energy will flow into its opposite. This is called *enantiodromia*. An example is the hyperrational person who develops irrational obsessions.

The polar structure of the psyche is significant for our interest in the feminine because images of masculine-feminine polarity frequently symbolize all the other psychic polarities, especially in decisive periods of growth when there is a struggle to unite opposites. Dreams of sexual union, marriage, or hermaphroditic figures often occur at such times.

Consciousness is that realm of psychic experience of which we are aware. The ego is only the center of consciousness, not the center of the whole psyche. Throughout childhood, the ego gradually develops out of the unconscious. The ego carries one's sense of I-ness and identity and personal continuity in space and time: it is the seat of willing, awareness, and memory. In order for a content to be conscious it must be connected with the ego.

3. Edinger, "Outline of Analytical Psychology," p. 9.
4. See Jung, *Two Essays on Analytical Psychology* (*CW*, VII, 1953), pp. 53, 72; and *Mysterium Coniunctionis* (*CW*, XIV, 1963), p. 3.

The Complex

CONTENTS THAT ARE UNCONSCIOUS first present themselves to the ego in the form of complexes.

> A *complex* is an emotionally charged unconscious psychic entity made up of a number of associated ideas and images clustered around a central core . . . [which is] an *archetypal image*. One recognizes that a complex has been struck by the emergence of an affect which upsets psychic balance and disturbs the customary function of the ego.[5]

Complexes disclose varying degrees of autonomy, ranging from those which hardly disturb psychic functioning to those which forcibly invade consciousness and resist assimilation.

An example is the ambivalent reaction of a young artist to women. Inwardly disgusted by women, he is nonetheless drawn to them like a magnet, becoming mute and fawning in their presence. Although sensitive to the feelings of others, he suspects that any interest taken in his feelings masks a desire to humiliate him, but he is nonetheless resentful if his feelings are not sought out. Anything faintly resembling maternal solicitude arouses his anger, yet he is irresistibly propelled toward maternal women, and into situations that call for the maternal virtues, either from him or in relation to him. One could say he has a "mother complex"; the maternal attracts him, and yet he cannot stand it. He is fascinated and repelled. It is as if an autonomous "mother" constellation operated in him, pulling him here, dragging him there, causing his reactions, whether he wishes it or not, likes it or not.

The complex consists of an associational "shell" and a nuclear core.[6] The shell is a network of emotionally charged

5. Edinger, "Outline of Analytical Psychology," p. 11.
6. See Jolande Jacobi, *Complex/Archetype/Symbol in the Psychology of Jung,* trans. Ralph Manheim (New York: Pantheon, 1959), pp. 8–9.

images, conditioned by childhood situations and personal history. In the case of this artist, inquiry disclosed similarity between the women he was attracted to, the feelings they aroused in him, and his original experience with his mother. He felt his mother was a talkative, possessive, invading person who showed interest in his feelings if they matched her mood, but who was scathing if they did not. With her he felt alternately enraged and compliant; and now everything that reminds him of her attitudes or behavior triggers this conditioned response.

At the core of every complex is a transpersonal, universally human pattern of experience; in the artist's case, it was the mother archetype. In its negative aspects this archetype is felt as devouring and castrating; in its positive aspects, it is felt as containing, nurturing, and grounding. The artist describes the negative aspect well: "When I get close to her, mother, she gets bigger than life. I go blank. She is like some primordial being who absorbs me into herself."

Jung says, "Everyone knows nowadays that people 'have complexes.' What is not so well known, though far more important theoretically, is that complexes can *have us*." [7] The way in which complexes "have us" is that the ego falls into a partial or total state of identity with them. There is no conscious separation between the ego and the impulsive, automatic energy drive of the complex. Hence there is no awareness of the complex as a separately existing entity. It is unconscious, and there is no differentiation between ego motivations and the driving elements of the complex. [8]

7. Jung, "A Review of the Complex Theory," *Structure and Dynamics of the Psyche*, p. 96.
8. Jung distinguishes between identity and identification: "Psychological identity presupposes its unconsciousness. It is characteristic of the primitive mentality, and is the actual basis of 'participation mystique,' which, in reality, is merely a relic of the original psychological non-differentiation of subject and object—hence of the primordial unconscious state. . . . Identity is primarily an unconscious equality with the object" (Jung, *Psychological Types*, trans. H. Godwin Baynes [London: Kegan Paul, Trench, Trübner & Co., 1946], p. 553). Identification, in contrast, is an unconscious imitation of an object (p. 551).

Three vivid signs indicate that the ego is undifferentiated from an unconscious complex.[9] The first is a compulsive quality of behavior. The artist we have been talking about was compelled repeatedly to involve himself in situations resembling his original relation to his mother and to reiterate the same old pattern of response. He had no choice and was full of rationalizations as to why it had to be so. He was unaware of the repetitive quality of his actions until after they had happened. The second sign that a complex "has us" is that we have an inflated sense of ourselves. We feel blown up, powerful, and right, as if fed by a power which is not our own and carried along by the urgent energy of the impulse. A corollary of this feeling is its negative version—we feel deflated and crushed by a power that is not our own. The third sign is that the complex is inevitably projected onto others and is seen as belonging to them rather than to ourselves. A clear indication that projection is occurring is the emotional agitation (positive or negative) which accompanies it. For the artist it was the feeling both of fascination and repulsion for maternal women.

Two methods are used to differentiate the ego from the state of unconscious identity with the complexes in order to gain conscious relation to their sources of energy. The first is a reductive analysis of the personal shell by exploring the original, conditioning situation. For the artist, this was his relation to his mother. The understanding that he was conditioned by past experience helped put his present difficulties with women into perspective but did not necessarily alter the dynamism of the complex. The second method is a symbolic or synthetic-constructive interpretation of the nuclear meaning of the complex that transforms its basic drive. For the artist, this was a confrontation with what Jungians call the archetype of the Great Mother in its

9. For a discussion of the complex, see Jacobi, *Complex/Archetype/Symbol*, pp. 14–18; and Edward C. Whitmont, *The Symbolic Quest* (New York: C. G. Jung Foundation, 1969), p. 58.

negative, devouring form. For the purposes of this discussion the archetype can be defined as a primordial image that lies dormant in the psyche until it is activated by a challenging experience. The archetype exerted upon him a regressive pull toward unconsciousness and toward an infantile state of being where he was passively contained like a child and unable to exist except in relation to a greater being. Like the heroes who slay the dragon, the artist had to kill this regressive tendency if he were to attain his own masculine identity. With the symbolic interpretation, the regressive drive of the complex is seen not only as a result of the relationship to his actual mother but also as the inevitable struggle of consciousness to maintain itself against the pull of unconsciousness. This has important results: the conflict is set in the present instead of the past. Instead of struggling with his mother as if he were still an infant, which makes him feel isolated from his peers and guilty toward his parent, the artist could accept this present conflict as a necessary fight for his manhood, and thus feel part of a common human experience.

To see one's problem in a larger human context frees the energy drive of the archetype to flow into new channels. Then the ego can relate to the energy in new ways. A complex is seen no longer as always pathological but rather as a fruitful and necessary source of energy.[10] A complex becomes pathological only when it is contaminated with personal material or when the ego is insufficiently differentiated from it. The artist's unresolved conflict with his mother, for example, prevented him from establishing satisfactory relationship to the archetype of the maternal because any person or situation associated with maternal qualities was automatically reduced for him to the terms of his original struggle with his mother.

10. See Jung, "Psychotherapy and a Philosophy of Life," *The Practice of Psychotherapy* (*CW*, XVI, 1954), p. 78; "The Psychological Foundations of Belief in Spirits," *Structure and Dynamics of the Psyche*, p. 313; and "Psychology and Religion," *Psychology and Religion: West and East* (*CW*, XI, 1958), p. 14.

THE EGO

THE EGO is the central complex of the psyche; it is a cluster of functions (willing, choosing, etc.), images (of the person and the world), and affects (feelings about oneself and others), which gather round the archetypal core of the self. The ego represents in spatial and temporal concreteness the unity and wholeness of the archetype of the self.[11] Other terms, such as shadow, anima, and animus, also designate psychic complexes, clusters of functions, affects, images, and energy drives that circulate around an archetypal core. Jung, therefore, speaks of the animus as an archetype, referring to its transpersonal, universal core, and also speaks of an "animus complex," indicating a disturbance of functioning in which the animus is operating without relation to the ego or the total personality. Complexes will appear in dreams in personified form if consciousness is insufficiently related to them.[12]

THE PERSONA

THE EGO has two functions: to relate the psyche to outer reality and to inner subjective reality. Jung uses the symbolic concept persona—"actor's mask"—to refer to the psychic function which mediates between the ego and the external world of people and society. It is as if the psyche develops a social role and assumes a public face when adapting to others. The persona develops out of personal propensities, teachings of parents, school, and church, and collective standards of behavior. The persona mediates between one's own individuality and the expectations of others. It tells one what role is

11. See Jung, "On the Nature of the Psyche," "Belief in Spirits," "Spirit and Life," *Structure and Dynamics of the Psyche*, pp. 224, 307, 323.
12. See Jung, "Review of Complex Theory," p. 98.

appropriate in the public situations and guards what is personal and vulnerable.[13]

Ideally, the persona is flexible, easily adaptable to changing situations and sturdy enough to protect what is intimate. It can be taken up and put aside at will. An inadequate persona is often revealed in dreams where one finds oneself naked in a public place, without any protective covering. Dreaming of doing housework in evening clothes might indicate a too exalted or affected persona, out of proportion to reality. Too rigid a persona results from such a complete identification of the person with his social role that there is no individual personality apart from "the minister," "the politician," "the mother."

THE SHADOW AND THE PERSONAL UNCONSCIOUS

THE SHADOW symbolizes the psychic function which mediates between the ego and the personal unconscious. The personal unconscious is composed of contents "which have at one time been conscious but which have disappeared from consciousness through having been forgotten or repressed. . . ." [14] It is analogous to Freud's concept of the unconscious as made up of the infantile mental life, repressed contents, unused information. The shadow is the image used by Jung to describe those contents in ourselves that we repress because they are unacceptable, such as tawdry thoughts, unbounded power aspirations, secret faults. On the collective level, the shadow is often personified as the devil; on the individual level it is always represented by someone of the same sex whom we dislike and find irritating or even hateful. Our first contact with our own shadow is usually through projecting it onto others; we see qualities we do not recog-

13. See Jung, *Two Essays on Analytical Psychology* (CW, VII, 1953), p. 281; and Edinger, "Outline of Analytical Psychology," p. 11.

14. Jung, "The Concept of the Collective Unconscious," *The Archetypes and the Collective Unconscious* (CW, IX, Part I, 1959), p. 42.

nize in ourselves as belonging only to them.[15] This projection can happen with positive or negative qualities, but usually what we reject in others is what we do not accept in ourselves. Racial conflict is a broader manifestation of this, as are the mutual projections of Communists and capitalists.

To face our shadow is a first step toward seeing ourselves as we really are and a shock to cherished or inflated notions of ourselves. Moreover, because shadow qualities exercise a kind of autonomy, they are not amenable to reasonable persuasion or good intentions. The frightening dream of a woman patient illustrates this: "A girl has done a hatchet murder in an asylum. I am living with her and reasoning with her to confess. I am very scared. She has a mysterious all-knowing quality about her." The dreamer must see this crazy, murderous woman as a split-off part of herself. The dreamer must recognize that she is not handling this split-off complex with the appropriate attitude. A psychotic person can never be reached through reasoning, but only through instinct and feeling. These are hard realizations to achieve:

> The shadow is a moral problem that challenges the whole ego-personality. . . . To become conscious of it involves recognizing the dark aspects of the personality as present and real. This act is the essential condition for any kind of self-knowledge, and it therefore, as a rule, meets with considerable resistance.[16]

Without a shadow we are flat, two-dimensional. The shadow's darkness grounds us, adding depth, perspective, and three dimensions. We take on substance and have a history. If conscious ego adaptation is around negative and inferior qualities, the shadow will then present us with neglected positive potentialities. It is not the shadow's own nature that occasions its menacing appearance, but rather our treatment of it. As we begin to give some attention and care to chan-

15. See Jung, "Conscious, Unconscious and Individuation," *Archetypes and the Collective Unconscious*, p. 284.
16. Jung, *Aion* (CW, IX, Part 2, 1959), p. 8.

neling these neglected aspects of ourselves, they become less
threatening and more and more helpful to us.

THE COLLECTIVE UNCONSCIOUS
OR OBJECTIVE PSYCHE

THE ANIMA AND ANIMUS are the symbolic concepts that Jung
uses to describe the psychic function that stands between the
collective and personal unconscious. The collective unconscious or objective psyche (a term later adopted when "collective" was becoming confused with "collectivity") refers
to that deeper layer of the unconscious which, unlike the personal unconscious, is ordinarily inaccessible to consciousness.
The contents of the collective unconscious are the archetypes
expressed in mythological motifs and primordial images; the
contents of the personal unconscious are repressed memories,
subliminal perceptions, and complexes.[17]

These archetypal contents are accessible to consciousness
only through symbols—such as dreams, fantasies, and myths.
They cannot be reified or observed except in their effect
upon a subject—hence the term "objective." The collective
unconscious cannot be translated in terms of personal history
alone because "it is not made up of individual and more or
less unique contents but of those which are universal and of
regular occurrence."[18] The collective unconscious is nonindividual, universal, suprapersonal. We experience it, therefore, as other than ourselves, as objective, acting upon us
quite independently of our conscious volition, intentions, or
ideas, as if it were an autonomous authority. Jung says: "No,
the collective unconscious is anything but an incapsulated
personal system; it is sheer objectivity. There I am the object
of every subject, in complete reversal of my ordinary consciousness, where I am always the subject that has an ob-

17. See Jung, "Concept of the Collective Unconscious," p. 42.
18. Jung, "Instinct and the Unconscious," *Structure and Dynamics
of the Psyche*, p. 134.

ject." [19] To catch the flavor of this objectivity, we need only recall dreams where we, the subjects, have been the object of scrutiny, attack, or the laughter of other dream figures, whether we have wanted to be or not. This collective or objective layer of the psyche exists prior to and independently of our subjective ego experience, but it forms and gives rise to the ego and seemingly demands that the ego relate to it. Contrary to our usual assumption that the psyche is the experience of the ego, the ego is secondary and is in fact an experience of the objective psyche.

The anima in the man's psyche and the animus in the woman's have the function of mediating to the ego this deeper objective psyche.[20] These terms do not refer to figures that "exist" as physical entities. These terms are symbolic concepts that describe clusters of psychic energy around an archetypal core which act as if they were subsidiary contrasexual personalities. Just as the objective psyche is experienced as "other" than the ego, so it presents itself to consciousness in images of the "totally other," that is, of the opposite sex. The opposite sex is human; hence we can communicate with it, but it speaks and moves and acts from a totally other frame of reference. The objective psyche is as familiar and as foreign to the ego as one sex is to another.

The polarity of consciousness and unconsciousness, then, is encountered symbolically in terms of the sexual polarity. Access to the objective dimension of the psyche is given to the conscious masculine ego through the anima, and to the feminine ego through the animus. The animus and anima personify those contents of the objective psyche which can be integrated into consciousness when taken back from projection onto dream or real persons of the opposite sex. When that happens the personification of those particular contents

19. Jung, "Archetypes of the Collective Unconscious," *Archetypes and the Collective Unconscious*, p. 22. See also Jung, "Psychology and Religion," pp. 39–40.

20. See Jung, *Aion*, pp. 13 ff.; and *Two Essays on Analytical Psychology*, pp. 186 ff.

ceases. We can expect that the images of the animus or anima will change as new contents are personified. We might even see a progressive and gradual development in anima figures, for example, from witch to seductress to beloved. What is significant is the role sexual polarity plays in helping us gain access and relationship to the wider reaches of the psyche. Sexual polarity introduces us to the mystery of otherness. The ego's meeting with the objective psyche is symbolized by one sex meeting the other; this is the spiritual function of sexual polarity.

The Anima

THE ANIMA, then, is an archetype symbolizing the feminine elements in a man's psyche; its function is to mediate the contents of the objective psyche to his conscious ego. Jung describes the archetype as comprised of a nuclear core which is represented by mythological and numinous images, which makes itself felt by occasioning certain patterns of behavior and emotion. This archetypal core becomes the center of a complex.[21] The archetypal images of the anima range from harlot, witch, martyr, sister, peasant, gypsy, beloved, muse, to saint, goddess, and spiritual guide.[22] The anima is represented mythologically in stories having to do with the eternal feminine in all its forms, such as Mother Earth, love, or wisdom, and as symbolized by animals such as the cow, dove, owl, cat, etc., that are traditionally associated with the feminine deities.

As a pattern of behavior, the anima archetype represents

21. Jung, "Mind and Earth," *Contributions to Analytical Psychology*, trans. H. G. and Cary F. Baynes (London: Routledge & Kegan Paul, 1928), p. 110. See also Jung, *Aion*, pp. 13–14; and "Concerning the Archetypes, With Special Reference to the Anima Concept," *Archetypes and the Collective Unconscious*, pp. 59, 69–72; Whitmont, *Symbolic Quest*, p. 73.

22. For an excellent description of these images, see Wolfgang Lederer, *The Fear of Women* (New York: Grune & Stratton, 1968).

instinctive drive behavior related to the feminine and symbolizing an elemental dynamism and energy; it is not to be
equated literally with the female as it appears in women.
Dr. E. C. Whitmont, an American Jungian analyst, describes
this "feminine principle" as composed of those

> drive elements which are related to life as life, as an un-
> premeditated, spontaneous, natural phenomenon, to the life
> of the instincts, the life of the flesh, the life of concreteness,
> of earth, of emotionality, directed toward people and things.
> It is the drive toward involvement, the instinctual con-
> nectedness to other people and the containing community or
> group.[23]

As a pattern of emotion, the archetype of the anima "consists of the man's unconscious urges, his moods, emotional
aspirations, anxieties, fears, inflations and depressions, as well
as his potential for emotion and relationship." [24] The anima
personifies the contrasexual elements in a man, expressing the
so-called feminine qualities of tenderness, sensitivity, devious-
ness, seduction, indefiniteness, feeling, receptivity, elusiveness,
jealousy, and creative containing and yielding. Sexual polarity
is part of inner personal experience as well as experience between persons. Just as relating to a woman opens a man to unguessed depths in himself, so relating to the "person" of his
own anima connects him to his inner femininity and the objective psyche.

As an archetype of the objective psyche, the anima exists
prior to consciousness and is not so much a definite content
of which the ego must become aware as it is a precondition of
ego consciousness. The anima causes *a priori* expectations and
emotional drives and reactions to people, objects, and situations.[25]

Like any psychic complex, the anima has a personal and an
archetypal aspect. Because it mediates between the personal

23. Whitmont, *Symbolic Quest*, p. 189.
24. *Ibid.*
25. See Jung, *Aion*, pp. 13–15.

and objective layers of the psyche, the anima has a foot on both sides. On the objective side, there is the anima as archetype, personifying the universal, transpersonal experiences of the feminine and the contrasexual elements in the masculine. On the personal side, the anima reflects the influence of the actual women in a man's life, especially in childhood, such as his mother, sister, and aunt. The personality of the anima is partially conditioned by the personality of those women. A man's choice of girlfriend or wife reflects the image of his anima; in some cases, his choice is totally determined by the anima. Just as each individual is unique, so his particular experience of the anima is a unique variant on the general theme of femininity.

TYPICAL ANIMA PROBLEMS

TYPICAL ANIMA PROBLEMS result when consciousness is not sufficiently differentiated from the subsidiary feminine personality in a man, but rather is in a partial state of identity with it. This shows itself in moods of compulsive touchiness, sentimentality, hypersensitivity, bitchiness, or self-pity, and in effeminacy driven to the point of homosexuality. Inflation by the anima shows itself in an exaggerated self-image, whether in a positive or negative direction. A man sees himself, for example, as a perfect lover, or an altogether incompetent one. It is as if the conscious ego personality were puffed up by energy not its own but belonging to the subsidiary anima personality. It is as if the man had been "seduced" by his anima.

Projection of the anima occurs in the experience of falling in love, which may lead to building a genuine relationship, or which may take a compulsive repetitive form that frustrates relationship. The projection can also be intensely negative, as in cases of instant dislike. A newspaper man's dream illustrates a disruptive anima: "I am putting the paper to press and my secretary is acting very helpfully and is full of praise for me. But at the same time she scatters the printing type, spilling ink, misspelling words, all the while protesting how helpful she is."

To establish contact with his anima, a man must treat her as though she were an actual, autonomous, inner woman who cannot be controlled or dismissed but must be met as a person.[26] In dreams the anima presents herself as a person. Jung cites an example: "The anima accuses the dreamer of paying too little attention to her. There is a clock which says five minutes to the hour." [27] Jung comments that it is as if the unconscious were pestering the dreamer, like an exacting woman. A sense of anticipation pervades the dream because there are only five minutes left to the hour. When the time is up something must be done.

To develop a relationship with the anima, a man must become conscious of the personal shell of the anima (the emotional and behavioral conditioning of the important females in his life) and make contact with the transpersonal energy and meaning of the archetypal core of the anima complex. In other words, a man must give due consideration both to his own ego demands and to the inherent intent of the anima archetype. If he does this, the anima will open to him the deepest aspects of the objective psyche. A visual impression from the same series as the previous dream is cited by Jung to illustrate this: "The veiled woman uncovers her face. It shines like the sun." The anima reveals herself (becomes accessible to consciousness) and, indeed, is a source of inner light and life-giving energy (the sun).[28] When a man takes a receptive attitude to the anima, the anima no longer appears in personified form. Instead, the anima itself becomes a means of relating the contents of the unconscious to consciousness.[29]

26. See Jung, *Two Essays on Analytical Psychology*, p. 201.
27. Jung, *Psychology and Alchemy* (*CW*, XII, 1967), p. 100.
28. *Ibid.*, p. 56.
29. See Jung, *Two Essays on Analytical Psychology*, p. 224.

THE ANIMUS

FOR THE WOMAN, the archetype of the animus symbolizes the masculine elements in her personality; its function is to mediate the contents of the objective psyche to her conscious ego.[30] The nuclear core of the animus archetype is represented by such male images as the laborer, judge, teacher, monk, Prince Charming, prophet, magician, or rapist. It is represented mythologically in tales having to do with the masculine in all its forms, such as the conquering hero, the great king, or the wise man, and is symbolized by male deities such as Zeus, Dionysus, Apollo, Pan, or the Devil, and the animals associated with male deities such as the bull, goat, dog, or eagle.

As a pattern of behavior, the animus archetype represents instinctive drive behavior related to the masculine as symbolizing an elemental dynamism of life. It is not to be confused with "masculinity" as it may be ascribed to specific men or women. The masculine symbolizes those drive elements related to active initiative, to aggressive assertiveness, to the search for meaning, to creativity, and to one's capacity for discrimination, separation, and judgment.[31]

As a pattern of emotion, the animus consists of woman's unconscious capacity to focus on, evaluate, and discern her own reactions, her unconscious rationality, her power aspirations, her opinions, her argumentativeness, her aggression, her capacities to differentiate, her expectations of how one "ought to be" and "what one should do," as well as her potential for relationship to creative meaning, clarity, self-expression, and the spiritual contents of her life.

The animus personifies the contrasexual elements in the woman, expressing qualities traditionally associated with

30. See Jung, *Aion*, pp. 14–15.
31. See Jung, *Two Essays on Analytical Psychology*, pp. 206–7.

man: the capacity to penetrate, separate, take charge, initiate, create, stand firmly and over against, to articulate and express meaning. It is interesting that in describing these masculine qualities the infinitives of active verbs are required, whereas for the feminine qualities represented by the anima nouns and intransitive verbs of being are used.

Because the animus, like the anima, is an archetype of the objective psyche, it exists prior to and as a condition for the development of consciousness and is therefore elusive to contact. The animus represents those unexamined, unquestioned emotional convictions and points of view of a woman which form the framework in which all her evaluations and judgments occur. She takes these standards for granted and assumes that everyone thinks this way. Consequently, the animus "is exceedingly difficult to contact because in searching for it, one tends to look for errors in judgment—which may be there—while neglecting the judging process itself." [32]

Like the anima, the animus has an objective aspect (as delineated above) and a personal aspect. The latter reflects the influence of the actual men in a woman's life, such as her father, brother, male cousin, or husband, those who concretize and condition her conception of man. Each woman's experience of her own animus is as uniquely varied as is her own personality from that of other women.

Typical Animus Problems

TYPICAL ANIMUS PROBLEMS arise when there is insufficient conscious differentiation of the "I" of the ego from the "Thou," or "other," of the animus. Where there is no separation of ego and animus, there is no conscious personal relationship to whatever the animus symbolizes. The woman opens her mouth, but the animus speaks. In this undigested state, the animus takes the form of emotional expectations of how things ought to be done or understood, expectations

32. Whitmont, *Symbolic Quest*, p. 201.

which are compulsively expressed and devoid of a sense of timing. The "oughts" are not understood or mediated by individual conscious experience but are delivered wholesale. Opinions exist ready-made, reflecting what is generally true but not necessarily what is relevant to specific issues, facts, or feelings.[33] An actual man may be expected by the woman to behave as if he were like her unconscious animus image. She might think to herself, for example, "If he really cared about me he would know what I felt intuitively, without my telling him. Because he doesn't, it proves he doesn't love me, and therefore I have a right to be hurt." The woman may direct these unexamined, unconscious expectations against ideas, situations, and against herself as well, giving the impression of over-generalizing, of being dogmatic and argumentative.

Another expression of a woman's ego in a state of partial identity with her animus can often be found in a primitive, unconscious power drive, a ruthless egotism masked by outward compliance or helplessness. She seems to be an interested listener but she hears nothing but a confirmation of her own opinions. She seems compassionate but she insists relentlessly on getting her own way. She forces her help on another to ensure that it is clear that she is needed. She is the one who seems to be trying to understand, but in fact she persistently misconstrues meanings and insinuates opposing purposes into conversations, thus seriously damaging her relationships with others. She has a primitive urge for prestige. She is concerned about how things look rather than how they really are. Any individual need, any real feeling of the moment, whether about herself or about others, is crushed if it interferes with good appearances. In the grip of such a drive, she will even forsake a man she loves in order to marry a collectively approved choice. This same power drive, if consciously integrated, could lead to creative assertion and discrimination of goals; it could stir a woman's initiative and give her courage to stand firmly on her own.

33. See Jung, *Aion*, p. 15.

Inflation by the animus shows itself in a woman's drive always to be right. There is, for example, the woman who argues to win a point, rather than to understand something or to arrive at the truth. Puffed up unconsciously with preconceived notions and assumptions, she feels that anyone who disagrees with her is "wrong," "stupid," even "immoral," about anything from child-rearing and cooking procedures to philosophical subtleties. An example of this is a woman who criticized her daughter-in-law as sneaky because she did not behave a certain way in a certain situation. In response to the comment that what the mother-in-law thought was right might be right for her but not necessarily for everybody else, the mother-in-law retorted, "But why not? That's the only honest way to be!" In other words, her inflated opinion of how things should be was the way they had to be.

The inflation of the ego by the animus may take a curious negative twist. The preconceived notions of what should and should not be may be directed not outwardly, toward others, but inwardly, toward a woman herself. She then becomes deflated—negatively inflated—always feeling inadequate, feeling that whatever she does is never enough. (Enough for whom or for what is left unspecified and hence unrelated to the individual circumstance. Thus her expectation can never be met because it is always abstract and not directed to a specific person, situation, or issue.) Instead of always being right, she is always wrong and feels constantly defensive and anxious to justify herself. Any situation, remark, or problem of relationship is felt as proof of her own inadequacy and may lead to tears, withdrawal, or depression. Any effort by someone else to point out the facts of the "deflation" she receives as criticism and attack.

Projection of the animus occurs when its qualities of discrimination, creative contact with meaning, articulation, and penetration are seen either as embodied in a succession of men with whom the woman falls in love or as the teacher with *the* truth. She is repeatedly disappointed because the real personality of these men falls short of the projected ideal. No man is ever good enough. Each candidate is weak and incompetent and not really a man as compared with her fantasy partner. If the projected animus image is negative, a woman sees men as enemies; she fears them and is hostile to them. Every man is greeted as if he had a gun in his hand and were about to shoot at her, and no matter what is said the answer is invariably "No, don't shoot!" This obviously makes relationship impossible.

In building a conscious relationship to her animus, a woman must treat "him" as if he were an actual inner person whom she must actively meet and speak with. This involves relating to both the personal, conditioning influence of father, brother, etc., as well as to the transpersonal archetypal core. Just as relating to a man opens a woman to hitherto inaccessible parts of herself, relating to this inner man puts her in touch with as yet unrealized capacities in herself. The animus puts a woman in touch with her capacities to focus upon and articulate the deeper aspects of her feminine being, to be assertive and to take definite stands in a feminine way rather than to imitate the masculine way. It helps her to distinguish her thought, feeling, and behavior from the expectations of the mob, and to use her judgment to further relationship with others rather than to dominate them. The sexual polarity both in and outside herself furthers a woman's growth to wholeness. As the woman becomes more related to her animus, its images disappear, and it assumes its automatic function, mediating between consciousness and the unconscious. The contents and effects of the animus and anima, but not the archetypes themselves, are integrated into consciousness.[34]

THE ARCHETYPE

AS I HAVE SAID ABOVE, the unconscious for Jung has, in addition to the personal layer of rejected, repressed material, an

34. *Ibid.*, p. 20.

objective dimension that is nonindividual, timeless, and universal. This "objective psyche" is accessible to consciousness only indirectly, through its effects on behavior and emotions and through symbols that belong to human history rather than to personal biography. On the basis of empirical observation, Jung noted that recurrent motifs in the myths, fairy tales, and religions of world literature repeatedly appear in the fantasies, dreams, and delusions of contemporary man. These typical images, associations, and related patterns of behavior and emotional reaction cannot be reduced to, nor be satisfactorily explained by, the influences of immediate circumstance or cultural context. It is as if an objective, nonpersonal, universal dimension of the psyche were expressing itself and addressing individual men through these stories, symbols, metaphors, and patterns. Jung uses the term archetype to describe the source of those symbols and to designate the contents of the objective psyche.[35]

"Archetype" is a symbolic concept. It conceptualizes our experience, but it is not a mere nominalistic designation. It has the symbolic function to mediate to consciousness the objective reality of the psyche that is not directly accessible to our sensory perception or to our logical reason. Archetypes symbolize the life of the nonindividual psyche that we all experience but which is not our personal possession.[36] We feel the drive effect of the archetype, its emotional patterns and images, but we do not experience the archetype *per se* because "an archetypal content expresses itself, first and foremost, in metaphors." [37] This is highly significant. In order to be in touch with the objective reality that archetypal symbols communicate, we must be willing to work hard with the imagination and intuition and to trust them.

We see here the polar structure of the psyche. The non-

---

35. See Jung, *Memories, Dreams, Reflections,* ed. Aniela Jaffé, trans. Richard and Clara Winston (New York: Pantheon, 1961), p. 380.

36. See Jung, "Psychology of the Transference," *Practice of Psychotherapy,* p. 169.

37. Jung, "The Psychology of the Child Archetype," *Archetypes and the Collective Unconscious,* p. 157.

rational unconscious is in polarity with the rational consciousness, and the psyche as objective (the archetypes which act
upon us) is in polarity with the psyche as subjective (one's
personal identity and experience). The necessary intercourse
of these opposites—their interchange of differing points of
view—generates one's psychic energy and influences one's
degree of richness and creativity as a person. Failure to develop symbolic modes of communicating diminishes one's
contact with vital aspects of reality both within and without.
The results of such diminished contact can be seen in individual cases of neuroses or psychoses that occur because unconscious contents have been excluded from consciousness
through such defenses as repression, schizoid splitting, or the
creation of a pseudo self. On the collective level, diminished
contact with the unconscious results in eruptions of mass
neurosis and psychosis, such as the Nazi persecutions, or a
widespread sense of futility and loss of meaning, with the
compensating rise of fanatical political movements.

Jung uses two polarities to describe the archetypes. They
have a biological and psychological aspect, and they have a
form and a content. The biological aspect, for example, denotes inherited modes of psychic functioning that correspond
to the inborn way a bird builds its nest. These modes are
preformed, instinctual, potential patterns of response that are
manifest in individual life as goal-directedness or purposeful
behavior, in patterns of emotional response and expectation,
and value systems.[38] Like the concept of sexual instinct that
is postulated to account for the observed similarities of sexual
behavior, Jung postulates the concept of the archetype to account for "the uniformity and regularity of our perceptions . . ."; he describes the primordial image as "the *instinct's perception of itself.*"[39] Just as instinctive reflexes act

38. See Jung, "Concerning the Archetypes With Special Reference
to the Anima Concept," p. 66; and Jacobi, *Complex/Archetype/Sym-
bol,* pp. 43–44.
39. Jung, "Instinct and the Unconscious," p. 136. See also Roland
Cahen, "Vingt ans après," in *Contact with Jung,* ed. Michael Fordham (London: Tavistock, 1963), *passim.*

autonomously and respond automatically to certain physical stimuli, archetypes react automatically to psychic stimuli. Just as the instincts determine the form but not the content and are the motivating dynamisms of biological behavior, so the archetypes determine psychic modes of apprehension and perception and are the motivating dynamisms for behavior on the psychic level. As the instincts are to the body, so the archetypes are to the psyche.[40] The archetypes, like the instincts, are part of the given structure of life, although their patterns may be modified over the centuries.[41] Jung calls them "organs of the pre-rational psyche."[42]

The special flavor of the objectivity of the objective psyche is due to the fact that it is not a "dead deposit" or a "rubbish heap" but is filled with archetypes which are a vital historical deposit of all human experience back to its origins. The objective psyche is "a living system of reactions and aptitudes that determine the individual's life in invisible ways—all the more effective because invisible."[43] The archetypes appear in the form of these inherited systems of readiness for action and readiness for images and emotions. The archetypal form is, then, a potentiality for experiencing, representing, and reacting to the world. It is the preconditioning framework for any kind of psychic awareness that can manifest itself anywhere at any time.[44] Although differing cultural contexts elicit the specific style of concretization of an archetype, the archetype itself is not reducible to cultural determinations because it "is empty and purely formal, nothing but a *facultas praeformandi*, a possibility of representation which is given *a priori*."[45] The objective psyche is conditioned by history but

40. See Jung, "Structure of the Psyche," p. 152.

41. See Jung, "A Psychological Approach to the Dogma of the Trinity," *Psychology and Religion: West and East*, p. 149 n.

42. Jung, "Psychological Commentary on *The Tibetan Book of the Dead*," *Psychology and Religion: West and East*, p. 518.

43. Jung, "Structure of the Psyche," *Structure and Dynamics of the Psyche*, p. 157.

44. See Jung, *Memories, Dreams, Reflections*, p. 381.

45. Jung, "Psychological Aspects of the Mother Archetype," *Archetypes and the Collective Unconscious*, p. 79.

is not reducible to mere historical conditioning because it is itself a source from which history flows. Its contents, the archetypes, are the forms which the instincts assume in history.

The form of the archetype has two aspects, a dynamic and a representational one. The form manifests itself dynamically as a pattern of behavior and emotional reaction. It manifests itself representationally as images, personifications, and motifs that are recorded in myths on the collective level and in dreams and visions on the individual level.

The content of the archetype is that specific emotional or behavioral pattern and cluster of images that become actualized through the environmental conditioning factors of personal biography and cultural context. The archetype becomes the core of a complex. The shell of the complex is built up from the interaction of the archetype with personal conditioning factors. The personal material in which the archetype is concretized is essential; it is the living stuff in which the archetype is incarnated and through which it is experienced. The archetype itself is not experienced; only its effects are experienced, for it is only a formal potential pattern of experiencing. The content of a particular person's experience of an archetype is not inherited—what is inherited is only a potentiality for experiencing such contents. Furthermore, although instinctual potential patterns of response are inherited, environmental factors determine which ones are activated and to what degree.[46] The form plus the personal material make up the experience of an archetype. Hence the criticism that archetypes are merely inherited ideas is fallacious. Jung says not that fixed representations are inherited but rather that the potentiality of representation is inherited.

A frequent misunderstanding and misuse of Jung's theory is to insist that it is "mystical." Such an interpretation attempts to avoid the exigencies of personal problems by focusing on the archetypes directly. A new patient once said, "I

46. See Jung, "Analytical Psychology and *Weltanschauung*," *Structure and Dynamics of the Psyche*, p. 372.

don't want to talk about why I can't make a living; let's talk about archetypes." It is equally foolish to focus exclusively on the personal aspect of problems. Meaningless suffering may result as the patient becomes hopelessly caught in the conflict between the ego's purposes and the instinctual drives. He may be caught in the conflict again and again even though he understands it "perfectly," because he is still controlled by unconscious forces.

What helps a person caught in such a conflict is for him to become conscious of the preconditioning archetypal forms of consciousness. These act like magnetic fields which, though unseen, arrange responses, emotions, and actions into specific patterns expressed in the form of symbolic images.[47] If the ego can relate to these archetypal centers of energy through their symbolic expressions, the use of instinctive energy can be consciously guided for the ego's purposes. Ideally, one should use two methods to achieve such an end. In the example that follows, the reductive method usually associated with Freud is used first, and Jung's synthetic-constructive procedure is used second. The first is a good beginning; it is no more than that, however. It requires the second to accomplish the resolution of the conflict.

A woman who is caught in a typical animus complex which shows itself in her nagging of others for never measuring up, is helped enormously by reductively tracing her present behavior to the conditioning influence of her father, whose temperament displayed just those characteristics. She sees that she has taken his misuse of authority as the model for her own idea of authority. This analysis, however, even though it results in some change in her behavior, cannot necessarily protect her from falling into another danger which is just as great. She may reject any claim to authority at all for fear of nagging, or worse, the nagging may now be directed toward herself. Nagging herself then becomes a remedy for nagging others. The conflict is not solved but only seen in a different

47. See Jung, "Psychological Approach to the Dogma of the Trinity," pp. 149 n, 150–51.

perspective. The conflict that heretofore was between the woman and other people, especially men, is now located in the past and present simultaneously. In the past, the conflict existed between herself and her father. In the present, the conflict exists between her own instinctive drive for self-assertion and her ego's drive to relate satisfactorily to others. The conflict, both past and present, goes on; the only difference now is its multilevel form of expression.

For a real solution to this kind of multilevel conflict, a different channel for the instinctual energy of the animus archetype is needed. This can come about only by the intervention of consciousness. The woman needs to become conscious not only of her specific judgments and their errors but also of the framework of the judging process itself—the assumptions from which she begins. To do this she must take the symbolic expressions of the animus archetype seriously. She might ask why the animus is so negative, what point is it trying to make? Where is it not getting sufficient attention so that it causes such a commotion? How could *she* respond in order to make the animus respond differently? The symbolic approach of the Jungian synthetic-constructive interpretation is necessary if she is to find new channels of expression for her archetypal dynamism.[48]

Just as the biological and formal aspects of the archetype denote its structural *a priori* effects on consciousness and behavior, and its content denotes its specific biographical experience in space and time, so the psychological aspect of the archetype denotes the experience of its meaning and its emotional impact and the expression of that experience in symbolic images.[49] The energy centers of the archetypes in the objective psyche translate the impact of natural physical occurrences into psychic factors by generating symbolic images that mediate to consciousness the psychological meaning of those natural occurrences:[50] "in the same way as the eye

48. See above, pp. 22–23.
49. See Jung, "On the Nature of the Psyche," pp. 211–14.
50. See Jung, "Psychology of the Child Archetype," pp. 153–54.

bears witness to the peculiar and independent creative activity of living matter, the primordial image is an expression of the unique and unconditioned creative power of the mind." [51] Jung tries in his hypothesis of archetypes to describe the psyche's mysterious spiritual activity. He is looking for a way to express the meaning of the ego's encounters with objective reality. This meaning is not accounted for solely in materialistic or biological terms. The admixture of the biological and psychological aspects of the archetypes faithfully portrays the inseparability of the physical and the spiritual aspects of life, Jung writes:

> For anyone acquainted with religious phenomenology it is an open secret that although physical and spiritual passion are deadly enemies, they are nevertheless brothers-in-arms, for which reason it often needs the merest touch to convert one into the other. Both are real, and together they form a pair of opposites, which is one of the most fruitful sources of energy. [52]

ARCHETYPAL SITUATIONS

THE EXPERIENCE of analysts and patients dealing with archetypes indicates that they tend to emerge in certain common situations. [53] Archetypes seem to occur when complexes have been dealt with on the personal level and there is a need to understand them on a level beyond their immediate personal origin. The case of a young man illustrates this. He came to his first appointment carrying Joseph Campbell's *A Hero with a Thousand Faces;* he was full of bravado about wanting to be a hero. His enthusiasm soon faded, and he confessed feeling unsure of himself, untrusting, helpless in fact, in most areas of his life. His relationship with his mother was un-

51. Jung, *Psychological Types,* p. 557.
52. Jung, "On the Nature of the Psyche," p. 212.
53. For additional discussion of archetypes, see Whitmont, *Symbolic Quest,* pp. 73–74. He cites three main kinds of situations in which archetypes emerge.

pleasant; he felt she was "a slob" and that she controlled him by giving him money which he was then unable to return. He dreamt: "I was in a Mediterranean country, as a peasant or fisherman. My friend S and I were working on my car; we were fixing the engine to try to get it to run. There suddenly appeared a burial mound covered by an ancient dolmen. From out of the mound rose a fiery red hand and a voice said 'The shade of Oedipus.'" The dreamer associated freedom of emotional expression with the Mediterranean climate close to the earth and the sea. He associated steadiness and honesty with the peasant fisherman, warmth and trustworthiness with his friend S, who he knew had the courage to follow his own way. The repair of the car was craftsman's work; the engine was the motor power, the energy source of his personal vehicle. A dolmen, he had learned, was an ancient stone structure associated with a burial site; it excited awe and a sense of mystery in him. The red hand was his right hand, his hand of executive functions (of writing, signing checks, dressing, etc.); its fiery color signified tremendous energy to him. He associated the words he heard in the dream with the Oedipus myth, summing it up to himself as the story of a man caught by his tie to his mother, who found his murder of his father and his marriage to his mother so ugly that he blinded himself. He turned these materials away from consciousness and became unconscious, thus turning his energy against himself.

The dream described his personal problem. The dreamer was, in fact, tied to his mother financially, and he did lack the clarity, purpose, and independence that might have proclaimed him a male adult. He was caught in a regression to infantile dependence on the maternal, on what was easiest, most pleasurable, and supporting. In fact, he had trouble living life under the power of his own initiative (the broken-down car) and was working on just this problem (repairing the engine). In the midst of repairing his personal vehicle something erupted from a deeper, archaic level that signified great energy (the red hand). It was necessary to recognize the significance of this deeper level and not to be unconscious of it (blinded) if he were to avoid fixation at an infantile level.

The major task in working on this dream was to relate the Oedipus archetype to the man's concrete life situation. It was also necessary to deal with the eruption of another dimension of experience that could lead to the realization of larger categories of meaning than the dreamer had yet acknowledged. Here, his childish yearning to become "a hero" found its appropriate expression, because the hero's task was to slay the dragon—the regressive hold of the unconscious (mother)—in order to achieve his own autonomous ego reality.

The point of view is what is crucial here. If one looks at the dream only in terms of the dreamer's difficulty with his mother, one simply repeats the obvious. One already knows of his situation with his mother. What one needs to know is why the dream associates the Oedipus archetype to the problem of repairing his broken-down personality. He did not dream of himself and his mother, but of Oedipus and repairing his car with a friend.[54] To deal only with the Oedipal myth and the hero's role to the exclusion of the dreamer's problem with his mother, however, would encourage evasion of the immediate issues. The myth would not be grounded; the problem would not be faced concretely. One needs both interpretations here.

54. Here we see a major difference between Freud's and Jung's methods of dream interpretation. For Freud, the dream symbols disguise the latent meaning of the dream, which is usually a repressed sexual wish, in this case the dreamer's incestual desire for his mother. The dream does not mention his mother but instead uses Oedipus and the repairing of the car to mask the dreamer's longing for his mother. For Jung, in contrast, the symbols used in a dream are the best possible expressions of an unknown content. The symbol does not disguise; it reveals. It must be met on its own terms rather than as a disguise for something that consciousness finds unacceptable. For an example of Jung's method, see "The Transcendent Function," and "General Aspects of Dream Psychology," *Structure and Dynamics of the Psyche*, pp. 75–76, 240–41. See also Jung, "Freud and Jung: Contrasts," *Freud and Psychoanalysis* (CW, IV, 1961), *passim*.

Another type of situation in which archetypes emerge is when outer or inner events are especially profound, shaking, or frightening. It is as if the archetypal image expressed the psychic meaning of such events. A clear illustration of this is the following dream, which occurred after a young woman had decided to seek help at a psychiatric clinic. She felt she was "coming to an end, losing herself," but the dream seems to point to a different meaning. It portrays her as beginning a trip: "I was on a train going to Russia with old Jewish peasant women. I reasoned with them not to go because they would be persecuted and suffer terribly. They said they had to go; they had to save something important."

The archetype of the transforming journey emerges in the midst of the dreamer's personal distress, as if to express an additional dimension of meaning in her decision. The dream puts the dreamer in the company of her personal problems: Jews, women, and peasants who would not listen to reason. In fact, she despised her own Jewish, immigrant origins and was violently antireligious. Her faith was in the power of reason. She had difficulty with her own feminine identity and with her mother. The more she reasoned with these problems, the more intense they became, until she felt she was losing her grip on herself and her familiar world. The dream put her in the company, for the sake of something of value, of those who leave what is familiar and journey to unknown places even at the risk of great suffering. This archetype of the transforming journey may also be found in Abraham's trip to the Promised Land or Jason's voyage for the Golden Fleece. Instead of rejecting her problems, the dreamer here must travel with them. Instead of losing herself, she must risk herself to save something important, her sense of her self. Her personal panic is thus set in the wider human context of losing oneself to find oneself. The panic does not vanish with this kind of analysis, but because one understands it one reacts to it differently.

Archetypes also emerge spontaneously in situations where the objective psyche takes over and the ego is swept away and assimilated by the archetype of the self. This results in brief psychotic episodes or even in a full-blown psychosis. An illustration of this is the dream and subsequent behavior of a schizoid woman who experienced a quasi-psychotic period when all ego functioning was virtually relinquished: "I was on a narrow path along a cliff by the sea. The wind was blowing and the waves rising. The water was purple-black and menacing. At a turn in the path I slipped and fell into the water. It was terrifying, the waves were so high. I had trouble keeping my head above water, and thought of just sinking into the sea."

Soon after the dream she felt as if she had fallen into choppy waters of emotion and could hardly keep her bearings, her life was so troubled. For a time she did "sink into the sea"; she could not go to work, nor even leave her house. She feared meeting people, and ordinary household tasks were too much for her. She sank under the covers of her bed, out of touch with people, with her feelings, with her reality. It is significant that the dream is devoid of any personal references to place, time, or acquaintances. It is as if the raw power of the archetype, undigested and unmitigated by personal ego-relatedness, swept over her and threatened to sink her. In dealing with such a situation, it is precisely these personal ego aspects that must be strengthened, so that there can eventually be an ego there to relate to the archetypes; otherwise, the nonpersonal, nonrelated power of the archetype will crash down as naturally and relentlessly as waves upon the shore.

Archetypes appear in the imaginative fable, the myth, the legend, the fairy tale. Parts of these, in turn, often reappear in dreams and visions. The recurring motifs in these expressions are called *mythologems:* "tales already well known but not unamenable to further reshaping." [55] On the collective level mythologems are stories of psychic events and their

55. Carl Kerényi, "Prolegomena," in *Essays on a Science of Mythology,* ed. C. G. Jung and C. Kerényi, trans. R. F. C. Hull (New York: Harper Torchbooks, 1949), p. 2.

meanings, whereas on the individual level bits of mythologems are fitted into personal material. Mythologems symbolize the meanings of psychic energy patterns and suggest ways in which one may relate to those meanings. Hence, to be in touch with mythologems can be very helpful in personal experience. For the woman with the dream of the journey, for example, a frightening breakdown becomes a significant breaking down of her orientation, one that will involve serious suffering, but suffering for the sake of something fundamental.

Jung thinks each individual psyche is shaped by emergent archetypal patterns that are conditioned and concretized by facts of personal biography. We each live out and fulfill our personal myth, experiencing our unique constellation of archetypal mythologems. The more experience we have, the more evident this is. We see our old impasses and problems coming up again in new forms and situations. Because the archetypes are preconditioning structures of the psyche, the recurrent mythologems shape the myth in terms of which we respond to our life situation. To catch sight of these invisible forces is to begin to piece together the mosaic of events that compose our inner history, where the meaning of experience unfolds: "the personality too desires to evolve out of its unconscious conditions and to experience itself as a whole. . . . What we are to inward vision, and what man appears to be *sub specie aeternitatis*, can only be expressed by way of myth. Myth is more individual and expresses life more precisely than does science. . . ." [56]

In a moving essay Jung writes about the experience of living in touch with one's personal myth. To do so is to be "called," to have a vocation. To hear and follow the law of one's own being is to achieve wholeness or "personality." To obey "one's own law" does not mean self-gratification or willful invention. The law is one's own only in the sense that it has been addressed to oneself and is inescapable. A call is

56. Jung, *Memories, Dreams, Reflections*, p. 3.

issued ". . . when the psyche, as an objective fact, hard as granite and heavy as lead, confronts a man as an inner experience and addresses him in an audible voice, saying, 'This is what will and must be.' " [57] This call is issued to everyone, but not everyone responds: "Though many are called few are chosen." Described religiously, one feels that this call comes from God and that fidelity to it is a daily devotion.

One of the ways such a call is voiced is through mythologems that appear in a bidding fantasy or dream, an arresting image or feeling tone which accompanies the appearance of an old difficulty. Too often, however, such mythologems are not seriously considered; they are rationalized away and their implicit guiding meaning is not seen. As a result, one feels arousing emotional urges and drives that are split off from their accompanying and potentially significant images. This split is augmented if one cannot accept the images at all because they conflict with traditional moral concepts. The essential importance of the symbolic approach again becomes clear. Through it the meaning of the mythologem is made accessible to us, and through the mythologems the objective psyche reveals meaning: "Myth is the primordial language natural to these psychic processes, and no intellectual formulation comes anywhere near the richness and expressiveness of mythical imagery." [58]

Archetypes also spontaneously emerge in the nonrational methods of therapy employed specifically to assimilate archetypal contents. Symbolic procedures are necessary because it is through images and symbolic patterns of behavior that archetypes make their effects felt. The conscious expression of archetypal contents might be encouraged, then, in the symbolic languages of painting, sculpture, music, dancing, poetry, etc.

The goal of the symbolic method is to bring about a conscious ego encounter with and relation to archetypal material.

57. Jung, "The Development of the Personality," *The Development of the Personality* (CW, XVII, 1954), pp. 177–78.
58. Jung, *Psychology and Alchemy*, p. 25.

When this happens benefits accrue to the patient. The heretofore general force of the archetype is channeled into concrete form, and that channeling relieves some of the pressure from the unconscious. The unconscious now has a spokesman, so to speak, a specific image or character to represent its point of view. Moreover, there is now a specific form through which the ego can relate to hitherto unrecognized aspects of the unconscious. This decreases the patient's anxiety in the face of the unknown and facilitates the arduous work of integrating unconscious contents.

A series of self-portraits sketched by a young woman illustrates this. She felt undefined, as if she always were adopting other people's viewpoints and merging with the surrounding emotional atmosphere. At the same time she felt "in touch with the universe." Her appearance was sweet and childlike; her eyes frequently brimmed with tears as unknown feelings swept over her. Her fear that "the light was going out" brought her to analysis. Early in treatment, she felt she wanted to draw her own face. The task of drawing helped her begin to define herself and to discover unguessed aspects of her personality.

The first pictures were striking in their aggressiveness: the eyes gleamed, the chin jutted forward, and the face was sharply defined and hard in appearance. We were both surprised. Here was a picture of what she had left out of her conscious adaptation—a face whose individuality was so strong it looked tough and power-driven. It showed clearly, however, what she needed to include in her conscious adaptation. The picture of this face impressed her more deeply and aroused her to relate to these unconscious power drives more quickly and effectively than a rational interpretation could have.

Active Imagination

"Active imagination" is a method Jung uses in certain cases to deal with archetypal contents. It is a method originated to give to unconscious contents an aesthetic formulation which expresses the "intent" of unconscious contents and to which the patient can consciously relate.[59] A concept without experience is empty, and an experience without an underlying concept is blind. The experience of depicting a fantasy or dream image and entering into active imaginative dialogue with a shadow figure, for example, involves one in direct exchanges with archetypal dynamisms, while at the same time preserving the conscious ego orientation so that the ego is not overwhelmed. What results from these exchanges is a full expression of the unconscious "viewpoint" that is related to by the ego's viewpoint of reality. From this interchange, what Jung calls a "third viewpoint" emerges that reconciles the opposing poles of the unconscious and the conscious ego by combining elements of both poles. Jung calls the psyche's tendency to reconcile its polarities in this way its "transcendent function." When this third viewpoint emerges, one feels urged to adopt it. If one does so, one neither falls into unwitting acting out of unconscious drives nor into a sterile, repressive position where the ego enforces its own particular view. Rather, one begins to act out of one's total psyche. There is, as a result, a conscious realization of underlying archetypal energies. The ego is thus able to differentiate unconscious collective elements from personal conscious elements and to avoid the confusion of trying to deal with collective problems on individual terms or vice versa.

EXAMPLES OF ARCHETYPES

BEFORE CLOSING my discussion of archetypes, I think it is important to give general examples of basic archetypal images. As we have seen, the unconscious "figures" enumerated above —shadow, animus, anima—are archetypes. Another example

59. See Jung, "The Transcendent Function," and "On the Nature of the Psyche," pp. 87, 211; and *Psychological Types*, p. 581.

is the archetype of the Great Mother. This is a manifestation of the feminine as concrete natural existence. It is succinctly described by Edward F. Edinger as

> . . . the fertile womb out of which all life comes and the darkness of the grave to which it returns. Its fundamental attributes are the capacity to nourish and the capacity to devour. It corresponds to mother nature in the primordial swamp—life being constantly spawned and constantly devoured. If the great mother nourishes us, she is good; if she threatens to devour us, she is bad. In psychological terms, the great mother corresponds to the unconscious which can nourish and support the ego or can swallow it up in psychosis or suicide. The positive, creative aspects of the great mother are represented by breast and womb. The negative, destructive aspects appear as the devouring mouth or the *vagina dentata*. In more abstract symbolism, anything hollow, concave or containing pertains to the great mother. Thus, bodies of water, the earth itself, caves, dwellings, vessels of all kinds are feminine. So also is the box, the coffin and the belly of the monster which swallows up its victims.[60]

The archetype of the Spiritual Father represents the masculine as the principle of consciousness symbolized by light, spirit, the sun, the heavens. Edinger explains:

> From this region comes the wind, *pneuma, nous, ruach,* which has always been the symbol of spirit as opposed to matter. Sun and rain likewise represent the masculine principle as fertilizing forces which impregnate the receptive earth. Images of piercing and penetration such as phallus, knife, spear, arrow and ray all pertain to the spiritual father. Feathers, birds, airplanes and all that refers to flying or height are part of this complex of symbols which emphasizes the upper heavenly realms. . . . all imagery involving light or illumination pertain to the masculine principle as opposed to the dark earthiness of the great mother. Shining blond hair, illumination of the countenance, crowns, halos, and dazzling brilliance of all kinds are aspects of masculine solar symbolism.

60. Edinger, "Outline of Analytical Psychology," p. 13.

The image of the *wise old man* as judge, priest, doctor or elder is a human personification of this same archetype. The positive aspect of the spiritual father principle conveys law, order, discipline, rationality, understanding and inspiration. Its negative aspect is that it may lead to alienation from concrete reality causing inflation, a state of spiritual hybris or presumption that generates grandiose thoughts of transcendence and results in the fate of Icarus or Phaeton.[61]

The archetype of the self is the central archetype expressing psychic wholeness, order, and totality. Jung defines it as "not only the centre but also the whole circumference which embraces both conscious and unconscious; it is the centre of this totality, just as the ego is the centre of the conscious mind." [62] The concept of self is difficult to define precisely because it symbolizes the psychic entity that encompasses and transcends the ego and conveys the indescribable nature of human wholeness. The self is the ground from which the individual personality originates and thus constitutes an *a priori* pattern of unfolding totality that operates upon ego consciousness in a compensatory and complementary way, as if to intend that all aspects of the psyche be taken into consideration and given their due.[63] The effect of the self's determining, organizing activity on the ego is never fully integrated because, however much of the contents and activity of the self is made conscious, there is always an indeterminable amount of unconscious material that remains hidden. The ego must take into account the self's point of view even when its intents are opposed to those of the ego. Ignoring the determining influence of the self can result in psychic disaster, where the ego is assimilated by the self (psychosis) or the self is assimilated by the ego (psychic inflation).[64]

The paradoxical unity of the self encompasses all the polari-

61. *Ibid.*, pp. 13–14.
62. Jung, *Psychology and Alchemy*, p. 41. See also Jung's words cited in Victor White, *God and the Unconscious* (Cleveland: World Publishing, 1961), p. 257.
63. See *Psychology and Alchemy*, pp. 78 n, 172–74, 340 n.
64. See Jung, *Aion*, pp. 24–25.

ties of the psyche which are symbolized most often in terms of the masculine-feminine polarity. The wholeness of the self is built up from the reconciliation of these opposite psychic poles, but not from their fusion, because the tension of the opposites remains the source of life's energy and the dynamism of the self. As the archetype of the self emerges, symbols of a centering process or a uniting of opposites emerge. Jung researched the alchemical symbols as examples of stages in this centering process. The medieval "philosopher's stone," for instance, was the product of the union of sun and moon, fire and water, king and queen. The paradoxical unity of such opposites is often represented in the imagery of the hermaphrodite. Again we see the masculine-feminine polarity employed to symbolize the psyche's urge to wholeness. A contemporary woman's dream illustrates this in striking ways:

> I go with A who in the dream is unhappily married to B to their house which is two rooms. In the second room there is a high table like an altar, yet it is also a bed. In it is their girl child. She is six years old, but big, has dark hair and a bright red dress and hair on her face. I realize she has three eyes; the third, on the end of her nose, is darkly lashed and lustrous. I realize she is abnormal and retarded. A is upset about her and embittered. A pulls down the covers and exposes the child's genitals. The child is both sexes. The child is terribly embarrassed. I feel sorry for her. I begin to befriend her and talk with her. I like her. She has great sensitivity and intelligence and is abnormal to me now in the sense of her exceptional development. She makes a few mistakes in grammar. She says she learned to talk at a special school of "phallic sound." I notice a picture on the wall. When I came in it was a fairy-tale castle, with a twilight landscape scene like Odilon Redon's work. When I look at it now, a second picture has been hung over it. It is of a city with a river running through it, with many bridges connecting the two banks of the river.

The dreamer associated with A that she was a woman of warm feeling who was anxious about her capacity to do intellectual work. The dreamer thought B was an opposite type: he was brilliant, logical, and organized, but emotionally immature. In the dream, A and B marry; a strong-feeling woman marries a strong-thinking man. They produce a child who is sensitive and intelligent, both feminine and masculine, both retarded and exceptional. The child is the center of the dream. The dreamer is led to the child, who is in the middle of the room on a table-altar. The focus is the interaction between the child and the dreamer. The child's third eye is stressed as its most beautiful eye—as if a third point of view were being hinted at, one which is a union of the other two. The dreamer associated with this eye "insight," "vision," seeing into the meaning of things; and with the placement of the eye on the end of the nose, she associated the most basic primitive sense, the sexual sense (smelling, sniffing). Here again opposites meet—the penetrating vision into the meaning of things is placed with the most elemental instinct. With phallic sound, the dreamer associated the *Phaedrus* of Plato, where the chariot of the soul mounts into the heavens and enjoys the music of the eternal circling of the spheres, and also a lecture she had heard some months before about the sound "Om" which is one of the essential syllables from which the gods and the universe are supposed to have come into being, according to Indian mythology.

The child is still in primitive form, however, as her age, her grotesqueness, and her mistakes in grammar show. Also, the marriage of A and B is unhappy, the union is not yet successful, though some reconciliation of opposites is occurring. The final detail about the picture emphasizes this: a magical, preconscious misty scene is replaced by the image of an actual city the dreamer knew, with which she associated a "combination of efficiency, order, productivity, and peace, where my feelings blossomed and I did creative work." The picture itself, of land and water and connecting bridges, conveys a quality of integration. This dream came a few days after the dreamer had risked acting on feelings that she had heretofore suppressed by reasoning away. However abortive, the uniting of opposites is beginning. The dream is a positive one, suggesting a more positive future for the dreamer, illustrating how the self is built up out of the reconciliation of opposites.

The self is often represented to us by such symbols as the "pearl of great price," buried treasure, or the water of life. The self is also represented by the mandala in its varied forms, as square, globe, rose, lotus, star, and the quadrated circle which combines an encircling centered totality with four cardinal directions, such as a circle with a cross in it. Examples of mandalas are the zodiacal circle, the Tibetan World Wheel, Christ surrounded by the four evangelists, and Navaho Indian sand paintings.[65]

Mandala symbolism appears in times of psychic confusion and intense conflict, as if to superimpose on chaos a psychological "view finder," as Jung calls it, that assigns each content its proper place and holds together the confusion within a protective circle.[66] Mandalas also appear after long periods of psychological development as if to symbolize release from the conflict of opposites and to convey the numinous impact of their reconciliation.

Because the self's imagery emphasizes wholeness and centeredness and because the self relates to the ego as a determining, integrating center, there are many parallels between the self and the imagery of religious figures. Jung understands the Christ symbol as of the greatest psychological importance because it is one of the most highly differentiated and developed symbols of the self. Furthermore, Christianity in its emphasis on original sin opens up in every individual the conflict of opposites. Jung says, "without the experience of opposites there is no experience of wholeness and hence no

65. See Jung, "A Study in the Process of Individuation," and "Concerning Mandala Symbolism," *Archetypes and the Collective Unconscious*, pp. 305, 355; "Commentary on the Secret of the Golden Flower," *Alchemical Studies* (*CW*, XIII, 1967), pp. 22–28. See also Marie-Louise von Franz, "The Process of Individuation," *Man and His Symbols*, ed. C. G. Jung (New York: Doubleday, 1964), pp. 213–17.

66. See Jung, *Memories, Dreams, Reflections*, p. 385.

inner approach to the sacred figures." [67] Jung's view of Christ is not the same as that of a theologian. For psychology, Christ points to the self; for theology, the self points to Christ.[68] Jung notes that Christ only represents the light half of the self archetype and that the dark aspect of the self is embodied in the Devil.[69]

STAGES OF PSYCHOLOGICAL DEVELOPMENT

IN JUNG'S VIEW, psychological development is the progressive differentiation of the ego, or consciousness, from unconsciousness and the building of a cooperative relationship between the ego and the unconscious and especially between the ego and the archetypal images that underlie the evolution of the human psyche. The need for the ego to relate to the unconscious is thus taken out of the pathological realm and is seen as a need of the normal adult.[70] Jung's general description of the stages of psychological development has been made more specific by such of his followers as Erich Neumann, Michael Fordham, and Edward Edinger.[71] Although characteristics of each stage of development can be outlined, in the process of growth the stages merge with one another and are not always correlated to the chronological ages as indicated below. It is also true that many people never progress beyond the first two stages so that though they are grown up physically, psychologically they are still children,

---

67. Jung, *Psychology and Alchemy*, p. 20.
68. *Ibid.*, p. 18.
69. See Jung, *Aion*, p. 44.
70. Edinger, "Outline of Analytical Psychology," p. 8.
71. See Jung, "The Stages of Life," *Structure and Dynamics of the Psyche*, pp. 387–404. See also Eric Neumann, *The Origins and History of Consciousness*, trans. R. F. C. Hull, 2 vols. (New York: Harper Torchbooks, 1954); Michael Fordham, *The Life of Childhood* (London: Kegan Paul, 1944); Michael Fordham, *New Developments in Analytical Psychology* (London: Routledge & Kegan Paul, 1955); Edinger, "Outline of Analytic Psychology."

or even infants. Psychic development is a lifetime process, and at no time can it be said that one has achieved maximum psychic growth, because the objective psyche is never fully encompassed by the ego, but is seemingly eternal and boundless.

In the early phase of development the ego is in a state of unconscious identity with the objective psyche—the world of archetypes—within, and with the external world without, and therefore has little autonomy. This stage corresponds to the prenatal period and early infancy in a person's chronological development. Jung used H. Lévy-Bruhl's term *participation mystique* to describe the quality of experience of this phase. The stage is symbolized, according to Erich Neumann, a distinguished disciple of Jung, by the mythical *uroboros*, the tail-eating serpent, which in psychological terms represents circular containment and wholeness. The ego exists in an undifferentiated wholeness; there is no distinction between inner and outer worlds, nor between image, object, and affect, nor between subject and object. The ego feels it is magically at one with its environment and with all of reality as a totality. This feeling can be observed in children, in primitives, and in mobs, where the individual's ego is swept away by the unconscious emotionality of the crowd. Reports of LSD experiments where boundaries disappear and the ego participates in "the essential reality" of all life may also be an example of this feeling. Because of its identification with and containment in the objective psyche, the ego feels as if it had an eternal, self-sufficient universe as its original core. This is one reason for the widespread notion of the divine origin of the soul.

Creation stories may be interpreted as descriptions of the birth of the ego. The ego becomes conscious of a world, a "me" and a "you," of a discrimination of inner and outer, etc. The central element in all these stories is the separation of being into opposites: consciousness seems to be the capacity to discern opposites. In the Genesis story there is a separation of light and darkness, of order and chaos, of earth and water. In some stories, the masculine and feminine are distinguished. Applied to individual psychology, the mythological images indicate psychic facts and the appropriate attitudes with which to deal with those facts. The first step in the creative process, for instance, is simply to withstand chaos ("the earth was without form and void"). For anything new to come to birth, we must first be open to shapelessness, to lack of form. Most of us find this formlessness so disagreeable that we avoid it. The image of the Spirit brooding over the waters seems like an appropriate attitude to take toward our own chaos—a staying with it and hovering over it, refusing to run away. This attitude encourages the human spirit to fecundate the chaos and to differentiate its polarities (day-night, earth-sea, etc.).

Neumann calls the second stage matriarchal. The ego has only indistinct consciousness and a precarious separation from the unconscious. The unconscious is personified archetypally as the Great Mother and is represented to the ego by the personal mother. As the child is passively dependent on its mother, the ego is passively dependent on the unconscious. The mother is all in all; she is both masculine and feminine, because the ego is not yet capable of differentiating the sexes. The ego's life is lived with the purpose of gaining the mother's support and avoiding her destructive maneuvers. (A frequent element in male homosexuality is precisely this subservience to the mother, both human and archetypal, where the man's feelings are not his own but are dictated by the approval or disapproval of his mother, or her surrogate, who receives the projection of the mother archetype.)

This matriarchal phase corresponds chronologically to early childhood. Interpreted symbolically, this is the phase of original incest, prior to the incest taboo, where the ego is immersed in the mother, and all life (emotional, sexual, mental, physical) is lived in relation to her. The Eden myth depicts the growth of consciousness that occurs at this time. One result of the eating of the fruit of the tree is the discrimination of the sexes ("they knew they were naked").

The net effect is that the ego becomes alienated from the pre-sexual source of contented wholeness. In its place comes the consciousness of duality, of an ego which is essentially different from other egos. The sexual polarity with all its symbolism comes to stand for this essential differentiation of individual consciousness from the unconscious. Sexual polarity is thus the primary means of experiencing otherness—of the other sex, of the unconscious, and of God.

The third stage, which Neumann calls patriarchal, corresponds to the prepuberty years and to the onset of puberty itself. Transition to this phase is represented in initiation rituals where the boy leaves the world of women, undergoes challenges, tests, and fulfills rules laid down by the men, and then joins their ranks as one of their own. The incest taboo is promulgated to prohibit regression to the mother-bound state of containing unconsciousness. In general, anything to do with the feminine is depreciated, rejected, or barely tolerated as inferior. When the transition to this new stage is successfully completed, the archetype of the Great Father becomes the sovereign deity and determines the values and goals of life. Consciousness, rationality, will power, self-discipline, adaptation to the demands of external reality, and a sense of individual responsibility become important. Full separation occurs between inner-outer, subject-object, right-wrong. The ego is now the source of action, and the sense of magical participation with the numinous dimension is lost. This is the time of separation from the original totality, alternately experienced as "estrangement" and as "being oneself."

In the patriarchal stage, then, the psychic polarities are not only distinguished from each other but are also experienced in opposition to each other. The values of the masculine are endorsed at the expense of feminine values; the principle of spirit is seen as opposed to earth; order and definition are seen as superior to creative fertility, commandments and obedience are valued over the virtues of acceptance and forgiveness, and becoming is seen as better than "just being."

The fourth stage is called integrative.[72] In this phase, the ego reclaims the elements of the nonrational feminine, as woman, as the unconscious, and as anima—characteristics that were all rejected and repressed in the patriarchal phase. These qualities must be recovered if the ego is to avoid sterile one-sidedness. Mythologically, transition to this integrative phase appears as the hero rescuing the maiden from the dragon. The hero represents an ego attitude strong enough to leave the safety of patriarchal standards and risk exposure to the dangers of regression, of diffusion of the ego's hard-won clarity, and of the threat of being swallowed up by the residual state of unconsciousness (the dragon). The maiden represents the anima—the feminine values in marriageable form which can be related to by the ego but which must first be separated in the myth, by the sword of consciousness, from the unconscious in its devouring aspects. If the ego succeeds in the task of freeing the anima from the unconscious, the ego's heretofore exclusive reliance on patriarchal values is complemented and modified by the feminine. As Edinger puts it: "This is a decisive step in psychological integration that amounts to a reconciliation of opposites: masculine and feminine, law and love, conscious and unconscious, spirit and nature."[73] In individual development this phase, at least on one level of realization, corresponds to puberty and adulthood when heterosexual relations become possible and the love of one woman and marriage may ensue.[74]

INDIVIDUATION

THE INTEGRATIVE PHASE of development by no means ceases at adulthood but recurs throughout life whenever nonra-

72. See Neumann, *Origins and History of Consciousness*, I, 411–13. See also Edinger, "Outline of Analytic Psychology," p. 16.

73. *Ibid.*

74. The stages of female development, which are somewhat different, will be dealt with in Chapter Twelve.

tional unconscious contents excluded by a conscious ego adaptation press for integration. As one gets older, integration increasingly has more to do with recovering an inner value than with establishing outer adaptation. Jung calls this ongoing process individuation, and his description of it is his main contribution to developmental psychology. Individuation is "a process by which a person becomes a psychological 'in-dividual,' that is, a separate, indivisible unity or 'whole.' " [75] Becoming whole includes realization of our innermost uniqueness, and hence the process also means becoming one's own self, as differentiated from having only a collective identity, as a member of a certain family, or group of people, or nation.

The process of individuation is not to be confused with the differentiation of the ego from the unconscious, as if individuation were simply ego-centeredness. Individuation is the process of the ego discovering, conversing with, and relating to the objective psyche, and realizing that it is subject to this more comprehensive psychic entity. The central representation of the objective psyche is the self; hence the successful individuation process leads to the self replacing the ego as the center of personality. Individuation is not individualism because "the self comprises infinitely more than a mere ego. . . . It is as much one's self and all other selves, as the ego. Individuation does not shut one out from the world, but gathers the world to oneself." [76] Although the relationship between the ego and the objective psyche evolves throughout life, it is not until the second half of life that the fruits of the individuation process usually appear.

The ego in this process of individuation discovers its limitations, learns that it is the center only of consciousness. Full ego development is found in accepting those limits and coordinating the attitudes and actions of the ego to the purposes of the total psyche. The ego has come full circle.

75. Jung, "Conscious, Unconscious, and Individuation," *Archetypes and the Collective Unconscious*, p. 275.
76. Jung, "On the Nature of the Psyche," p. 226.

It has separated itself from its original identity with the unconscious, obtained definition and strength, and now is ready to turn again to the unconscious to encounter and relate to the self.

Whereas in the patriarchal phase the power of being was experienced in terms of the ego's personal goals and meanings, in the integrative phase the power of being is experienced symbolically as the mystery beyond the ego and the ego's powers. The intangibles of inner life and the questions of one's relation to the meaning of life press for attention. Ego values are no longer the central concern. Now it is a question of what the ego is devoted to, revolves around, and serves; the ego seeks to correlate its purposes with the intentions of the whole psyche. This experience of relating to the larger center of the self is felt as the subordination of one's personal wishes to a greater power and meaning. There is a religious quality to this experience that is often expressed as "finding one's way," "following the will of God," "serving not oneself but Christ within," etc.

This quality of experience, of an ego relating to a self, is sometimes confused with the earliest phase of ego containment in the unconscious, prior to the birth of the ego. The language describing the two states is similar: it stresses unity, wholeness, and the subordination of the ego to an encompassing psychic entity, in the case of the integrative phase to the self, and in the case of the matriarchal phase to the archetype of the Great Mother. As a result, ego differentiation from containment in the unconscious, at the earliest stage of ego development, may be resisted because the necessary ego emphasis on "I, me, or mine" is seen as selfish and self-centered. Frequently, language that describes the later phase of ego devotion is used to support this resistance to ego development with such religious formulations as "I should deny myself and follow Christ."

The aggressive and sexual instincts bring the ego into being. They accent the personal—"my body," "my will," "my desire." The appearance of these instincts brings to an end the matriarchal phase of the ego in which it is passively contained. In this phase of passive containment, the ego feels as if it is serving a higher authority. Actually, this is not the case, because there is not yet a sufficiently developed personal self to be devoted to anything. The ego is passively held, not devoted.

Some ascetic writers in the Christian tradition have tended to equate the use of self-assertive sexual instincts with opposition to the service of God. As a result, some patients feel that the suppression of these instincts is the way to salvation. For people who consciously identify themselves as Christians, every step toward strengthening ego identity, which means accepting and using these instincts, may be experienced as a betrayal of their essential values.

In such situations, an analyst may find himself in the curious position of having to interpret or reinterpret the Christian faith to his patients. For instance, it may be necessary to point out that genuine devotion to God presupposes an authentic ego identity, developed as a result of full contact with life. The mere election of a religious identity is not the same thing as having fleshed out an ego, with the inevitable accompanying guilts, exhilarations, and estrangements. All this may demand a major readjustment and re-evaluation of faith on the part of the patient. The patient must come to the point of accepting self-assertion, sexual enjoyment, striving, willing—in short, the ego functions—as desirable and coherent with his religious values.

The young woman who drew portraits of herself is an example. Although she was vague and had weeping spells, she did feel "in tune with all that is," and "somehow connected to the real meaning of life." What was left out of her rhapsodies, however, was everything that was in the self-portraits: assertion, anger, greed, power, fire, competence, confidence, passion; namely, the as-yet undeveloped ingredients of a well-functioning ego. Initial attempts to encourage ego development failed; they were enveloped in a cosmic mist. A decisive step toward ego development occurred after the analyst asked her where *she* was, and where was *her* point of view, *her* wishes, pointing out her strong identification with her husband's ideas, the Jungian school of psychology, the analyst herself, etc. The woman responded with a furious letter full of feeling. The analyst had attacked and depreciated everything that was most important to her, she said. The letter ended with two significant statements: "I don't care what you think. Your way does not have to be my way!" and "I hope this letter disturbs you and hurts you!" Instead of fusion, differentiation had occurred. The night after sending the letter she dreamt that the analyst had come to see her in her house and had there met her husband. The analyst was not interested in the husband whom most visitors to that house immediately responded to, seeming to forget the wife entirely. The analyst was absorbed instead in the colorful autumn leaves the dreamer had brought in from outdoors. The analyst said they would have their session in the dreamer's own room from now on. The dream, in essence, said that the analysis was now to be conducted within the context of the dreamer's own space, her personal room, her unique identity, not as an echo of her husband or some school of psychology.

One can say, well, this was all to the good, what then was all the fuss about? But for both patient and analyst it was a turbulent time. Some weeks passed before what the dream described could become a reality. What all the fuss was about was that the young woman felt as if the demands of her own identity had set her against her deepest feeling of unity with life. Her conflict was acute, and the process of ego emergence was tantamount to leaving Eden.

ALCHEMY

JUNG'S STUDY OF ALCHEMY relates to the process of individuation. He saw in the alchemical stages of producing the "opus" parallels to stages of individuation. This led him to interpret the whole movement of alchemy across the centuries on a symbolical level. He saw the work of the alchemists as descriptive of the processes of psychic transformation: "Alchemy describes, not merely in general outline but often in the most astonishing detail, the same psychological phenomenology which can be observed in the analysis of the unconscious process." [77] Alchemy was concerned with the transformation of base metals into gold. Jung saw this as very much like the transformation of personality from base servitude to the unconscious, culminating in the shining clarity of conscious integration of unconscious contents. Jung thus recovers the significance of a movement which heretofore had been dismissed as little but tawdry hocus-pocus.

SYNCHRONICITY

IN HIS STUDY OF THE SELF as it is increasingly manifest in the individuation process, Jung formulated the concept of synchronicity which postulated an acausal connecting principle between coincidences.[78] For Jung, causality, which functions within spatio-temporal dimensions, does not apply to unconscious processes, particularly when the objective psyche has been activated. Instead, events are connected

> through another principle, namely the contingency of events. This connection of events seemed to me essentially given by the fact of their relative simultaneity, hence the term "synchronistic." It seems, indeed, as though time, far from being an abstraction, is a concrete continuum which contains qualities or basic conditions that manifest themselves simultaneously in different places through parallelisms that cannot be explained causally, as, for example, in cases

77. Jung, "The Psychology of the Transference," p. 198.
78. See Jung, "Synchronicity: An Acausal Connecting Principle," *Structure and Dynamics of the Psyche*, p. 441.

of the simultaneous occurrence of identical thoughts, symbols, or psychic states.[79]

The determination of the event as synchronistic depends on whether or not the coincidence is experienced by the subject as having meaning. Therefore, objective statistical methods cannot be used. The empirical material from which conclusions are drawn are just subjective experiences of psychic and physical events and their parallel states. A dream may refer to life events that happen after the dream rather than before it, or analysis of certain unconscious contents may be accompanied by outer events which to the subject have a significant simultaneity, but not in terms of cause and effect. On this subjective basis it is known that synchronistic events occur, and often with profound effect upon us. The full significance of synchronicity on the objective level—of the meaning of an acausal connecting principle for the nature of reality itself—is yet to be discovered. Jung is on the borderline of knowledge here. Still, on the basis of a good deal of evidence, we can say that what we have called "subjective" experience may really be a doorway to objective reality; and that nonrational coincidences grasped by our intuitive, emotional, faculties may convey aspects of objective reality which are inaccessible to our reason.

Psychological Types

Jung also constructed a theory of psychological types. These types classify the innate patterns of ego adaptation which determine a person's habitual frame of reference to the world and people. There are two fundamental attitude types, those of extroversion and introversion.

> Introversion or extroversion, as a typical attitude, means an essential bias which conditions the whole psychic process, establishes the habitual reactions, and thus determines

79. Jung, *Memories, Dreams, Reflections,* p. 388.

not only the style of behaviour, but also the nature of sub-jective experience . . . it also denotes the kind of com-pensatory activity of the unconscious which we may ex-pect to find.[80]

The extrovert is characterized by the tendency of his libido to flow outwards toward the object: to people, external ac-complishments, and things. His libido functions primarily to connect him to the external world; his greater interest and comfort is found in functioning in external adaptation. He is less certain and more uncomfortable in relating to his own inner world than to the outside world. He tends to de-preciate subjective experience as mere fancy or selfish pre-occupation. The introvert is characterized by the tendency of his libido to flow inwards to subjective experience, into feelings, images, fantasies, thoughts, and intuitions. His libido functions primarily to relate him to the inner world, and his greatest interest is in these inner experiences. He is most at ease when alone and free from the pressures of external adaptation. He habitually relies on what an outer object con-stellates in his subjective experience, in contrast to the ex-trovert who constantly refers to what reaches him from outer objects. He is less certain in large groups and public functions and tends to regard the extrovert's charm and social abilities as shallow, manipulating, and insincere.

Everyone contains some of both of these attitudes, but in each of us one is more developed as our accustomed mode of response. Each type tends to undervalue the attitudes of the other. To the introvert, the extrovert seems superficial, two-faced, and without conviction; to the extrovert, the introvert seems withdrawn, egotistical, and aloof. The attitudes are opposites, and if two people of the different types marry their different frames of reference are a frequent cause of misunderstanding.

The law of enantiodromia regulates extroversion and in-

---

80. Jung, *Modern Man in Search of a Soul*, trans. W. S. Dell and C. F. Baynes (New York: Harcourt, Brace & Co., 1933), p. 86. See also Jung, *Two Essays on Analytical Psychology*, pp. 54-56.

troversion within each of us. Excessive development of one attitude, say extroversion, gives rise to the expression of its opposite, introversion, but in a primitive, unadapted form. If a conscious attitude is too one-sided, the neglected attitude falls into the unconscious and begins to exert itself there to compensate for the one-sidedness. For the extrovert, subjective factors will behave like suppressed minorities, issuing in infantile, egotistical moods, obsessive ruminations, even nervous collapse.[81] For the introvert, objective factors gain a disproportionate influence which may induce compulsive attachment to objects, inferior relationships, and obsessive defenses to protect him from objects.[82] Conscious recognition and clear development of an inferior attitude may relieve it of its regressive archaic form and further fuller adaptation to both inner and outer reality. Because all perception involves both the object and the perceiving subject, both attitudes are necessary.

There are four fundamental function types: thinking and feeling (which are rational functions)—and sensation and intuition (which are nonrational functions). Psychic elements are rational insofar as they are logically and causally related; they are nonrational insofar as they make their presence felt simply by their direct givenness. A "function" for Jung is a "certain form of psychic activity that remains theoretically the same under varying circumstances." [83] We cannot choose which function will be our main mode of adaptation to life, he says, but only whether we will become conscious of which function is, in fact, dominant. Thinking is the capacity to organize experience conceptually and logically; feeling is the capacity to give value to experience; sensation is the capacity to perceive and adapt to experience through the senses; intuition is the capacity to perceive connections, conclusions, or representations which

81. See Jung, *Psychological Types*, pp. 423–24.
82. *Ibid.*, pp. 471–72.
83. *Ibid.*, p. 547.

have not yet been experienced, perceiving as it were via the unconscious. The four functions form two pairs of opposites. The first is thinking-feeling. We are not able to react simultaneously to experience through thinking *and* feeling because each process cancels out the other. One gives order, the other gives value. They may follow each other swiftly, but they cannot operate at precisely the same moment. The second pair of opposites is intuition-sensation. The factual perception of concrete realities, i.e., sensation, is antithetical to the flash of insight, whose origin is obscure to consciousness.

Potentially each person has all four functions at his disposal, but one becomes most developed, because it becomes one's habitual way of reacting and adapting to life. This is the "superior function"; it may not necessarily be what an individual does best. Environmental factors may encourage the development of a function that coincides with individual gifts or may be antithetical to them. Carried to an extreme, an ego which is formed in opposition to a person's superior functional type of adaptation will be a pseudo-ego, and all the real strengths and potentials of that person will reside in the shadow.

The least developed function in a person, which is therefore his most primitive and unconscious function, is the opposite of the superior one and is called the "inferior function." Because it is the most unconscious, the figures in dreams may be flavored by this inferior function in its ill-adapted form. A thinking type, for example, may find himself dreaming of hysterical women, or of highly charged emotional situations. A feeling type may dream of opinionated intellectuals. The inferior function is usually lived out symbolically rather than concretely, because it is so opposed to the superior function—the person's habitual pattern of adaptation.

Two other functions remain. One is called the "auxiliary function," because it achieves sufficient development to become an alternative to the superior function as well as an enrichment of it. The last function is unnamed. It can be developed by hard work and integrated to some degree in a person's conscious adaptation to reality.

Because any of the four functions may become a person's superior function, Jung formulated a theory of four personality types—the thinking, feeling, sensation, and intuitive types. These are also correlated to the attitudes of extroversion and introversion. Hence, there are eight possible variations among the psychological types, the extroverted-feeling type, the introverted-feeling type, the extroverted-thinking type, the introverted-thinking type, etc. For purposes of brevity, it is best to outline only the four main types.[84]

The thinking type finds his habitual adaptation to reality oriented by the thinking function. His first response to events is to perceive logical interconnections or the lack of them, and to formulate what he perceives in the form of orderly concepts and generalizations. If fully identified with the thinking function, his thinking will tend to be rigid and dry, and experiences which do not conform to his formulas will be dismissed as frivolous. His inferior function is feeling, which, if totally undeveloped, will express itself in primitive or even negative forms—in inadequate relationships, in sentimentalism, tactlessness, gauche behavior, and in the repression of nonrational interests such as art or religion.

For the feeling type, the habitual adaptation to reality is oriented by the feeling function. His first response is to determine the personal value of what he perceives, whether he likes it or dislikes it, accepts it or rejects it, and to order events according to his subjective response. For the feeling type, thinking is the inferior function. In extreme form, the feeling type is totally immersed in personal reactions—incapable of detailed perceptions, blown from one reaction to another, astounding in his contradictoriness. His thinking will be primitive, often negatively expressed, erupting in dogmatic judgments of a "nothing but" character or an exaggerated concern over others' opinions.

84. For a description of the eight variants, see Jung, *Psychological Types*, pp. 428–68, 480–518.

The sensation type is oriented in its habitual adaptation to reality by the sensation function. His strength is in his realism, his reliable relationship to concrete reality. He responds to what he sees without unnecessary complications or subtleties. Such a person is matter-of-fact and down-to-earth but also capable of great sensual enjoyments and aesthetic appreciation. People of this type may also be absorbed in subjective sense impressions to the point of detachment from objects. Their weakness is their lack of lightness and imagination. They may seem heavy and dull. Intuition is their inferior function, which they often depreciate as mere whimsy, and which is most often expressed in negative forms, such as forebodings, suspicions, and compulsive neuroses.

The intuitive type is oriented in his habitual adaptation to reality by intuition. He has a keen feeling for new possibilities, unseen connections, and unsuspected developments. He is filled with images, ideas, insights. If he is of an introverted bias, concrete reality for him is the inner psychic world of archetypes. If he has a bias to the extroverted attitude, he may have something like extrasensory perception. The weakness of this type is his difficulty in seeing anything through, for he is always attracted to the new and feels bored, impatient, and caged by the familiar and old. He lives intensely but often without fulfillment; he is vital but also irresponsible because commitment feels like entrapment to him. His inferior function is sensation, which will make itself felt by its absence. The intuitive type fails to take facts into account and will consequently misjudge situations, or be unable to arrange things satisfactorily where they concern money, career requirements, and the like. He may even fear external facts and withdraw from any dealings with them. The repressed sensation function may take its revenge in the form of hypochondriacal symptoms and bodily sensations. Impulsiveness and dependence on the immediate impression of objects will typify his actions and may result in a compulsion neurosis.

The theory of psychological types concludes this presentation of Jung's analytical psychology. The presentation has been made in detail in an attempt to offer a clear, concise, and systematic examination of Jung's thought in a brief conspectus.

Jung's theory of the psyche grew out of his treatment of patients. Behind every theory here presented is the living experience of therapist and patient. In closing this section it is important to note again the originality of Jung's approach to the psyche of his patients. His vocabulary, his concepts, and his method of treating the psyche are all based on what he thought was its own objective nature. He saw the psyche as objectively "there" as a precondition of consciousness, as operating autonomously, and as speaking its own symbolic language. Because a theory of the psyche structures our knowledge of it by giving us a way to talk about our encounters with the unconscious, we may conclude that the person guided by Jung's theory will have a different experience of the psyche than will persons who subscribe to other theories. What will stand out about that experience is a recognition that psychic wholeness is not simply a goal we choose but is a demand issued to us from the psyche itself. The symbolical style in which that demand is presented to us, and our feeling of being summoned to strive for wholeness, as if in that pursuit we would participate in a dimension of meaning beyond the simply personal aspects of our life, associate psychological development with religious growth. This leads us to our next section.

PART II
Religion and the Psyche

[The soul] has the dignity of a creature
endowed with, and conscious of, a
relationship to Deity. The soul must
contain in itself the faculty of
relation to God.

C. G. Jung

The Religious
Function of the Psyche

J UNG WAS THE FIRST among the pioneers of depth psychology to point out that the psyche has a religious function. He based this conclusion on clinical data and on his understanding of the nature and structure of the psyche.

As we have seen, the psyche, Jung thinks, is structured in polarities. In order for the psyche to achieve wholeness, the ego must recognize and reconcile these polarities. The process of reconciliation occurs through conscious participation in symbols which emerge from the unconscious and bring together the two opposing poles in a third form. This new symbol, by performing the work of reconciliation, puts consciousness in deeper touch with the rest of the psyche, thus, in turn, enriching a person in his relationships with other persons and making him feel more fully in touch with life.

The experience of reconciliation carries with it a sense of being guided by and related to the source and power of being. It is this kind of experience that is felt as religious. This native capacity of the psyche to produce symbols that have this reconciling effect and stirring presence is what Jung calls the religious function.

The symbols of the masculine-feminine sexual polarity are central to the process of individuation because they represent the opposition of all the polarities of the psyche and their mutual attraction as well. The symbols of the union of masculine and feminine stand for the sense of new being and wholeness that is felt when the tension of opposites is resolved. We must recognize, therefore, the significance of the sexual polarity for the religious life. We cannot recognize that significance, however, without taking into account the feminine, which has been the neglected pole of sexual polarity. Historically, women have had second-class citizenship; they have had to fight for suffrage; they have been given little chance to participate in the world through equal employment opportunities. In psychoanalytic literature, women have too often been dealt with as inadequate males, and almost exclusively from the point of view of masculine psychology. The result has been to translate sexual differences as inferiorities. Jung initiates a completely new approach to the female. He sees the feminine as a category of being with its own unique values and strengths. The feminine represents one half of the central psychic polarity of masculine-feminine, which symbolizes all the other psychic polarities in both sexes. We must, therefore, recognize the feminine if we do not want to lose access to half of all those psychic polarities we must have if we are to become whole persons. Since the drive to produce symbols that reconcile opposites is the essence of the religious function, and since the fundamental human polarity is sexual, the connection between the religious function and the feminine is of the closest kind.

DEFINITION

EARLY IN HIS CAREER, Jung recognized the irreducible nature of the psyche's religious function. He rejected Freud's view that religion is only the result of repressed sexuality: "Can anyone show us those 'normal' peoples or races who are free from such silly repressions? But if no one can . . . then I really do not see how one can justify the argument that religious phenomena are not genuine and are merely repressions of sex." [1] In later works, Jung puts it more bluntly: "*I* did not attribute a religious function to the soul, I merely produced the facts which prove the soul is *naturaliter religiosa,* i.e., possesses a religious function." [2]

The "facts" which Jung produced came from clinical materials and their correspondence to dogmas, creeds, and religious symbols. The facts may be classified in three categories. The first is an examination of neurosis itself; Jung observes that a component of most illnesses, especially in patients over thirty-five, is the loss of religious meaning: "A psychoneurosis must be understood as the suffering of a human being who has not discovered what life means for him." [3] The second fact is the appearance of dream images which arouse and compel a reverent, fearsome, and awed attitude in the dreamer and make him feel vitally in touch with transpersonal meaning. These dream motifs often correspond to aspects of religious creeds and traditions. The third fact is the process of individuation (evident to a greater or lesser extent in all analyses) which indicates that a goal of wholeness is integral to the psyche.[4] Inherent in the drive to wholeness is the production of symbols that fulfill and reconcile opposing polarities of the psyche that are the source of the psyche's energy. These symbols depict images of God (or images to which

1. Jung, "Analytical Psychology and Education," *The Development of the Personality (CW,* XVII, 1954), p. 83. See also Jung, *Two Essays on Analytical Psychology (CW,* VII, 1953), p. 71.
2. Jung, *Psychology and Alchemy (CW,* XII, 1967), p. 13.
3. Jung, *Modern Man in Search of a Soul,* trans. W. S. Dell and C. F. Baynes (New York: Harcourt, Brace & Co., 1933), p. 225.
4. See Jung, *Psychology and Alchemy,* pp. 4–5; and Jung, "Conscious, Unconscious, and Individuation," and "A Study in the Process of Individuation," *The Archetypes and the Collective Unconscious (CW,* IX, Part I, 1959), pp. 275–76, 348–49.

the psyche relates as to a god) and unify and center the psyche.

Therefore, the religious function of the psyche, according to Jung, can be described as a drive for clear relation of the personal self to the transpersonal source of the meaning and power of being. If this drive does not find adequate expression, it produces neurosis as surely as does the repression of the sexual or self-preservative instincts. The description of this drive is close to the language that expresses the theological view that man is created in the image of God. Jung seems to agree with this view when he writes that the soul ". . . has the dignity of an entity endowed with, and conscious of, a relationship to Deity." [5]

In Jung's view, the religious function expresses itself in distinct ways. One way is through a direct personal experience of the numinous, unmediated by dogma or creed. The numinous imposes itself on the individual and in no way can it be contrived or produced. The form of imposition is often a dream, a drawing one makes, a vision, or a stark event; in short, one feels its impact through images and affects rather than concepts. Experience of the numinous is for Jung the essential element in religion, and it is to be distinguished from creedal belief. Jung defines religion as:

> a careful and scrupulous observation of . . . the *numinosum*, that is, a dynamic agency or effect not caused by an arbitrary act of will . . . it seizes and controls the human subject, who is always rather its victim than its creator. The *numinosum*—whatever its cause may be—is an experience of the subject independent of his will.[6]

Experience of the numinous is nonrational, without logical coherence or apparent meaning. Nonetheless, the individual feels that in the mysterious symbolism he is drawing near to some meaning greater than himself which, if yielded to, will grant peace of mind despite the initially terrifying or over-

---

5. Jung, *Psychology and Alchemy*, p. 10.
6. Jung, "Psychology and Religion," *Psychology and Religion: West and East* (CW, XI, 1958), p. 7.

whelming character of the image. The numinous image exerts an irresistible power of attraction and sense of mystery on the individual. In an astonishing way it can express a synthesis of all the dreamer's conflicting tendencies and bring about a period of psychic equilibrium. Jung writes: "No matter what the world thinks about religious experience, the one who has it possesses a great treasure, a thing that has become for him a source of life, meaning and beauty, and that has given a new splendour to the world and to mankind." [7]

Jung concerns himself exclusively, so he protests, with the empirical description of the psychological aspect of such an experience. The origin and nature of the numinous symbols outside the realm of the psyche are the concern of the theologian, not of the psychologist. Jung observes that the experience of the activated archetypes in the individuation process is similar to what Rudolf Otto describes as the experience of "the holy," an experience which produces a sense of dependence, energy, majesty, mystery, and fascination, and which changes men's lives for the better. These effects of the experience of the numinous testify to its truth not by logical formulation but by lived confirmation:

> Where is the criterion by which you could say that . . . such an experience is not valid. . . . Is there . . . any better truth about the ultimate things than the one that helps you to live? This is the reason why I take careful account—"religio!"—of the symbols produced by the unconscious. They are the one thing that is capable of convincing the critical mind of modern man . . . for a very old-fashioned reason: They are *overwhelming*, which is precisely what the Latin word *convincere* means. . . . And if such an experience helps to make your life healthier, more beautiful, more complete and more satisfactory to yourself and to those who love you, you may safely say: "This was the grace of God." [8]

7. *Ibid.*, p. 105.
8. *Ibid.*

The religious function also expresses itself in the attitudes of careful consideration and trust that develop as a result of an experience of the numinous. Religion itself is described psychologically by Jung in terms of these attitudes.

> Religion appears to me to be a peculiar attitude of the human mind which could be formulated in accordance with the original use of the term *religio*, which means a careful consideration and observation of certain dynamic factors that are conceived as "powers": spirits, daemons, gods, laws, ideas, ideals, or whatever name man has given to such factors in his world as he has found powerful, dangerous, or helpful enough to be taken into careful consideration, or grand, beautiful and meaningful enough to be devoutly worshipped and loved.[9]

The religious function expresses itself in translating the original numinous experience into dogmas and creeds. Creeds are different, for Jung, from religion. Creeds are built up over the centuries as a part of organized religions and give expression to a definite collective belief in ritualized form. Creeds are essentially related to religion, however, in that "every creed is originally based on the one hand upon the experience of the *numinosum* and on the other hand upon πίστις, that is to say, trust or loyalty, faith and confidence in a certain experience of numinous nature and in the change of consciousness that ensues."[10] The symbols of dogma express an intensely lived psychic reality for its formulators and adherents and thus provide a valid form of religious experience within a stable framework. In addition, dogma protects its adherents from a direct, unritualized experience of God, an experience which can be terrifying. Hence, creedal symbols channel the dynamic psychic forces which must be "carefully considered" and substitute themselves for the unmediated confrontation with those psychic forces. If we grasp this, then we can understand the power of dogma as

9. *Ibid.*, p. 8. See also Jung, "Psychology of the Transference," *The Practice of Psychotherapy* (CW, XIV, 1954), p. 195.
10. Jung, "Psychology and Religion," p. 8.

well as respect its value and necessity; it is also clearer why dogma can die. The symbols lose their meaning in proportion to their decreasing ability to quicken awareness of the original numinous experience out of which they arose and to carry the projection of that experience. Symbols that convey peace to generations of believers can slowly lose their content until, sometimes centuries later, people suddenly discover they are meaningless.

PHILOSOPHICAL CONTEXT

JUNG'S DESCRIPTION of the psyche's religious function is best understood, in my opinion, in the context of a development in the history of Western thought that focuses on the shaping power of symbols in human life. In the seventeenth century, with Descartes, philosophy took a decisive turn away from asking questions about what we know to asking questions about the processes by which we know. Epistemology thus replaced metaphysics as philosophy's main work. In the eighteenth century, Hume concluded that there is no certain basis of knowledge but only bombardments of sense data and the fictions of "causality," "continuity," "substantiality," and "self" which the mind creates to fill in the gaps between the sense data. Kant's investigations, in the same period, continued to focus on how we know more than on what we know, but he rescued the knowing process from extreme empiricism with his formulation of the unalterable categories of reason. These forms of the knowing process combine with sense data to yield knowledge. Hence, for Kant, "causality," "substance," "time and space" are categories through which the knowing subject perceives and constructs reality. These are the forms which structure the raw sense data and to which the data must conform if they are to be "experienced" at all.

Kant focuses on the interaction between the knowing subject and the known object. The focus is on the forms of apperception through which the subject experiences the world and which, by implication, structure the world. The mind cannot know sense data directly, but only as they are arranged in spatio-temporal, causal terms. Kant puts this strongly by saying that we never know reality as such (*das Ding an Sich*); we know only our perception of it through the categories of reason.

The significance of Kant's new focus on the interaction between subject and object is that a new concept of reality is implied. Reality is no longer seen as something objectively and unequivocally given "out there," to which the subject must connect and adjust, nor is reality seen as a given reasoning process "in here," which is reflected in the objective world. Instead, reality is seen by Kant as a product of the interpenetration of subject and object. It is not given (either as outer facts or inner reason) but is created, constructed, and made perceptible through the interpenetration of subject and object. Reality emerges.

Ernst Cassirer carries Kant's emphasis on the thought forms further by examining prelogical conception and expression out of which develop reason and factual knowledge. The mythical-symbolical mode is the primary form of experience. From it are won the empirical and rational viewpoints. Mental processes fail to grasp reality itself, and in order to represent reality at all the mind must use symbols that are always mediators or interposers and thus obscure as well as reveal. Symbolic forms, such as art, religion, myth, language, or science, gradually evolve and express the interpenetration of subject and object. Moreover, these symbolic forms are themselves forces which produce and posit a world and make it accessible to man. These symbolic forms are not, therefore, mere imitations or mental copies of reality but are "organs of reality," because it is solely by their agency that anything real becomes an object for intellectual apprehension. Man's experience of reality is gradually built up through the emergence of different symbolic forms (art, science, religion, etc.), which make reality accessible to him.

It is irrelevant to ask what reality is apart from these forms because every form of existence has its source in some peculiar way of seeing, some intuition and intellectual formulation of meaning.

This point of view avoids the subject-object dualism and the endless variations of the arguments of the idealism-realism debates. When religion, language, myth, art, and science are seen as ideational forms, the basic philosophical question is no longer their relation to an absolute reality which forms their substantial substratum. The central problem now is their mutual limitation and supplementation. They all function organically together in the construction of spiritual reality, yet each organ has its individual assignment.[11]

After Kant, one can no longer appeal to an absolute given reality as the standard of reference for the truth or falsity of one's judgments. Jung recognizes this when he says that we can only investigate the psychological processes of religious experience and our projections on to God, never the objective reality of God himself. We know only these images and projections, never the *Ding an Sich* of God. Jung rejects the old criterion of truth correspondences—that a statement or a percept is true if it matches an external fact. He disclaims knowing the external objective fact to which the archetype of God corresponds, for example. As an empiricist, Jung thinks he can only show that dogmatic images correspond to psychic facts, that is, that they are images that have certain functions in the psyche. But what these functions, in turn, refer to, he cannot say. The psychic images (or archetypes) contribute to the emergence and shaping of what comes to be called "reality."

After Cassirer, however, things change in philosophical thought. Today, we cannot escape metaphysical questions by saying that we know not reality "in itself," but only how we perceive it, because, as Cassirer himself points out, our perceptions are part of what emerges as objective reality. The

11. Ernst Cassirer, *Language and Myth*, trans. Susanne K. Langer (New York: Harpers, 1946), pp. 8–9.

dualism Jung sees between psychic processes and "reality itself" is not easily acceptable to a mind trained in later twentieth-century thought. Such a mind must challenge Jung's implicit positivism and must insist that the psychological mode is itself a symbolic form and an "organ of reality" which shapes reality.

When one focuses on the shaping power of symbols, a picture of man emerges as primarily *homo symbolicus* rather than *homo rationalis*. Kant focused not on the content but on the forms of apperception. Cassirer focused on the mythical and prelogical dimension out of which emerge the symbolic forms that posit a world. Jung researches the structure, dynamics, and effect of these symbolic forms in the psychic dimension, through the archetypes and the religious function. Like Cassirer, Jung asserts that mental processes fail to grasp reality itself and thus are driven to use symbols, however obscure, to reveal what "emerges" as reality as the result of the interpenetration of the subject and the object. This is illustrated in the interpenetration of the personal and objective dimensions of the psyche and in the necessity for both personal associations and archetypal themes in dream or fantasy interpretation. Jung carries further Cassirer's view that man's use of symbols is not an alternative to reason but is the very basis of reasoning. The necessity which man feels to produce symbols is the psychological basis of the religious function. In producing images of God, the psyche tries to express its subjective relation to the source of life and to meaning itself. The symbols that reconcile psychic polarities build up an inner psychic unity that interpenetrates with the unity posited and perceived in God.

The importance of symbols and the religious function for the nature of one's world suggests that theology, too, is a symbolic form of perception.[12] Statements about God, then,

---

12. Jung criticizes the theologians' failure to deal with symbols in his words to Upton Sinclair: "It is tragic that science and its philosophy discourage the individual and that theology resists every reasonable attempt at an understanding of its symbols. They call their creed 'sym-

must be understood as formative modes of reality by whose agency God becomes an object for apprehension. Hence, theology is like an art form; it often consists of picture-making and myth-creating. In criticizing theologies one must consider the images used in terms of their ability to organize experience and, indeed, make it possible.

Because an image speaks to the whole person—his mind, heart, senses, experience, and imagination—it engages him more fully than does a mental concept. Hence, implicit in the symbolic mode is a relational aspect: we are touched and we respond. We are in-the-midst, not abstracted; this anchors our, by now, almost autonomous conceptualizing faculties in a total human response. Theology is thereby spared its usual reception as a theoretical system addressed only to the intellectually adept and becomes, like psychology, a world of total human experience, accessible to all sorts of human beings.

---

bolism' but they refuse to call their 'truth' symbolic, yet if it is any-thing, it is . . . symbolism and therefore capable of reinterpretation" ("Letter to Upton Sinclair," *New Republic,* February 21, 1955, p. 20).

CHAPTER FIVE

The Symbol
and Theology

B ECAUSE SYMBOLS are so central to the religious function, it is profitable to look at Jung's view of the symbol more closely as a preface to an examination of Jung's view of the relation of psychology to theology. It is also useful to note that Paul Tillich's views of the symbol are remarkably similar to Jung's.

JUNG AND TILLICH

BOTH MEN ASSERT that symbols are figurative constellations which point beyond themselves to objective reality.[1] The reality is called "ultimate" by Tillich and "psychic" by Jung.

1. See Paul Tillich, "The Religious Symbol," *Daedalus* (Middletown, Conn.: Wesleyan University Press, 1958), vol. LXVIII, no. III, *passim*. See also Jung, *Symbols of Transformation* (*CW*, V, 1956), pp. 77–78, 231.

Both men agree that the symbol makes perceptible that which is hitherto unknown and opens within man corresponding depths of response. Both men think that the symbol is invested with the innate power of that which it represents and is a live and effective symbol only insofar as it bears this power to people. If the symbol fails to reveal the power to the beholder, then it is dead. Both men agree that the symbol cannot be produced at will but instead is spontaneously generated in an encounter with reality itself. For Jung, symbols are "spontaneous products of unconscious psychic activity." [2] Both men agree that the symbol, in contrast to the sign, is essentially, not arbitrarily, related to that which it represents. Tillich speaks of this essential relation as the symbol's participation in the reality to which it points. The symbol cannot be replaced or exchanged at will; it is intrinsically related to that which it represents. Jung speaks of this essential relation of the symbol to the reality it represents by saying: "the symbol always presupposes that the chosen expression is the best possible description, or formula, of a relatively unknown fact; . . . which cannot conceivably, therefore, be more clearly or characteristically represented. . . ." [3] Finally, both men emphasize the mediating function of the symbol: it makes us aware of the reality to which it points. Symbols have a revelatory character.

Jung, more than Tillich, strongly emphasizes the defending function of the symbol: it protects us from the terror of immediate encounter with reality.[4] Jung, more than Tillich, investigates the psychic function of the symbol as a releaser and transformer of energy. The symbol frees libido that is blocked on one level and redirects it along new channels and

2. Jung, "The Soul and Death," *The Structure and Dynamics of the Psyche* (*CW*, VIII, 1960), p. 409.
3. Jung, *Psychological Types*, trans. H. Godwin Baynes (London: Kegan Paul, Trench, Trübner & Co., 1946), p. 601. See also Jung, "On the Relation of Analytical Psychology to Poetry," *The Spirit in Man, Art, and Literature* (*CW*, XV, 1966), p. 70.
4. See Jung, "Brother Klaus," *Psychology and Religion: West and East* (*CW*, XI, 1958), pp. 318–19.

on to a higher level. For example, the symbol "Mother Church" can release energy bound up in infantile mother fixation and channel it to a religious level. Jung says, "With the birth of the symbol, the regression of the libido into the unconscious ceases. Regression changes into progression, blockage gives way to flowing, and the pull of the primordial abyss is broken." [5]

This is a more daring conception of the symbol's function, I think, than is Freud's concept of sublimation. In the theory of sublimation, psychic energy is redirected, but the nature of the basic drive does not change and can always, therefore, revert to its original infantile form. For Jung, however, the symbol effects a change in the drive itself and acts as a bridge from the old to the new and transformed state of the drive. Jung thinks that symbols can effect this change because they are an intrinsic part of the energy drive. As I have tried to show in Part I, archetypes are the symbolic representations of the instincts. Therefore, if the symbols change, the energy changes too, and conversely, if the drive changes, so will its symbolic expression. In the concept of sublimation, on the other hand, symbols are merely the package in which the drives present, conceal, or disguise themselves. For Freud, symbols are not essentially related to the drives as, I believe, they are in reality, and as Jung so clearly demonstrates.

For Jung, then, the symbol has a healing function. It unifies the psyche by providing a bridge from less adapted to more adapted functioning and by reconciling the various psychic polarities. A dream symbol sometimes initiates such a redirection of energy. Let us consider, for example, the dream of a young man who was caught in unsatisfactory relations with women because of compulsive anima projections behind which stood an unresolved dependence on his mother: "C has died. I am standing before her grave gazing at her statue which is like the Virgin Mary." At the time of

5. Jung, *Psychological Types*, p. 325.

the dream, the dreamer was still completely involved with the woman (C) and had only a dim awareness that he was again caught in the same old pattern of relationship. In the dream, however, the woman is no longer alive but already dead. Instead of worshipping her, the dreamer stands beneath her statue, which is like that of the Virgin Mary. The symbol of the statue reveals the dreamer's anima content, which he may then begin to deal with much more directly. The dreamer had some negative associations to the Virgin Mary. In exploring those, he gradually became aware of the negative element in his feelings and in his actions toward the women of his many relationships. Through the dream symbol of the statue, the libido that was projected onto successive women was now made available, in a new form, to the dreamer's own consciousness.

A symbol's meaning is opaque and complex because it includes elements known in the past, but repressed, and elements that have not yet come to consciousness. The symbol expresses, therefore, a unity of the conscious and the unconscious, of the known and the unknown, of the rational and the nonrational, of past and future. The meaning is grasped if the conscious, known, rational, past elements are perceived in their essential correlation with the as yet unrealized and hence unknown unconscious elements. The symbol then makes use of an earlier orientation to carry development to a higher stage. Without this correlation, the psyche is stuck in reiterations of the known ("the same old problem," often called "resistance"), or in vagaries or theorizings about the unknown. For a symbol to mediate the unity to which it points, and thus to remedy the neurotic's lack of psychic equilibrium, the unknown must be incarnate in the known and touch the person through his most familiar experience. This is the way the known reveals new dimensions and becomes transformed.

Dream symbols must be interpreted synthetically on the subjective level, as well as analytically on the objective level, if the energy which they embody is to be put at the dreamer's disposal. Interpretation that equates dream images with real objects is objective interpretation and analytic, too, for it "breaks down the dream content into memory-complexes that refer to external situations." [6] Interpretation that refers dream images back to the dreamer himself is interpretation on the subjective level; it is synthetic "because it detaches the underlying memory-complexes from their external causes, regards them as tendencies or components of the subject, reunites them with that subject." [7] The dream refers to both subject and object and therefore unites both aspects of the person.

The following dream illustrates this unifying and healing function of symbols: "I was at my college dorm. Y had returned from the hospital, after having had a serious breakdown, and L was with me. We entered a large eight-sided room that faced the sea. The top half of the room was black; the bottom half white. Sitting around the room were girls in harem costumes and men in Spanish dancers' costumes who were smoking. There were huge black dogs, that looked like Great Danes. L said to me, 'This is good; it brings out your animal beauty. You are less willful and less volitional.' " The dreamer said that on waking she felt deeply rested, even blessed by her dream experience. She had felt tormented by two things: Y's attitude of "bear-trap intelligence" that analyzed everything to pieces and stressed will power as the way to change, and upsurges of sexual attraction to men she barely knew, moods of willfulness that her reasoning could not subdue.

Compulsive reasoning (Y) has broken down and been restored in this unifying octagonal room that faces the unconscious (the sea). Reasoning and disciplining powers have not been discarded, as the college setting suggests, but simply put in a new context in which the darkness often associated with the unconscious and the feminine is stressed, as shown

6. Jung, *Two Essays on Analytical Psychology* (CW, VII, 1953), p. 84.
   7. *Ibid.*

by the decoration of the room in which black predominates. Harem costumes accent the sensual in the dream. L is the dreamer's lover by whom she felt accepted just as she was, not for anything she had accomplished. He affirms the unity of two conflicting tendencies in her: her rationality and will power on the one hand and her nonrational instinct on the other hand. These unite in a setting which brings out her animal beauty and her basic feminine qualities.

Allusion is made to what the Jungian analyst sees as possibly the mythological figure of Hecate through the presence of the giant dogs, her messengers. The figure thus conjured is the three-formed goddess of Luna or Selene in the heavens, of Artemis or Diana, the chaste huntress on earth, and Hecate the goddess of the dark of the moon, of earth and of the underworld.[8] In contrast to the masculine figures of the Christian Trinity from which emanate order, light, and goodness, this feminine trinity represents the ambiguity of good and evil, the crossroads of beauty, chasteness, hunting, revenge, the deeds of darkness and of evil magic. The Jungian analyst amplifies a passing figure in a dream in this way because his experience has taught him that passing figures in the dream worlds of his patients really do refer to archetypes whose imagery abounds in mythological materials.

The allusion to Hecate and the ascendance of the dark powers over the light, of black over white, hints at a larger meaning. Sensuality—harem, lover, animal beauty—and disciplined reason (Y, college) are reconciled under the ascendancy of a feminine deity. She encompasses reason and instinct instead of segregating them (as does the masculine Christian Trinity). Instead of clarity, the feminine deity represents brooding darkness which holds both good and evil. Instead of decisive either-or action, she stands at the crossways of a "both-and" inclusiveness. Instead of "mere sex" or "mere intellectualizing," body and mind are raised to a higher power.

8. Edith Hamilton, *Mythology* (New York: New American Library, 1942), p. 32.

An attitude of devotion is suggested in the dream by symbolic reference to a feminine deity and by the dreamer's feeling of having received a blessing.

Within the context of devotion, the dreamer finds a way between her twin dangers of rigidity and impulsiveness. The dreamer's conflict between personal relationship with L and impersonal sensuality (urges for sex with men to whom she was unrelated) also finds a different context which is hinted at in the allusion to a deity, Artemis, who is one form of the three-sided goddess. Artemis' loyalty is not to man; her sensuality is impersonal in the sense that it does not unite her in a personal relationship. She is chaste, true to her own law of being and not subjugated to another. The dream hints that the solution of the dreamer's sexual conflict is to be found not in repression or sublimation but in directing the dreamer's sexual energy along new channels. The dream symbols correlate known conflicts with as yet unknown and unrealized possibilities. The impersonal sensuality (harem girls and men) is now to be seen as part of a devotional attitude to the deity (within the octagonal, black-dominated room); there, it does not conflict with her personal relation to L, and in this setting he affirms the rightness of this approach for the dreamer because the setting evokes her essential beauty. The dream suggests that sexuality has two aspects: a nonpersonal aspect, connecting the dreamer with her basic instinctuality and femininity, and a personal aspect, connecting her with another person. Both are good. Complementing the dreamer's conscious Christianity which, she thinks, emphasizes that sex is good only under the aegis of personal relationship ("commitment") is the dream's symbolic reference to the feminine deity of mythology, which suggests that connection with the dreamer's own instinctuality and essential femininity is part of her proper response to the transpersonal dimension.

The very richness of the symbol's meaning contributes to its lack of clarity. Because it includes unconscious aspects that look only to future realization, it cannot be exhausted by conscious analysis. The only suitable attitude toward a symbol, therefore, is one of receptive waiting, where one allows oneself both to be penetrated by a symbol's meaning and drawn by its power of attraction. Tillich enjoins: "Wait in quiet tension of openness to what can only be received." [9] This attitude of receptive waiting has often been called a feminine attitude. On the other hand, consciousness can adopt an attitude toward symbols in which it either comprehends and assimilates them, so that they become part of one and are no longer alive as symbols, or is unable to comprehend the symbols at all. In the latter case, the symbols are set against consciousness and cause dissociation, such as autonomous hallucinations, in the psyche.[10]

Jung and Tillich agree that there is a serious impoverishment of symbolism in present-day Protestantism because of its radical iconoclastic spirit, a spirit that rejects all symbols but those of God's transcendence, and because of a general emphasis on an objective world view to the exclusion of attention to anything subjective.[11] This impoverishment has serious consequences. In Jung's opinion, the modern Protestant is dangerously vulnerable to the ravaging effects of an immediate experience of reality. He is without the mediating power of traditional symbols and the protective, intercessory role of such symbolic figures as the Virgin Mary, the saints, the angels, etc. Tillich points out that for many people Protestantism has become a husk of intellectual forms and moralistic precepts, without an informing core, because religious symbols are taken too literally. The symbols no longer convey the richness and vitality of a living religion which is expressive of man's relation to ultimate reality.

Both Tillich and Jung seek a revitalized spiritual life

9. Paul Tillich, "Hope" (Sermon delivered at Union Theological Seminary, New York, April 4, 1965).

10. See Raymond Hostie, S. J., *Religion and the Psychology of Jung*, trans. G. R. Lamb (New York: Sheed & Ward, 1957), p. 68.

11. See Jung, *Modern Man in Search of a Soul*, trans. W. S. Dell and C. F. Baynes (New York: Harcourt, Brace & Co., 1933), p. 232; and "Psychology and Religion," *Psychology and Religion: West and East*, p. 48. See Tillich, "Religious Symbol," pp. 17–19.

through return to and reinterpretation of symbols.[12] Symbols elicit a response and an involvement from depths within us which cannot be evoked by reason. Symbolic language is used to communicate psychic truth, which Jung insists exists just as much as does logical truth or empirical truth. The criterion for a logically "true" statement is its correspondence to the rules of logic. The criterion for an empirically "true" statement is its correct correspondence to an empirically demonstrable fact. The criterion for a psychically "true" statement is its correspondence to psychically demonstrable facts—to facts that recur and are experienced by many people. The recurrent motifs in different religions, or recurrent archetypal images, are just as "true" as the recurrent facts of physical nature. They are "there," and when we make statements about them, we feel confident that we are talking about something that is real.

Jung recommends that we look at dogma and traditional religious symbols from this standpoint of psychic truth. Jung does not believe that religious experience is "invented" and therefore untrue, or that God is "nothing but" a projection and therefore illusory. Religious experience happens; it is not contrived. Its facticity is based on assertions of the unconscious that state the inner reality of truth. The unconscious speaks of our actual experience of God—as guiding, as tormenting, as absent—rather than giving a statement about what God is in himself. The attempt made by any one person to define his concept of God is inevitably involved with projections of his own experience. Jung is not calling God a projection of man; he is saying that all our symbols and concepts of God are projections onto unfathomable mystery. Since we do not know this mystery in itself, the recurrent religious symbols are simply the best possible descriptions of something unknown or unknowable. Hence, rather than saying that God is nothing but a projection, Jung is reasserting

12. See Jung, *Symbols of Transformation*, pp. 226–27. See Paul Tillich, *Systematic Theology*, 3 vols. (Chicago: University of Chicago Press, 1951–63), I, 60–63.

the transcendent mystery of the deity. Luther and Tillich make the same point in the words, "As you believe him, so you have him." [13]

Tillich seeks revitalization of the spiritual life through reinterpretation of symbols and exposure of their literalistic distortion. Tillich's method is to set the symbols in their original context by tracing their etymological roots, and to free the symbols from their present distortion by offering "equivalent" conceptual formulations—for example, "transition from essence to existence" for "the Fall." By his insistence on the necessity of symbols, Tillich also reasserts the transcendent mystery of the deity; it cannot be known directly. Jung renews our participation in religious symbols by offering "equivalent" psychological formulations.

There are, then, three similarities between the views of Jung and Tillich on the symbol: their understanding of the nature of the symbol (although Jung investigates its psychic function more than Tillich); their agreement that Protestantism is at present dangerously impoverished of its symbolism; their agreement that revitalization of the spiritual life is to be found in the recovery and reinterpretation of symbols.

IMPLICATIONS FOR THEOLOGY

JUNG'S TREATMENT OF THE SYMBOL has, I think, important implications for Christian theology. The relation of symbols to archetypes is of decisive help in solving problems associated with Protestant relativism.[14] Tillich distinguishes between Catholic and Protestant views on the creation and

13. *Ibid.*, II, 77.
14. The Protestant is faced with the dilemma of how to hold on to a permanent element in his religion while also stressing the need to redefine symbols in terms of the contemporary world. The Catholic solves this problem by seeing everything contemporary, no matter how far removed from traditional symbols, as directly analogous to an unchanging religious reality. These issues are often discussed in terms of "the problem of relativism" and "the analogy of being."

transformation of symbols. For the Catholic, the symbols are produced in terms of the "analogy of being," which stresses the rational character of theological statements about ultimate reality: the symbols touch something that is true in itself whether or not they are subjectively received.[15] The analogy of being is, therefore, essentially static because its symbolic content is final—known once and for all—after its discovery. Changing human experience does not participate in the symbols' creation or transformation. The Protestant attitude is different; it is iconoclastic, existential, and dynamic. Symbols are born out of the revelatory experience of individuals and groups and die when they are no longer expressive of the power of the reality which they represent. Changing human experience participates in the creation and transformation of symbols. Protestantism thus recognizes the need for a genuine vitality in symbols but is threatened by a relativism and a lack of continuity and permanence in its symbolism. Tillich suggests that Jung's theory of archetypes points a way out of this dilemma.

In Jung's distinction between archetypes that are underlying and constant and symbols that are varied ways of expressing the archetypes, Tillich sees an implicitly ontological distinction. Tillich recognizes that Jung tries to refrain from making metaphysical statements but notes that, nonetheless, Jung does just that. By referring to the archetypes as primordial, Jung is saying that they belong to the early and eternal past. Jung also says that archetypes can be known not in themselves but only through the symbols which express them. Tillich understands these as ontological statements: the archetypes are potential whereas the symbols are actual; the archetypes are eternal and unchanging whereas the symbols are temporal and varied. The primordial archetypal forms "belong to the mystery of the creative ground of being of

15. See Paul Tillich, "Paul Tillich," *Carl Gustav Jung: A Memorial Meeting* (New York: The New York Association for Analytical Psychology and The Analytical Psychology Club, 1962), p. 29.

everything that is." [16] By understanding the changing symbols of Christianity as different expressions of continuous, unchanging elements of being, Protestants might resolve their dilemma. Although symbols are continuously transformed and thus retain their own vitality, they express those constant elements of being, the archetypes.

Jung's theory that symbols are produced by the unconscious state, the factual truth of our inner experience, that is, the way it actually is as contrasted to the way we might like it to be, is a strong counterargument to those who feel that traditional religious symbolism is empty or dead. His theory demands that we confess our spiritual poverty, that we recognize that we are the beggars, the poor in spirit, who seek the kingdom of heaven.[17] Such a confession would enable us to take seriously the symbols of emptiness and deadness that haunt our dreams and intrude upon our daily experience. By confessing our spiritual bankruptcy—our recognition that the traditional way to God has become inaccessible— we show our trust in the belief that such poverty is blessed with the experience of God: "Blessed are the poor in spirit, for theirs is the kingdom of heaven." Such trust means an openness to full experience of the present and a vital contact with God that generates its own appropriate symbols. Such openness is part of "being in Christ."

Jung's work with symbolism also challenges the Christian claim for the finality of revelation in Jesus Christ. While treating Christianity with the utmost seriousness, Jung does not accept its claim to be the final revelation and the only way to God. Although in psychological terms Christ offers one of the fullest disclosures of the self, and although Jung's psychology insists that Western man, rooted psychologically in Christian soil, must come to terms with this revelation, for

16. *Ibid.*, p. 32.
17. See Jung, *The Integration of the Personality*, trans. Stanley Dell (New York: Farrar & Rinehart, 1939), p. 63.

Jung Christ is still but one of many manifestations of the Spirit. Jung cautions against the destructive megalomania that can result from thinking "that Christianity is the only truth, and the white Christ the only Redeemer." [18] Jung thus relativizes Christianity, suggesting that it is one of several ways to truth. Jung does recognize, however, that it is not enough for an individual to find his own truth; he must also reconcile his "individual realization—or whatever one may choose to call the new insight or life-giving experience— with the collectively valid opinions and beliefs . . . [because] that which is *only* individual has an isolating effect, . . . He would still be neurotically unrelated and estranged from his social group." [19]

Tillich's interpretation of the finality of revelation in Jesus Christ seems to build a bridge between Jungian psychology and Christian theology. According to Tillich the revelation in Jesus Christ is not final quantitatively—there may be other revelations—but it is final qualitatively; all further revelations are implicit in the revelation in Jesus Christ.[20] Tillich's view encourages a wider interpretation of the Christ figure and successfully avoids both the narrowness of ancient readings and the disturbing relativism of our time, especially in its dealings with the doctrine of revelation. Tillich's view of the Christ figure answers Jung's criticism of that figure as failing to include the feminine element or the element of evil. In Tillich's view, Christ includes every possible element which might belong to such an all encompassing divine and human figure. Then one can say, perhaps, that such elements are not absent in Christ but rather in our interpretations of the Christ figure. Then we can ask ourselves, is our experience and interpretation of the Christ flexible enough to expand and include these elements, or do we need a totally new symbol?

18. Jung, *Modern Man in Search of a Soul*, p. 213.
19. Jung, "Foreword to White's *God and the Unconscious*," *Psychology and Religion: West and East*, p. 301.
20. See Tillich, *Systematic Theology*, II, 119–20.

THE FEMININE

A REBIRTH of vital religious symbolism, in my opinion, may result from recovery of the feminine element both in individual experience and in the religious symbols themselves. Because the feminine element is by and large de-emphasized in religious symbolism, the fullness of human experience is not represented. Many people criticize religion as irrelevant to life. They do not feel that religion speaks to all of experience. For them, religion has become dry and academic, too self-conscious and not enough fed by its roots in the unconscious. Church congregations do not feel the mysteries of their religion; they are not really grasped by them. There is too much intellect in their religious exercises and not enough ecstasy. The symbolism of Protestantism is predominantly masculine; the Trinity consists of Father, Son, and a masculine or asexual Holy Spirit. Tillich says that this traditional one-sided emphasis on the male element is one of the reasons for the success of the Counter Reformation, for the many conversions to Roman or Greek churches and to Oriental mysticism, and for the effeminate picture of Christ in pietistic Protestantism. Symptomatic of the effort of many to renew contact with the nonrational and affective dimensions of experience is the effort to reach the unconscious through drugs.

Tillich himself encourages an emphasis within Protestantism that could recover the feminine element. The concept of "Ground of Being," for example, symbolizes "the mother quality of giving birth, carrying, and embracing, and, at the same time, of calling back, resisting independence of the created, and swallowing it." [21] Recovering this feminine element would balance the overemphasis on God as the demanding Father that has so unbalanced the moral conscience and re-

---

21. *Ibid.*, III, 294.

ligious consciousness of so many Protestants. The self-sacri-
fice of Jesus the Christ does not exclusively belong to either
of the sexes, but includes both. The ecstatic experience of being grasped by the Holy Spirit includes and transcends both
the rational and emotional elements which have been attributed to the male and female sex respectively.

Jung's insistence that the anima is intrinsic to every man
(as is the corresponding animus to every woman) makes us
newly aware of the male-female dialectic within each of us.
Integration, or spiritual wholeness, is the incarnation and
expression of the self which includes and transcends the male-
female alternative. Thus Jung reminds us that we cannot attain to spiritual health by neglecting either one of these elements. This reminder reproaches moralistic Protestantism for
its suppression of the feminine element. Too often, consciousness ignores the feminine element so that the whole
dimension of experience that has to do with the ecstatic, nonrational, sexual, embracing, carrying, devouring, passionate,
sensitive, feeling qualities is either repressed or acted out. We
often see in Protestantism, for example, the rigid, judg-
mental attitudes that combat feeling and pleasure. We also
see eruptions of emotionalism in revivalist meetings, sudden
conversions, and lapses that are just as sudden. By pointing
to the potentials for growth that may be found in the energy
constellated as the anima, or in the woman whose animus is
well channeled, Jung tries to counteract the disparaging of
the feminine that has so afflicted Christianity, and to offer
new vistas to those of its religious persuasion.

CHAPTER SIX

Analytical Psychology and Religion

JUNG'S WRITINGS on the relation of analytical psychology to religion generally, and to Christianity specifically, have evoked controversial reactions. Some critics think Jung is trying to replace Christianity with his own form of psychology. Other critics think Jung replaces psychology with a gnostic type of religion. I think that Jung has developed a specific psychological tool that can have a useful function in relation to Christianity, but it is only a tool; it does not compete with or replace religion. Still it has a very valuable instrumentality to offer. In the following pages, I present an interpretation of Jung's thought which stresses its important implications for Christian theology, with particular emphasis on those elements in his thinking which indicate that the impoverishment of the interior life of contemporary Christians and the decreasing vitality of Christian symbolism result in large part from a loss of connection with the feminine mode of being.

Psychology's Function for Religion

ANALYTICAL PSYCHOLOGY, focusing on the symbolic aspects of our experience, can be a device to indicate the psychic equivalents of religious symbols. "Psychology," Jung writes, "is concerned with the act of seeing and not with the construction of new religious truths, when even the existing teachings have not yet been perceived and understood." [1] We do not yet perceive the meaning of religious symbols because ". . . far too many people are incapable of establishing a connection between the sacred figures and the psyche: . . . they cannot see to what extent the equivalent images are lying dormant in their own unconscious." [2] Analytical psychology can perform the useful function of reopening people's eyes to the psychic meaning of religious symbols. "To see," in this context, is to connect the religious symbol with its correspondent psychological experience of archetypal motifs and images.

To understand this view, we need to appreciate the context out of which it arose. Jung was a doctor who was concerned with what helped his patient. He observed that a recurrent theme in neurosis is the loss of a vital sense of life's meaning and that healing involves its rebirth. Jung has said of the patient that "he has to undergo an important change through the reintegration of hitherto split-off instinctivity, . . . the modern mind has forgotten those old truths that speak of the death of the old man and of the making of a new one, of spiritual rebirth and similar old-fashioned 'mystical absurdities.' " [3] Individual neuroses make explicit the problems embedded in modern culture and religious tradition. Modern man searches for his soul as well

1. Jung, *Psychology and Alchemy* (*CW*, XII, 1967), p. 13.
2. *Ibid.*
3. Jung, "Psychology and Religion," *Psychology and Religion: West and East* (*CW*, XI, 1958), p. 35.

as for his split-off instinctuality. Piecing together Jung's various descriptions of modern man's spiritual malaise, it is fair to say, I think, that Jung has seen him as suffering from too much reliance on reasoning and on the outer forms of religion, as well as from a loss of inner connection to the reality that religious symbols represent. Analytical psychology tries to correct all this.

Too much reliance on external forms in all areas of life gradually brings about a leanness of experience. Jung thinks that the psychic life of Western man presents an uninviting picture intellectually, aesthetically, and morally. Too much of our energy has gone into building the external world around us. No doubt that world is impressive, "But," writes Jung, "it is so imposing only because we have spent upon the outside all that is imposing in our natures—and what we find when we look within must necessarily be as it is, shabby and insufficient." [4]

Christianity, too, emphasizes the outer forms of religion too much and therefore fails to perform its important educative task: "So long as religion is only faith and outward form, and the religious function is not experienced in our own souls, nothing of any importance has happened. It has yet to be understood that the *mysterium magnum* is not only an actuality but is first and foremost rooted in the human psyche." [5]

The Christ figure, for example, has come to represent an ideal that is external to our own persons. Because symbolically Christ carries our sin, that too becomes something outside ourselves. As a result, our souls are left empty: "if the supreme value (Christ) and the supreme negation (sin) are outside, then the soul is void; its highest and lowest are missing." [6] We hardly feel capable of evil or of good. Impotence and moral laxity go together. The individual "is

4. Jung, *Modern Man in Search of a Soul*, trans. W. S. Dell and C. F. Baynes (New York: Harcourt, Brace & Co., 1933), p. 214.

5. Jung, *Psychology and Alchemy*, p. 12.

6. *Ibid.*, p. 8.

more of a fragment then ever, since superficial understanding conveniently enables him, quite literally, 'to cast his sins upon Christ' and thus to evade his deepest responsibilities—which is contrary to the spirit of Christianity." [7] But without the soul's participation, "religious life congeals into externals and formalities." [8]

Too great a reliance on the outer forms of religion occurs when symbols turn into mere signs. Rituals and images no longer bring spiritual reality to the soul, and the soul's aspirations are no longer enacted in the ceremonies or expressed in the symbols of religion. The libido withdraws, finding no adequate channel in these symbols, and no new channel within the psyche. But the unused libido continues to make its demands, comes pouring back, and "the waters rise, and inundating catastrophes burst upon mankind." [9] The catastrophes may be individual breakdowns, collective breakdowns (such as mob violence), or a widespread indefinable sense of malaise and senseless drifting.

Psychology deals with this spiritual problem in its attention to our inner world. Jung goes so far as to say that modern spiritual impoverishment has led to the "discovery" of psychology.[10] Psychology compensates for the exaggerated insistence upon outer forms of religion by stressing the necessity for inner realizations. In contrast to the blind acceptance of religious traditions, psychology stresses the need for personal experience of the contents of those traditions. Jung, however, is not recommending that we correct excessive reliance on outer forms by an exclusive reliance on inner worlds. Jung attends to the psychic world because that is the one that is neglected and, because of the neglect, it is the one that causes trouble. In our time the psychic world is to be found deep down within us. But this has not always

7. Ibid.
8. Ibid., p. 10.
9. Jung, The Integration of the Personality, trans. Stanley Dell (New York: Farrar & Rinehart, 1939), p. 71.
10. See Jung, Modern Man in Search of a Soul, p. 201.

been the case: "the psyche is not always and everywhere to be found on the inner side. It is to be found on the *outside* in whole races or periods of history . . ." [11]

Modern man's excessive use of reason reinforces his reliance on the outer forms of religion. Jung uses "reason" to stand for the process of reasoning according to logic and the positivistic standards of truth and falsity that developed from the eighteenth-century Enlightenment. Gone is the "reason" of Plato that embraced the passion of deeply felt experience and articulated presentiments of unseen mysteries. Instead, reason has become a method of analysis subservient to the aim of establishing what is "certainly true" according to syllogistic logic, and pertaining even then only to its own statements and not to the disclosure of any larger facets of reality. Reasoning can also be used to establish the "truth" of empirical statements by measuring their correspondence to observable facts. Reason measures and orders facts and matches statements to facts, according to prescribed and severely limiting rules.

Jung contrasts "rational," which describes the logical and causal relationship of items to each other, with "nonrational," which describes that which makes its presence felt by its factitiousness or direct evidence, unmediated by any logic or sentiment. Modern man, in Jung's view, too often equates rational with "rationalistic" and develops an excessive reliance on the reasoning process as the sole source of knowledge and as the fundamental criterion in the solution of all problems. In contrast, modern man equates "nonrational" with blind, uncomprehending acceptance, as in the case of "faith." Faith is given, or not given, and is exclusive of reason. Jung may himself contribute to this misunderstanding of the nature of faith by narrowly interpreting it as an acceptance of something on the authority of tradition rather than on the authority of personal experience, or as a gift of grace in which truth is accepted but not really understood.

11. *Ibid.,* p. 200.

Jung understands modern man to be caught between this narrow kind of reasoning and this narrow kind of faith. Either he has faith—blind acceptance of something without comprehension of it—or he has reason—understanding through the logical progressions, causal connections, and outer forms of things without direct experience of them.[12] A divorce ensues between head and heart; the former becomes excessively mental and rationalistic and the latter almost completely inaccessible. Consciousness is more and more cut off from its roots and becomes increasingly manipulative. It tries to deal with its uprootedness through a show of power or through a projection of its despair onto scapegoat enemies. Unconsciously, our unclaimed, untamed energy prowls restlessly like a beast, only to break out in sudden attacks of violence that reason "knows all about" but is powerless to prevent. This force was evident in the case of a young woman who had made two suicide attempts. She rationalized these as threats made by her to secure attention. Although she was conscious of the reason for her suicide attempts, her consciousness was in fact impotent—analysis showed she could not really choose to do otherwise.

If the reasoning process is directed to religious contents that have been accepted blindly "in faith," the effect can be

12. Jung's own use of "reason" and "faith" aggravates the split between them. It is closer to Jung's intentions, I think, to understand that he objects to the rationalistic use of the reasoning process rather than to reason itself. This understanding avoids the facile dismissal of Jung as anti-intellectual or as mystical. Jung's stress on knowledge in preference to faith has aroused the criticism that he is a gnostic. When we are clear that Jung objects to faith as a substitute for actual participation in the object of belief, that knowledge, for Jung, is the knowing which results from experience, and that such knowledge is always symbolic of and never identical with God, then it is clear that Jung is not a gnostic. Tillich's view of faith, as being grasped and transformed by a power that heals our brokenness, would be nearer, I think, to Jung's understanding of faith. See Jung, *Psychological Types*, trans. H. Godwin Baynes (London: Kegan Paul, Trench, Trübner & Co., 1946), p. 583; *Psychology and Alchemy*, p. 31; and Victor White, *God and the Unconscious* (Cleveland: World Publishing Co., 1961), p. 271.

devastating to the religious life. All religious assertions contain logical contradictions; this is the essence of religious assertion. The rhetoric of paradox is a good example. It is one of our most precious spiritual possessions because it alone ". . . comes anywhere near to comprehending the fulness of life. Non-ambiguity and non-contradiction are one-sided and thus unsuited to express the incomprehensible." [13] When the mind that relies too heavily on reasoning tries to make "the paradoxical nature of some tenet of faith the object of its lucubrations, as earnest as they are impotent, it is not long before such a one will break out into iconoclastic and scornful laughter, pointing to the manifest absurdity of the mystery." [14] The result is the loss of the rhetoric and emotional tone of paradox as a spiritual possession. It becomes first a stumbling block rather than a mode of disclosure, and finally, only a curious relic of the past. Examples might be the paradoxes of the Virgin Birth and of the Trinity. Like a vicious circle, the more we "reason" with the paradoxes contained in dogma, the more we fail to understand what they mean. The more external our understanding becomes, the more affronted we are by the irrational form of paradoxes. As a result, Christianity becomes inwardly impoverished, and we are left with a choice between "faith" or "reason," but without a vital religious life.

By its focus on the symbol, psychology, in Jung's view, helps to correct exaggerated reliance on the reasoning process. The conflict of reason and faith is based on a split between the rational and nonrational elements of the psyche. Psychic elements are rational insofar as they are logically and causally related; they are nonrational insofar as they make their presence felt simply by their direct givenness. Both kinds of elements are necessary to the psyche, and psychic wholeness depends on their reconciliation. The symbol unifies the rational and the nonrational and the conscious

---

13. Jung, *Psychology and Alchemy*, p. 15.
14. *Ibid.*, p. 16.

and the unconscious in man. The symbolic attitude stresses image-making, image-using, and the nonrational functions of sensation and intuition that disclose reality just as much as the rational functions of feeling and thinking do. Frequently, qualities of the nonrational, and the fear and irritation that these elements arouse, are projected onto women or associated with the feminine. Clichés show this: "Women are so illogical, so emotional!" "Women are intuitive; they are never rational." "One can never tell what's going to pop out of them."

Neglect of the feminine mode of being means, then, a loss of touch with nonrational elements of the psyche and therefore of those aspects of reality which these elements disclose. Because religion is so full of nonrational elements, our neglect of the feminine has had direct, destructive effects upon our religious life. To recover the value of the feminine means, also then, to bring back nonrational values.

If we accept this emphasis on the need for both the rational and nonrational, we may better understand some of the problems in Jung's style of communication. His writings abound in contradictions, ready generalizations, and unclear and unspecified transitions and exemplify what Avis Dry calls the *sic et non* quality, where mutually exclusive attributes are ascribed to the same entity.[15] An emotive tone pervades Jung's writing; it is often characterized by explosive value judgments and passionate imprecations against minds that must "understand" everything about a subject in order to conclude that it is "true." Jung's style is often directed to vivid imagery rather than to precise concepts. These stylistic problems do not make for clarity, but Jung is groping for a clarity beyond the cool precisions of logic, a clarity that will include the whole psyche, not just rational consciousness.

Too much reliance on the outer forms of religion and too

15. Avis Dry, *The Psychology of Jung* (London: Methuen & Co., 1961), p. 89.

much reasoning about its symbols go hand in hand with a loss of inner connection to the reality that religious symbols and dogma mediate: "In his soul the Christian has not kept pace with the external developments. Yes, everything is to be found outside—in image and in word, in Church and Bible —but never inside. Inside reign the archaic gods, supreme as of old; . . ." [16] As a result, "There is a religious sentimentality instead of the *numinosum* of divine experience. This is the well-known characteristic of a religion that has lost the luring mystery." [17] Jung sees that a religion of this kind is useless both morally and psychologically.

Loss of inner connection to the symbols of religion results when the psychic factor—the archetypal image—is projected onto, and thought to be identical with, the dogmas, rites, and images of religion that are external to the psyche. The archetypal image thus remains unconscious as a psychic factor, that is, the ego sees it not as part of the psyche but rather as belonging only to the outer forms of religion. All the libido connected with the archetypal image remains in its primitive form, because it flows outward and is neither related to directly nor influenced by the conscious mind.[18] Then, when the symbols no longer channel the libido, it comes flowing back into the psyche, still in its archaic form.

One of psychology's functions is to redirect the libido. The Jungian analyst encourages his patient to give attention to—i.e., invest libido in—the psychic meaning of religious symbols and to their correspondence with any symbols which may emerge from the patient's unconscious and compel his interest. Instead of allowing the patient to project outward both the archetypal images and the libido connected with them, seeing them exclusively as properties of entities quite outside the psyche, the analyst encourages the patient to see the archetypal images as part of the psyche and then to relate to them consciously. This may result in

16. Jung, *Psychology and Alchemy*, p. 12.
17. Jung, "Psychology and Religion," p. 32.
18. See Jung, *Psychology and Alchemy*, p. 11.

experiences of intense emotional impact. Libido is then used to absorb this impact and to realize its inherent meaning. The person is thereby inwardly connected to the meaning of the symbol. The religious symbol that was once a dried-up relic or a sentimentalized curio now becomes a precious spiritual possession. Through a recognition of the parallels between symbols that appear in one's own dreams and visions and those in religions and mythologies, the patient can "relate so called *metaphysical* concepts, which have lost their root connection with natural experience, to living, universal psychic processes, so that they can recover their true and original meaning. In this way the connection is reestablished between the ego and projected contents. . . ." [19]

Jung gives the imitation of Christ as an example. The meaning of the affirmation is to be found not in copying Christ's life in its outward form but in realizing one's own deepest conviction and meaning with as much courage, persistence, and trust in one's direct experience of God as Christ did.[20] Only by inwardly experiencing something can we understand it. Jung uses the masculine-feminine polarity to describe that inner connection: "It is in the inward experience that the connection between the psyche and the outward image or creed is first revealed as a relationship or correspondence like that of *sponsa* and *sponsus*." [21]

To make men "see" this inner connection of their own interiority with the Christ figure is not to reduce the mystery of Jesus to something known and accountable. Just as it is disastrous to see Christ only as an outward form onto which libido is projected and to which one never consciously relates, it is a serious mistake to see the Christ figure only as an inner psychic factor. Jung, therefore, is equally opposed to those who externalize the image of Christ and cut off the

19. Jung, *Aion* (CW, IX, Part 2, 1959), p. 34.
20. See Jung, *Psychology and Alchemy*, p. 7; "Commentary on *The Secret of the Golden Flower*," *Alchemical Studies* (CW, XIII, 1967), p. 53; and *Modern Man in Search of a Soul*, p. 236.
21. Jung, *Psychology and Alchemy*, pp. 13–14.

soul's participation in it and those who say that if one deals with the psychic experience of the Christ image religious experience is reduced to nothing but a psychic process. Jung protests that to talk about images of God in the soul is not to replace God: "How could any man replace God? I cannot even replace a lost button through my imagination, but have to buy myself a new real one." [22] The archetype of the self, which the figure of Christ represents in Jung's opinion, is an inner objective fact whose symbols disclose the reality of the psyche's growth to wholeness and its relation to meaning. Similarly, the existence of Jesus Christ is an outer, historic, objective fact; as a symbol, it discloses an objective psychic reality. To reduce the figure of Christ to mere historic reality or to an archetype of the self, one or the other, is a falsification and is only half the story.

The Empirical Study of the Soul

In re-establishing inward connection to religious symbols in this way, Jung began a strikingly original task, the empirical study of the soul. The life of the soul and the manifestations of the Spirit have been studied for centuries, as the saints' manuals and reflections indicate, but the study has been in religious terms.[23] Jung uses an empirical method to study the soul and the workings of the Spirit, a method heretofore used only with respect to the world of outer nature and the structures of physical energy. Jung observes, classi-

22. Cited by Victor White, *God and the Unconscious*, p. 267 n.
23. What the ancients called "soul" (which included many subsidiary classifications that described the activities and personifications of the soul's life), Jung calls the "psyche." He also notes, as we have seen in Part I, Chapter Three, the subsidiary classifications of the various psychic functions to which he gives separate names. The concept of anima, for example, which Jung often calls a man's "soul-image" describes specific psychic functions of a man's personality. See Jung, *Aion*, p. 13; *Psychological Types*, p. 588; and *Psychology and Alchemy*, p. 8 n.

fies, and formulates hypotheses about the facts and processes of the Spirit as they occur within the experience of the subject. He talks about these facts as "psychic facts" and about these processes as "psychic energy." What have been called spiritual phenomena become, therefore, part of the world of empirical investigation and as accessible to study as "external" objects.

It is just here that Jung's hypothesis of the objective psyche makes its weight felt. There are not only objective outer facts in the world of the psyche but also objective inner facts that happen to and impinge on the conscious experiencing subject. What is interior to the experiencing subject and felt as coming from within him cannot be reduced to a subjective origin. For just as the soul's yearnings and religious assertions correspond to exterior objective facts—that there was a man Jesus who to his followers was the Messiah, and that there are religious rites and mythologies that have elicited devotion—so do these yearnings and assertions correspond to interior objective facts, to the archetypes. The figure of Christ represents the archetype of the self that demands from the ego recognition and relationship. "Objective," therefore, no longer refers to nonsubjective, external events, and "subjective" to nonobjective internal events. Jung instead studies the "objective" within the "subjective" interior life. In deciding whether or not something is true, if we follow Jung, we must add to the traditional correspondence theory of truth (a judgment is "true" if it correctly correlates subjective experience or ideas with external facts) the new criterion that the subject's experience or idea must also correspond with inner objective facts. A subjective perception must correspond to outer phenomena, which we observe. In the same way, a subjective perception must also correspond to an objective psychic fact which can be verified by human experience.[24]

24. For an example of this kind of interpretation, see Edward F. Edinger, "Christ as Paradigm of the Individuating Ego," *Spring* (New York: The Analytical Psychology Club, 1966), p. 22.

Dogma performs the task of relating the world of subjective experience to the corresponding inner and outer objective events. That is why it is such a catastrophe when the bridge from dogma to inner individual experience breaks down. Subjective experience loses its connection to spiritual reality and thus becomes an easy prey to delusions, despair, and the dissociation of reason from feeling. The best way out of this trouble is to take seriously the inner psychic images, because "with the knowledge and actual experience of these inner images a way is opened for reason and feeling, so that both gain access to those other images the teachings of religion offer to mankind." [25] By establishing the correspondence of archetypal images to religious images one does anything but "psychologize away" religion. This procedure "opens people's eyes to the real meaning of dogmas, and, far from destroying, it throws open an empty house to new inhabitants." [26]

THEOLOGY AND DEPTH PSYCHOLOGY

JUNG'S RELIGIOUS POSITION is sharply criticized by both theologians and psychologists. Psychologists think he takes religion too seriously. Many psychologists reject Jung's symbolic approach to the psyche, particularly his hypothesis of the objective psyche and its contents, the archetypes. But no one, in my opinion, has yet formulated a more adequate hypothesis with which to describe the "psychic facts." Jung's theories are dismissed as "too complicated," I think, because, clumsy as they are, if we give them serious attention we are forced to give even more serious and searching attention to our own interiority. This is clearly contrary to the temper of this time—perhaps of all time. People prefer to deal with psychic reality in its external projected forms—

25. Jung, *Psychology and Alchemy*, p. 14.
26. *Ibid.*, p. 15.

prefer to change "the system," to change the other, not themselves. As a result, whenever a person appears who *does* deal with his own psychic life directly, he achieves a compelling presence and an extraordinary authority, and very often becomes the source of a genuine revolution in social life. Christ, Ghandi, Martin Luther King are examples.

Theologians say Jung does not take religion seriously enough. Some theologians are disturbed by Jung's view that no single religious position can claim final authority, and by his tendency to treat the Christian message as a religious myth which provides archetypal content to be investigated. Jung defends himself by saying he is a doctor who must deal empirically and objectively with his patients' material: "my point of departure is not any creed but the psychology of the *homo religiosus*, the man who takes into account and carefully observes certain factors which influence him and, through him, his general condition." [27] The analyst cannot dictate to his patient where values are to be found: "The difficulties of our psychotherapeutic work teach us to take truth, goodness, and beauty where we find them. They are not always found where we look for them: often they are hidden in the dirt . . . 'In stercore invenitur' (it is found in filth). . . ." [28] Consequently, an analyst must start with the images which grasp the patient and must not intrude his own point of view or insert dogmatic recommendations of what "should be." Otherwise, the patient will suffer: "Were psychology bound to a creed it would not and could not allow the unconscious of the individual that free play which is the basic condition for the production of archetypes. It is precisely the spontaneity of archetypal contents that convinces, whereas prejudiced intervention is a bar to genuine experience." [29]

Jung defends himself against criticism that he treats Chris-

27. Jung, "Psychology and Religion," p. 9.
28. Jung, "Psychology of the Transference," *The Practice of Psychotherapy* (*CW*, XVI, 1954), p. 189.
29. Jung, *Psychology and Alchemy*, p. 16.

tianity merely as a myth by saying that to him that does not mean a depreciation of value. To an empiricist a myth is " 'a statement about processes in the unconscious,' and this applies equally to the religious statement. He has no means of deciding whether the latter is 'truer' than the mythologem, for between the two he sees only one difference: the difference in living intensity." [30] The objection that one myth may be "true" and another "false" only impedes psychological understanding. The empiricist must deal with what is there: "Mythologems *exist*, even though their statements do not coincide with our incommensurable idea of 'truth.' " [31] A doctor must carefully observe when, where, and how a sick person "feels a healing, living quality, which can make him 'whole.' " [32] Only after the patient recovers his personal stability does the reconciliation of his own individual belief with collective belief become vitally important to him, and so an analyst must often insist on putting his patient's beliefs aside to concentrate on those problems of imbalance and neurosis which make it impossible for the patient to give any serious consideration to belief at all. [33]

In contrast to his focus on the archetype, Jung thinks the theologian's focus is on the source of the archetype: "The religious point of view understands the imprint as the working of an imprinter; the scientific point of view understands it as the symbol of an unknown and incomprehensible content." [34] The psychologist does not know the origin of the archetype or of the psyche. Psychology can only ascertain by its comparative research whether or not there is such an

30. Jung, "Foreword to White's *God and the Unconscious*," *Psychology and Religion: West and East*, p. 301.
31. Jung, "The Transcendent Function," *The Structure and Dynamics of the Psyche* (*CW*, VIII, 1960), p. 91.
32. Jung, "Foreword to White's *God and the Unconscious*," p. 301.
33. This is what Husserl calls "epochē" and what Jung, who in fact calls himself a phenomenologist, did in his work as an analyst.
34. Jung, *Psychology and Alchemy*, p. 17. By "theologian" Jung means the nineteenth-century theologian whom Jung indiscriminately lumps together with the metaphysician and the philosopher.

imprint in the psyche, one that can perhaps be properly described as a God image; but "Nothing positive or negative has thus been asserted about the possible existence of God, any more than the archetype of the 'hero' proves the existence of a hero." [35]

Even the recurrence of the symbolism of the divine is to be taken as proof not of God's existence but only of the existence of the idea of God in the psyche. For Jung, "God" designates a psychic, not an ontological reality, even though he does not always make this clear. The empiricist is limited to what is observable; beyond that resides mystery, which he does not presume to classify. For the empiricist, metaphysical truth and religious experience are essentially psychic phenomena, that is, they manifest themselves as such and must therefore be investigated, criticized, and evaluated from a psychological point of view. Jung writes: "As a science of the soul, psychology must confine itself to its subject matter, and avoid overstepping its boundaries by any metaphysical assertions or by any other expressions of belief or opinion." [36]

CRITICISM OF JUNG

A SERIOUS CRITICISM of Jung's insistence on separating the empirical from ontological statements is that his own theories and results do not support the separation. Jung's adherence to "what works" for the patient, and to what is "true psychologically" simply because it exists must be related to what the Dominican priest Victor White calls the "psyche's deep yearning for true *judgment* concerning facts, whether attributed to faith or reason." [37] White adds, "Yet it must always be found to be itself a psychological fact that a religion which is not 'true'—or at least apprehended as

35. *Ibid.*, p. 14.
36. Cited in White, *God and the Unconscious*, p. 246. See also Jung, "Psychology of the Transference," p. 192 n.
37. White, *God and the Unconscious*, p. 87.

'true'—does not even 'work' "[38] Projections and paranoid delusions "exist" too, and Jung is quick to realize that their "truth" is vastly different from the truth of symbols that promote healing. In the depths of truth what heals and what simply is, must be and are the same. To insist on their separation is an evasion.

Jung's investigations into man's symbol-making and symbol-using capacities in apprehending reality, his hypothesis of the objective psyche operating within the personal psyche, his detailed observation of the formative influence of the archetypes in creating one's context of perception and action—all nullify the segregation of reality into empirical facts and ontological speculations that he urges on his reader. Jung's theories contradict the implicit positivism of his position that psychology deals only with phenomena as they appear and can never offer judgments of their ontological value. Empirical psychology, as we have seen, is itself a mode of perception; it is one of the symbolic forms which posit and shape reality, while in turn (according to Cassirer) it is posited and shaped by what it tries to describe. Both what "is" and what "works" emerge from the interpenetration of the modes of perceiving and of the perceived. The kinds of hypotheses Jung brings to his work influence his gathering of facts, just as the facts shape the hypotheses. Ontological assertions are unavoidable because one's mode of approach, in all its details, is itself a piece of the reality one perceives as well as one of the means of giving it its shaping and identifying qualities. One must agree with Jung, I think, that it is not the work of the doctor to concern himself with explicit description and criticism of ontological postures and their values, but it seems to me an untenable assumption that a doctor is exempt from dealing with any implicit ontology that may affect his treatment of his patient. Jung's own work is the best evidence for this conclusion.

38. *Ibid.*, p. 88.

CHAPTER SEVEN

Remythologizing Life

Psychology's function for religion is to make men see—
see what is there, see into things, and see what is beyond the
sense of sight. In the pursuit of this goal Jung's psychology
joins with much of recent theology—for example, Tillich's
vision of existential categories that illuminate the mystery of
being, H. Richard Niebuhr's interest in the inner history of
revelation, the death-of-God theologians' focus on prophetic
revelation and on the imaginative discourse of the poet
William Blake.

The result of seeing into and seeing beyond the "seen" is
the remythologizing of life. Facts are set in their full contexts, and their contexts are seen to become parts of stories.
Events fall into themes. One's life gradually makes visible
one's myth. One sees one's own particular truth both as one
creates and shapes it and as one is created and shaped by it.
An old religious dimension of life comes alive again—
Providence. One begins to live *sub specie aeternitatis*.

128

One of the special strengths of Jung's insight into symbols and their role in psychic life is this remythologizing of everything to do with man's imaginative life, not the least of which are elements gathered from the Christian gospels. Christian truths are made visible in the context of personal experience and psychic functioning. Jung's treatment of the parable of the sheep and goats is an example of this. Christ tells those who marvel at finding themselves among the elect that inasmuch as they show compassion to "the least of the brethren," they show it to him. The essential question to ask, however, is *who* is the least of the brethren: "What if I should discover that the least amongst them all, the poorest of all the beggars, the most impudent of all the offenders, . . . are within me and . . . that I myself am the enemy who must be loved—what then?" [1] Instead of giving kindness, Jung notes, to this inner enemy (the "shadow" in his special vocabulary), we scorn it: "Had it been God himself who drew near to us in this despicable form, we should have denied him a thousand times before a single cock had crowed." [2]

We cannot give to others what we do not have ourselves. The compassion we deny ourselves is also denied our neighbor, as is all too evident when we are so quick to condemn in him the shadow aspects we do not accept in our own personalities. The healing aspect of "remythologization" lies not in translating the story into psychological jargon, but in pointing out that our personal struggle with self-rejection is part of the human struggle described in the parable. Our eyes may be opened to see anew the "truth" of this story. This central part of religious tradition may become alive again and bring us the grace to accept fully our own humanity.

1. Jung, *Modern Man in Search of a Soul*, trans. W. S. Dell and C. F. Baynes (New York: Harcourt, Brace & Co., 1933), p. 235.
2. *Ibid.*

THE EXPERIENCE OF THE NUMINOUS

REMYTHOLOGIZING CHRISTIAN DOCTRINE is possible only if we take seriously our immediate personal experience of the numinous. Jung focuses on this possibility rather than on the theological intricacies of dogma which are customarily inspected in this sort of discussion in the religious world, or on the sublimations of instinct which are customarily dealt with in the analytic world. Jung looks at the heart of dogma: the consuming, inchoate, and numinous elements which become transmittable through its guardian images. For those who wonder what relevance dogma has to their personal lives, Jung's thought has the power to reconnect psychic experience to the life- and light-giving currents of religion. It is no wonder Jung is suspected of schizophrenia, for he himself warns of the danger of sudden sharp contact with the divine.[3] He stresses the necessity of discovering the connections of dogma with deliberate slowness if this primary experience is to be made digestible.

Immediate experience always includes both conscious and unconscious life. The effect of this understanding for Christianity is the focus on the individual as the locus and carrier of meaning and the extension of the mode of revelation to unconscious life. How a person comes to terms with the unconscious is for Jung "the fundamental question, in practice, of all religions and all philosophies. For the unconscious is not this thing or that; it is the Unknown as it immediately affects us." [4] The unconscious, just as much as anything else, may be an avenue for God's presence. To say that God cannot show himself in the human soul would be blasphemy:

3. See Jung, "A Psychological Approach to the Trinity," "Transformation Symbolism in the Mass," and "Answer to Job," *Psychology and Religion: West and East* (CW, XI, 1958), pp. 150, 246, 363.

4. Jung, "The Transcendent Function," *The Structure and Dynamics of the Psyche* (CW, VIII, 1960), p. 68.

"Even the believing Christian does not know God's hidden ways and must leave it to Him whether He will work on man from outside or from within, . . . the believer should not boggle at the fact that there are *somnia a Deo missa* (dreams sent by God). . . ."[5] The danger of equating the medium of revelation with the revelation itself is overcome by Jung's insistence on the symbolic mode of knowing. The language in which we discuss revelation is that of analogy; we can only speak about God in terms of "as if."

THE RECOVERY OF IMAGINATION

IN ORDER TO REMYTHOLOGIZE our experience we must recover the value of imaginative thought. Prior to Jung, "fantasy thinking" was considered pathological, was scornfully called "autistic" and associated with retarded development, primarily because it was the kind of mental process observed in psychotic patients and very young children. Jung's work with symbols recovered the value of what he called "non-directed" fantasy or imaginative thinking.[6] Imaginative thinking, Jung showed, is subconscious, spontaneous, and non-directed; it pursues aims which are not yet conscious and adapts to an inner reality which is expressed in images. It is concerned with creating an image world and with satisfying desires rather than with establishing truth; it is individual in its orientation and all but incommunicable, except through images that evoke rather than describe the reality they express. Imaginative thinking is controlled by principles of contiguity, correspondence, and association and is determined by concrete emotions, by intimations of unknown

5. Jung, *Psychology and Alchemy* (*CW*, XII, 1967), p. 10. Paul Tillich's words are also apt: "There is no reality, thing, or event which cannot become a bearer of the mystery of being and enter with a revelatory correlation." (*Systematic Theology*, 3 vols. [Chicago: University of Chicago Press, 1951–63], I, 118).

6. See Jung, *Symbols of Transformation* (*CW*, V, 1956), p. 7.

intents, and by subjective states of meaning.[7] In contrast to this kind of thinking, a person is also capable of the logical and "directed thinking" which pursues a conscious aim.[8] It is willed and intelligent, adapting to an outer reality apprehended in concepts. Directed thinking is concerned with influencing the real world and focuses on whether things are true or false. Unlike the evocations of imaginative thinking, its perceptions are communicable through a shared language and are controlled by laws of logic and shared experience. Directed thinking inhabits a world of abstract logic and outer reality.

Jung's work emphasizes the validity and necessity of the nonconceptual, undirected, image thinking which adapts to inner reality. Loss of relation to this mode of consciousness produces pathology just as much as a loss of directed thinking, which would separate the person from external reality. One kind of thinking counterpoints the other. An image conveys to consciousness the personally felt significance of something perceived, whether in the outside world or in the soul. A concept abstracts, generalizes, and makes communicable a perception and its inherent meaning. Loss of contact, therefore, with the image-making functions (the symbol or

7. The principle of contiguity asserts the close association of symbols and events. Any item that happens to be present or coincident with the occurrence of a strongly felt image or event, especially of an archetypal nature, becomes associated with that image or event and may therefore evoke it. For example, to see a lady in a blue dress of a certain shade may evoke powerful emotions, images, and behavioral reactions in one whose mother was wearing that color when she suddenly had a heart attack and died. The principle of correspondence describes a process of image construction. The meaning of one series of images is presented in analogous terms with another series of images. For example, if one feels gloomy and forlorn, one may imagine oneself as sitting all alone in a public place on a gray day with everyone else rushing by occupied with his own business. The principle of association describes the process by which one image may recall an entire experience, affect tone, and reaction pattern; or where one image may call to mind a correspondent situation that is different in outward detail but similar in meaning to the original one. These three ways of structuring experience are very often found in dreams.

8. See Jung, *Symbols of Transformation*, p. 16.

the religious function) results in loss of meaning in life as it is immediately lived. Symbols are the means through which meaning discloses itself.

THE RECOVERY OF THE FEMININE

REMYTHOLOGIZING EXPERIENCE cannot occur if we cannot reach out to all of our humanness, a wholeness of being that is only available through full recognition of the masculine-feminine polarity. If we accept the implications of Jung's work, we are brought time and again to see the complementarity of the sexes and of the masculine-feminine structure of each individual—the anima-animus relationship. The religious saints knew this too. Their use of the conjugal metaphor for the soul's meetings with God makes clear their perception, at least in terms of imaginative thought, of the polarity of sexual characteristics in each human being. Jung uses the terms "anima" and "animus" to indicate that the soul (used here in the religious sense of the place of the eternal within the temporal, the presence of God within man) makes itself known to consciousness through the language of masculine-feminine polarity.

We cannot see into the dark recesses of human experience if we think persons are entirely and literally male or female. That is like building a structure on only one support: it tips over. We need two supports, those of the masculine and the feminine. We do not know human beings unless we know them as male and female, with a polarity of sexual characteristics. In his works, Jung does not discover the centrality of sexual polarity as if it were not known until he found it; he rather retrieves this knowledge from obscurity, from worlds where it was once known, and he does so by his rigorous attention to the feminine.

The feminine mode of being has been too long neglected. We are as familiar with the masculine as it is possible to be familiar with something that is as truncated as the masculine must be without the feminine. We have dealt long and thoroughly with the rhetoric, the imagery, and the special vocabulary of the masculine. If we accept Jung's thesis of sexual polarity, however, then we must conclude that even though we know all this, we still do not really know the masculine and will not until we see it in its full complementarity with the feminine. The feminine is the missing link in our chain of connections to the knowledge and deepened experience of man's psychic life. There is no access to full conscious and unconscious life without the feminine modality. The feminine must be worked on, probed, examined, meditated upon, conjectured about, and contemplated, for the feminine is the completing element in every effort we can make to become a fully human person. Recovery of the feminine would restore sexual polarity to its central function, making possible through its symbolic discourse the psyche's growth to wholeness. Recognition of the centrality of sexual polarity would restore to men what is feminine and to women what is masculine, which would not make for homosexuality but on the contrary would make the male more masculine and the female more feminine. Loss of the feminine means loss of all those aspects of life associated with it, loss of a fullness of interiority, loss of a full spiritual life, loss of a true sense of the human person.

For many Christians, and especially Protestants, there is a loss of touch with the feminine. Too little attention is given the feminine for its own sexual and psychological strengths, for its symbolizing of the divine, or for its role as a transcendent dimension of life and therefore a central part of the religious life. There are many examples of how this lack of attention causes psychic difficulties. We can imagine the confusion felt by a man who in a dream was moved to worship a mysterious goddesslike woman. He was conditioned by his religious upbringing—as so many of us are—to see this kind of worship as a throwback to a primitive pre-Christian idolatry that is somehow surviving in the unconscious. To interpret the dream only reductively would have severed all connection between his "soul" (used both in the religious sense and as anima) and the potential transformative powers which the goddess symbolizes.

Many other case histories reveal the same impoverishment of the psychic and religious life. Repression of the feminine element in Christian symbolism contributed enormously to the compulsive affairs, for example, of a minister's son who saw unknown women as the embodiment of the unknowable mysteries of life. In another instance, a man of Puritan upbringing dreamt of an ecstatic sexual meeting with his girl in a church, while the church elders frowned and intoned dramatically, "No; this is forbidden." Thus, although his ecstasy of standing outside himself and surrendering with his girl to something beyond them both, occurred in a holy place, the means of surrender was condemned by his faith. To condemn his religion in turn, as psychoanalysis often does, as nothing but repressive, does not really solve the problem but simply moves it around in place. For today sexuality is no longer the repressed element; religion is. The dreamer's struggle with the relation between the mystery of sexuality and the mystery of the divine must be seen as a double conflict. It might be a healing comfort to such a dreamer to hear of the ancient temple rites which embraced sexuality as a means of congress with the divine, for this ancient association would offer him a context which gives meaning to his struggles. The lack of such a context in his own religious tradition effects a destructive isolation in him that, instead of making his psyche whole, splits it apart.

Jung is strongly critical of the Christian tradition for omitting the feminine as part of the Godhead. He suggests that the Trinitarian symbolism is incomplete: a fourth person, the feminine, the *mater* and *materia* and hence the dark substance of the flesh and the Devil, should be added. Jung is ambiguous about whether he sees the feminine and the Devil on the same plane. One would prefer to think not. But he does imply an associative link through the feminine as flesh, as matter, as the dark and the earthy, to the black

evil of Satan; and he refers to both as the missing "fourth."
Perhaps it reflects the denigrated status of the feminine to
see it linked with the demonic.[9]

What relation has the feminine to the religious life—as it
appears in dreams, in the love of a woman and in woman's
love, in the impersonality of the feminine instinct, in the
sexual images of opening, conceiving, and giving birth?
Jung's attention to the central role of masculine-feminine polarity in psychic life makes that question unavoidable. We
must also ask: is there no relationship in Christianity commensurate with our experience of the feminine, or is it
there and as yet hidden and undeveloped? If we say there is
no such relationship, then it is questionable how adequately
our experience can be guided by Christian doctrines and
images, for it is clear that continued neglect of the feminine
is not tolerable. If we say that the feminine elements in
Christianity are still to be developed, then we must bring into
a Christian context our burgeoning experiences of the feminine—the increase of homosexuality, the decrease of contact
with feelings, the plunge into the unconscious through drugs,
the medical translation of one sex into another, the scientific
study of the female orgasm, the organizations of angry
women insisting on their own qualities of person, their own
independent experiences, determined to make the world see
that they are far more than men have seen them to be. From
both sexes and from our culture at large come great and
demanding questions now about the nature and place of the
feminine.

9. See Jung, *Psychology and Alchemy*, pp. 23, 144, 148, 150, 160, 167,
186. See also Jung, "A Psychological Approach to the Trinity," *Psychology and Religion: West and East*, p. 177. See also Victor White,
God and the Unconscious (Cleveland: World Publishing Co., 1961),
pp. 260–61.

PART III

The Psychology of the Feminine

The girl and the woman, in their new, their own unfolding, will but in passing be imitators of masculine ways, good and bad, and repeaters of masculine professions. After the uncertainty of such transitions it will become apparent that women were only going through the profusion and the vicissitude of those (often ridiculous) disguises in order to cleanse their most characteristic nature of the distorting influences of the other sex. . . . This humanity of woman, borne its full time in suffering and humiliation, will come to light when she will have stripped off the conventions of mere femininity in the mutations of her outward status . . . some day there will be girls and women whose name will no longer signify merely an opposite of the masculine, but something in itself, something that makes one think, not of any complement and limit, but only of life and existence: the feminine human being.

Rainer Maria Rilke

CHAPTER EIGHT

Descriptions of the Feminine

I<small>N THE LAST THIRD</small> of the twentieth century we are experiencing many revolutions—in race relations, sexual mores, and educational institutions—all of which are of the profoundest importance for the future of our lives together. In my opinion, the revolution that is taking place in our understanding of the nature of the feminine is the most far-reaching of all. The change in our consciousness of the feminine and in our relation to it is so radical because it changes our consciousness of what it means to be human. When we talk about the feminine, we talk about our concepts of the human person and of relationships between persons. We touch the most intimate aspects of our lives—our relation to sexuality, to our wives, our daughters, our mothers, to feminine elements in the male personality, and to the unconscious; we touch on our notions of marriage and of the relationships between the sexes.

Three Approaches to the Feminine

In the short time that the psychology of the feminine has been a subject of study from the point of view of depth psychology, three dominant approaches have emerged: the biological, the cultural, and the symbolic. The biological approach is to be found primarily in the Judeo-Christian tradition and in the thinking of Freud and the Freudians. This is the approach to the feminine through the biology of the female: anatomy is destiny. The psychology of the feminine derives from the contours of the female body and, for Freud especially, from what the female body lacks—a phallus. Thus the entire psychology of the wounded female is built upon the lack of the phallus. In this view, the psychological is thus dependent on the physical and is a derivative of the physical; the psyche is not recognized as an autonomous element in itself.

The cultural approach is represented by such figures as Karen Horney and Margaret Mead. Their psychology of the feminine derives from the influences of cultural tradition, from the custom and habit that have molded if not entirely recreated the psychological propensies of women and society's definition of the feminine. Horney valiantly defends women against Freudian premises, saying that anatomy does not determine a woman's nature and asserting instead the primacy of sociological facts. Although woman's traditional subordinate position has created in her a psychology of dependence and passivity, these are traits that are not intrinsic but may be changed if our culture changes. In recent years the more radical implications of this cultural view have been made explicit. The more militant women's groups, formed for the conscious purpose of "liberating" women from this inferior cultural position, claim, on the basis of Horney's argument, that there is no real difference between men and women, only the differences created by unjust male cultural standards.

The symbolic approach to the feminine is represented by Jung and the Jungians. My focus is on Jung's original contribution to a psychology of the feminine, and it is best seen by contrasting Jung's view with the first two approaches. Three striking differences are: Jung's notion that the feminine is not confined only to females; Jung's description of the nature of the feminine in the language of symbol and myth; and Jung's notion that personal wholeness can only be achieved by a full awareness of contrasexuality.

THE FEMININE IN BOTH SEXES

THE BIOLOGICAL AND CULTURAL APPROACHES understand the feminine literally, as belonging only to females, to women. Jung's symbolic approach not only understands the feminine as referring to a female anatomy that culture then expands into larger systems of sexual differentiation, but also sees the feminine as a psychic element quite apart from its biological or cultural existence, however much it may influence or be influenced by that existence. The symbolic approach to the feminine adds an essential dimension to its understanding:

> Only half of feminine psychology can be covered by biological and social concepts. But . . . woman possesses also a peculiar spirituality very strange to man. Without knowledge of the unconscious, this new point of view, so essential to the psychology of woman, could never have been brought out in such completeness.[1]

Jung's approach to the feminine, in other words, grows out of his symbolic approach to the psyche as a whole (see above, Chapter Two). In addition to the defining influences

1. Jung, Introduction to Esther Harding, *The Way of All Women* (London: Longmans, Green & Co., 1936), pp. x–xi.

of anatomy and the shaping influence of society and cultural history, there is for Jung a third element or force that defines and shapes our lives at least as powerfully as the other two. This third element is the psyche. Jung recognizes the psyche as an autonomous entity, a presence in itself which is not simply an offshoot of the body, nor determined merely by culture. We owe to Jung the clinical probing and empirical documenting of the presence of the psyche and its shaping influence on our cultural history. In his concept of the objective psyche, Jung tries to describe this facticity; in his concept of the archetype, Jung tries to describe the language in which the psyche speaks and the means through which it exerts its influence. The means are the symbol, the image, the drama, the texture of dream, the compelling fascination of legend or myth. The language of the objective psyche is not knowable in itself but can only be described in terms of the images, behavior patterns, and emotional responses which the archetypes arouse in us.

For Jung, the feminine and its psychology describe not only factors which form a specific female sexual identity but also certain modalities of being which belong to all human beings. These modalities are styles of being and of awareness, ways of relating to reality, digesting reality, and making judgments about it. These modalities express themselves in their own characteristic images, behavior patterns, and emotional responses. For Jung and his symbolic approach, the feminine and its psychology describe, point to, and symbolize certain aspects of psychic or spiritual reality. In that sense, the feminine and its psychology represent, in addition to physical and cultural reality, aspects of objective psychic reality. In learning about the feminine and its psychology, we learn something about the objective psyche, about styles of being human that apply to both men and women, although in different ways.[2] The feminine seen symbolically is under-

2. The different ways in which males and females experience and relate to the feminine will be taken up in Chapters Eleven and Twelve of Part III.

stood as an archetypal aspect of the human psyche. Like any archetype, the feminine cannot be known in itself as something simply equatable with something else, such as anatomical structure or specific cultural traditions, but can only be understood through images and through the behavioral and emotional responses that it arouses in us. To understand the feminine in this way is to see it as a symbolic form that shapes as well as articulates our meeting with the reality that it seeks to express, not unlike what Cassirer calls an "organ of reality" (see above, Chapter Four).

Jung argues from the following premise. The psyche is structured in polarities of opposites whose interchange of energy is the life energy of the psyche for the human being (see above, Chapter Three). These polarities—conscious-unconscious, flesh-spirit, reason-instinct, active-passive—are most often characterized in masculine-feminine terms and are perceived by us, whether we are male or female, as a confrontation with an "other." When we consciously encounter aspects of the psyche hitherto unknown or unconscious to us, we experience that encounter as a meeting with an opposite, with something different from ourselves and our own conscious point of view, and yet something quite accessible to us and fully bound up with us.

Jung reasons that, as we grow to wholeness and struggle to overcome the oppositions within ourselves, we engage in an endless process of reconciling our indwelling opposites and polarities. Out of a series of successive reconciliations, the self is gradually constructed. The self is thus built up out of the repeated process of encountering the otherness of the opposing pole of a psychic polarity, and the reconciliation of the two poles. In this way we become individual persons with unique identities and not just a collection of stray qualities or a mere pasting together of the various influences in our lives.

Jung tries to demonstrate that the psyche speaks in symbols as the best possible expressions for little-known or all-but-unknowable facts. He observes that the symbols most frequently employed by the psyche to convey to us the process of reconciliation of opposites and the successive stages in the building up of a self are the symbols of the masculine-feminine polarity: "This primordial pair of opposites symbolizes every conceivable pair of opposites that may occur: hot and cold, light and dark, north and south, dry and damp, good and bad, conscious and unconscious." [3] Our own experience constantly gives us evidence for Jung's conclusion. Those aspects of ourselves with which we struggle are most often personified in sexual terms. An example is the dream of a man who constantly hides his feelings from others and avoids becoming involved with others. He dreamt of a woman who challenged him to show himself as he really was. In the next scene in the dream the man was naked except for a towel and terribly anxious lest he expose himself to the woman.

The sexual elements of our being also have a spiritual function: to convey to us the fact of otherness, of that opposite point of view or tendency within ourselves that we cannot ignore but to which we must establish a clear relation. Understood symbolically, then, the psyche uses the biological differences between male and female to speak about psychic opposites or polarities. It is in this sense that the feminine symbolizes and is the best possible representation for certain modes of consciousness and of spirit. The feminine is one pole in the central masculine-feminine polarity that symbolizes all psychic polarities.

Put in extreme form one could say that the objective psyche chooses to make its different modes of being and of awareness known through sexual differences, but this would make all the physical and cultural aspects of human life dependent upon the psyche. Jung does not go that far. What is exciting about his approach is that he does not take that easy way out. Jung considers the psyche to be just as

3. Jung, *Psychology and Alchemy* (CW, XII, 1967), p. 144. See also Jung, *Mysterium Coniunctionis* (CW, XIV, 1963), p. 89.

powerful a determining element of human life as are the physical and cultural elements; yet he does not reduce everything to the psyche. That would be as fallacious as it would be to reduce everything to the physical. To reduce everything to psychic causes would be to psychologize away the physical facts of sex, or to consider the actual persons to whom we relate as mere figures who trigger our own inner dramas. Jung opens the psychic world to us not so that we can escape the everyday world, but so that we can enrich our daily life with access to this darker psychic world, strengthen our ability to penetrate the darkness, and thus develop the ability to live more fully in the world of everyday life.

SEXUAL DIFFERENCE

JUNG'S SYMBOLIC APPROACH answers the strong challenges of the cultural school of psychology and of the women's liberation leaders who say that there is no basic difference between the sexes that is not simply the product of cultural influences. The implication of these challenges is that, given new cultural traditions, the sexual differences will disappear and with them their psychologies. For Jung, sexual differences reflect inherent structural polarities of the psyche, and therefore he finds any expectation that we could ever be free of sexual differences naïve. To be without sexual distinctions would be to be without psychical structure. Instead of the freedom that the representatives of the cultural school seek— from sexual roles that dictate styles of identity to men and women—Jung's view asserts that the denial of sexual differences would lead to a lack of structure that would prevent a person from achieving any identity at all. The structuring of the psyche in various polarities is not simply a product of cultural influence, although, of course, the way those polarities are conceived and evaluated is indeed subject to cultural forces. Thus Jung might answer the current chal-

lenges to sexual distinction by saying that the way we con-
ceive of and value psychic polarities, which are symbolized
most often in masculine-feminine terms, may vary according
to historical time and cultural influence, but the fact of
psychic polarities and the centrality of the masculine-feminine polarity is a basic structure of the human psyche.

Jung is not proposing a psychic determinism that would
replace the biological determinism of woman's fate. To say
that the psyche has a stable structure is not to conclude that
the feminine pole of that structure is now equatable with
certain unchanging characteristics that should be taken ab-
solutely as the norm that defines what a woman should be.
In Jung's approach, the feminine is understood symbolically
as an archetype which cannot be directly known in itself and
therefore cannot impose a set of characteristics on individual
persons. Rather, it is the task of the individual person to deal
with and integrate in his or her own way the images, feelings,
and behavior patterns that seem to arise from within and express this feminine pole of being, and to decide whether the
culture's way of dealing with these factors helps or hinders
the development of a personal identity. The same would
hold true of the influence of the masculine pole. This way,
there feed into the culture the archetypal factors of the objective psyche, the personal factors of the individual, the biological factors of gender, and cultural traditions.

To say that we can do away with sexual difference by developing new cultural standards, is naïve not only for the
reasons mentioned above but also because it ignores the reasons for the development of the cultural traditions that rested
upon and enforced sexual differences. It is too easy to say
that sexual differences were simply the result of the male's
fear of the female and his wish to tyrannize over her. If we
push the cultural approach far enough we come back to the
biological view that all sexual differences arise from differences of anatomy. Different cultural traditions grew up
around the two sexes because of different physical functions.
The culturalists fight this viewpoint, I think, because they

equate difference with discrimination. They are afraid that from the recognition of woman's child-bearing capacities will come a whole psychology that will keep her confined to the home, to homemaking, and to child raising. In the light of the history of discrimination against women, that fear is only too well justified. The answer, however, is not to deny sexual difference for fear it will automatically bring discrimination but to respond to it differently.

When we recognize that there are differences between the sexes and their psychologies, we are faced with the task of differentiating ourselves and developing identities as female or male persons. Difference, then, does not necessarily imply discrimination. To deny sexual differences is destructive; we evade the tasks of personal, sexual, and psychological differentiation. To be a whole person we must come to terms with our own physical, sexual identity and with all those psychic factors which are represented to us by means of the symbolism of the masculine-feminine polarity. Without wrestling with this task of differentiation, we fall into formlessness and a cheap imitation of current persona roles. We miss our chance to become unique persons. Furthermore, we miss the spiritual significance of physical sexuality. If we deny sexual differences we deny the fact of otherness that is so strikingly conveyed to all of us through sexual experience. If we say that we are really all alike, we fail to respond to the effect otherness has upon us. Otherness challenges our viewpoint by confronting us with a different one; otherness calls us out of ourselves and our egoism by demonstrating that we are not complete in ourselves; otherness lures us to new perspectives from which the possibility of a new unity with ourselves and with others and with the divine may result.

Finally, we must speculate on the significance of having the kinds of bodies and psyches that we do have. The culturalists too blithely pass over the inescapable fact that it is in a particular human body—which is male or female—that we live and in which we meet others and enjoy those deep satisfactions of union and reunion. It is in this body and psyche that we struggle with obstacles and suffer their divisive effects. To say that bodies and psyches are all alike is to defend against the facticity of human being with which individuals must come to terms. To say that by changing cultural conditions we can erase sexual and psychological differences is to defend against the task of working out our own identities, and also to assume that culture is only the project of our conscious design. Culture also expresses, in Jung's language, the collective aspects of the objective psyche with which we must inevitably deal.

THE BIOLOGICAL AND CULTURAL APPROACHES

THE FIRST MAJOR CONTRAST, then, between Jung's symbolic approach to the feminine and that of the cultural and biological schools is that for Jung the feminine does not describe only physical differences or cultural roles of women; it is understood symbolically and thus as representing certain psychic modalities that belong to both sexes and to all cultures. The second major contrast between the three approaches is in the content of their descriptions of the feminine.

According to the biological approach, feminine psychology is understood literally as belonging only to women, and woman is seen as merely a deficient male. F. J. J. Buytendijk describes the prevalence of this opinion in antiquity: "le fruit naturel de la fécondation devrait être un individu masculin. Le fruit féminin résulterait donc d'une déficience dans l'acte de la procréation." To substantiate his interpretation of antiquity, Buytendijk quotes Thomas Aquinas: "Femina est mas occasionatus." [4] An extreme example of this thinking is Otto Weininger's idea that woman is a souless and immoral creature, and, he reasons, "If . . . womanliness is simply

4. F. J. J. Buytendijk, *La Femme*, texte français d'Alphonse de Waehlens and René Micha (Bruges: Desclée de Brouwer, 1954), p. 34 n.

immorality, then woman must cease to be womanly and try to be manly." [5]

Freud strengthens this view. Feminine psychology, he thinks, is based on the little girl's traumatic discovery that she lacks a penis, which she sees as castration; thus she sees herself as irreparably deprived.[6] This lack is a mortal blow to her self-esteem, and she compensates for her essential inferiority by developing a lifelong narcissism stronger than that of men. Awareness of her deficiency arouses her infamous penis envy, which is eventually transformed into a wish for a child, especially a male child, again to compensate for her bodily defect. This discovery of her inferiority effects a change from mother to father as the object of her affections; mother cannot be penetrated because the equipment is lacking, but the vital genital equipment can be obtained indirectly through an affectionate relationship with her father. Mother, however, is held responsible for sending her into the world so ill-equipped—an understandable basis for hostility between women. Penis envy is also responsible for a woman's eventual shift from an active to a passive orientation psychologically and from a clitoral to a vaginal focus sexually. Penis envy is the basis of her feminine mental characteristics. Her inferiority feelings and fear of losing love are at root the castration shame; her capacity for greater jealousy than the male grows from this original penis envy. Her ambition is an effort to surpass and challenge men who have a penis. Her happiness during pregnancy comes from having the penis-child, and her menstrual depression stems from the constant reminder of her lack. Her modesty is an effort to hide the imperfection.[7]

5. Otto Weininger, *Sex and Character* (New York: Putnam, n.d.), p. 341. See also p. 189.

6. See Sigmund Freud, *New Introductory Lectures on Psychoanalysis*, trans. James Strachey (New York: W. W. Norton & Co., 1965), pp. 124–27. See also pp. 114–15 for Freud's discussion of human bisexuality.

7. See Sigmund Freud, "Female Sexuality," *Collected Papers*, 5 vols. (London: The Hogarth Press, 1956), V, 252–72.

Helene Deutsch develops Freud's penis-envy concept at some length. The basic "feminine core" is characterized by narcissism, passivity, and masochism.[8] Femininity derives from the continuance of narcissism beyond adolescence, and this self-loving, wanting-to-be-loved narcissistic quality is the basis for much of a woman's charm. Mortification over her genital inferiority makes narcissism stronger in women than in men, which is illustrated in woman's constant demands for gestures and reassurances to compensate for her offended self-love. Her erotic power results from an interplay of masochism and narcissism—her sexual and self-preservative instincts.[9]

Passivity is an inherent and primary factor of femininity that is rooted in anatomical structure.[10] The penis envy that for Freud is primary is for Deutsch a secondary rationalization and projection onto external reality of a lack the girl already feels.[11] The genital trauma is due to the focus of the lack upon the penis and the subsequent awareness that the vagina has no autonomous responsiveness but depends on male activity to awaken it. To lessen the disparaging connotations of "passivity," Deutsch defines it as "activity directed inward," and she distinguishes masochism from its perverted self-punishing form in neuroses by considering it to be the aggressive energy that accompanies this passive "activity directed inward." Masochism as the destructive impulse turned against the ego, however, is still an "elemental power in feminine life."[12] Narcissistic self-love must master this destructive impulse so that it does not assume the perverted self-punishing form of "moral" masochism.[13] Moreover, masoch-

8. Helene Deutsch, *Psychology of Women*, 2 vols. (New York: Grune & Stratton, 1944), I, xiii, 139, 187, 239.

9. *Ibid.*, p. 193.

10. *Ibid.*, p. 226.

11. *Ibid.*, p. 238.

12. *Ibid.*, pp. 191, 240, 278.

13. *Ibid.*, p. 240. Freud distinguishes between erotogenic or feminine masochism and the moral masochism of neuroses. See Freud, "The Economic Problem in Masochism," *Collected Papers*, II, 255–68.

ism helps a woman adjust to reality through the necessary consent to pain (of menstruation, intercourse, defloration, childbirth, etc.).

Erik Erikson makes a provocative contribution in describing the Freudian dictum that "anatomy is destiny" in more positive terms. On the basis of clinical observation of how girl children construct space with blocks, as compared with boy children, Erikson concludes that there are "two principles of arranging space which correspond to the male and female principles of body construction." [14] Girls' scenes were interiors or enclosures, rooms with people or animals in static positions, with low walls, doorways for entrance, all expressing peaceful atmospheres. The boys constructed exterior scenes with people and machines in action or created sudden arrests of action outside enclosures with elaborate walls, protrusions, and high towers that were being erected or were collapsing. The different constructions of space parallelled the differences in sexual organs, following the female's internal and static ova and womb and the male's external erectible penis that penetrates, channels active sperm, and collapses.

Erikson shifts the emphasis on what is missing that is characteristic of Freudian penis-envy theory to the more compelling reality of what is present: "a *productive inner-bodily space* safely set in the center of female form and carriage. . . ." [15] He challenges Freud's stress upon passivity, asserting that a woman's activity is of a different kind from a man's, attuned to inner bodily processes, developing a self-contained intensity of feeling that furthers intimacy. A woman's fear of loss of love is felt as emptiness and is related not to the lack of a penis but to the fear of her inner space being unproductive, barren, left empty of warmth, blood, and new creation. Erikson asks, too, whether masochism really is central to woman, cautioning against confusing masochism with

14. Erik Erikson, "Inner and Outer Space: Reflections on Womanhood," in *The Woman in America,* ed. Robert Jay Lifton (Boston: Houghton Mifflin Co., 1965), p. 11.
15. *Ibid.,* p. 6.

a woman's ability to endure the unavoidable pain of menstru-ation or childbirth and her ability to endure pain in order to understand and alleviate suffering.

At every juncture of Freudian feminine psychology, Erikson accents the positive, summarizing his views as turning

> from the loss of an external organ to a sense of vital inner potential; from a hateful contempt of the mother to a solidarity with her and other women; from a "passive" renunciation of male activity to the purposeful and competent activity of one endowed with ovaries and a uterus; and from a masochistic pleasure in pain to an ability to stand (and to understand) pain as a meaningful aspect of human experience in general, and of the feminine role in particular.[16]

Erikson comes closest among those in the Freudian tradition, I think, to recognizing feminine qualities as originating from a direct feminine source rather than from a failure to possess something masculine. This is particularly impressive, I think, because Erikson works from that Freudian basis which favors the "l'homme manqué" view. This basis is sometimes limiting to Erikson, however. For all the special suasion of Erikson's views, the reader still senses in him a valiant defense of woman against Freudian attack that implies that the feminine still needs defending and justification. As Freud himself said, his psychology "cannot solve the riddle of femininity." [17]

Karen Horney challenges the "biological standpoint" of Freud and Freudians. She accepts as fact the assertion that differences in sexual constitution and function influence mental life but finds it more helpful to focus on "the way specific and cultural conditions engender specific qualities and faculties, in women and men. . . ." [18] Horney challenges the centrality of penis envy in feminine nature. She questions the

16. *Ibid.*, p. 13.
17. Freud, *New Introductory Lectures*, p. 116; see also p. 135.
18. Karen Horney, *New Ways in Psychoanalysis* (New York: W. W. Norton & Co., 1939), p. 119.

evidence for penis envy, noting that tendencies to dominate, to be ambitious and envious, to dream in phallic symbols, occur equally in neurotic men as well as women. Furthermore, she sees such behavior in women as directed toward other women and children as well as against men. Horney also objects that penis envy is not really an essential characteristic of feminine psychology. Rather, its rhetoric may provide a convenient rationalization for the inability of a woman to realize that she has an inflated self-image which is punctured whenever her excessive demands on her environment are not met. Cultural factors that grant to men the values of independence, strength, sexual freedom, and the right to choose a partner aid the neurotic woman in associating these qualities with the wished-for penis. Horney contends that, while it is true that the wish to be a man may in fact occur in neurotic women, it cannot be considered as a necessary trait of all women.

Horney also questions just how central masochism is to feminine nature. Masochism is not a sexual phenomenon; therefore it is not an anatomical predisposition of women but rather a strategy to gain satisfaction and security through inconspicuousness and dependency. Cultural emphases on women's weakness and frailty—"the ideology that it is in woman's nature to lean on someone and that her life is given content and meaning only through others"—foster masochistic attitudes in feminine neuroses.[19] Horney agrees with Freud that the overvaluation of love and the dread of losing it are central to feminine nature—but for cultural, not biological, reasons. For centuries the life of woman was restricted to the emotional sphere, which was her only avenue to happiness, status, and security. This restriction resulted in the excessive valuation of love. Thus Horney offers a direct challenge to Freud's three touchstones of feminine psychology—penis envy, masochism, and passivity (or longing for love)—and with her challenge offers an alternate explication of female psychology based on cultural factors. Still, how-

19. *Ibid.*, p. 113. See also Karen Horney, *Feminine Psychology* (New York: W. W. Norton & Co., 1967), *passim*.

ever, the symbolic meaning of the feminine is left unexplored in Horney; it is treated only by contrast with masculine psychology and as determined by cultural deprivation.

THE SYMBOLIC APPROACH

IF WE SEEK FROM JUNG a precise definition of the feminine, we will still seek in vain. His presentation is limited in quantity and uneven in quality. Jung glances over profound truths, repeats the obvious ones, loses threads of arguments, and is often inaccurate in his observations. At the same time, however, a mere passing comment will reveal a new depth; a chance remark will inspire a whole field of research, and for all his disjointed, unsystematic method, Jung fundamentally pays serious attention to the feminine as an original psychic mode of being rather than as a deficient masculinity. The positive result is not so much what Jung accomplishes as what he has inspired others to do with his aperçus. To gather the full wisdom of the Jungian psychology of the feminine, therefore, it is necessary to piece together a mosaic of quotation and paraphrase from Jung and his followers.

In contrast to the cultural and biological descriptions of the feminine, Jung's method is to capture the feminine as a psychic as well as a sexual and a cultural determinant of human being. He describes the feminine symbolically as a principle of being. The symbolic approach is necessary because the feminine cannot be known directly as a thing in itself but only indirectly as it is encountered in images, actions, and emotional responses. To describe the feminine as principle is to refer to it as an inner law or essence, a primary source inherent in the nature of things, like the law of gravity.[20]

Jung describes this feminine principle as eros, whose nature

20. See Jung, "Woman in Europe," *Civilization in Transition* (*CW*, X, 1964), *passim;* see also Esther Harding, *Woman's Mysteries* (London: Longmans, Green & Co., 1935), p. 20; Eleanor Bertine, *Human Relationships* (New York: David McKay Co., 1958), pp. 98–99.

is most clearly seen in contrast to logos, the symbolic concept representing the masculine principle. Jung most often discusses the feminine and masculine poles in complementary relation to each other. This approach derives from the emphasis Jung puts on the importance of contrasexuality, which I will take up later. Jung writes, "The concept of Eros could be expressed in modern terms as psychic relatedness, and that of Logos as objective interest." [21] Jung sees the feminine principle of eros as a major shaping factor of a woman's consciousness and of the anima in a man's sexuality. The masculine principle of logos, with which Jung associates discrimination, judgment, insight, and relation to nonpersonal truth, is seen as determining masculine consciousness, and as represented by the animus in female sexuality. The concept of eros describes symbolically the psychic urge to relate, to join, to be in-the-midst-of, to reach out to, to value, to get in touch with, to get involved with concrete feelings, things, and people, rather than to abstract or theorize.

The psychic urge for relatedness does not have the same meaning as *relationship*. Relatedness means being connected to, in the middle of, involved with, part of; relationship refers to a consciously developed and worked upon relation to an "other" that needs both distance and differentiation as well as closeness and sharing. Relatedness describes an unconscious drive that operates upon and within a person—especially female persons. Relationship presupposes conscious intention. To feel related to someone, in Jung's sense of the word, is not, then, necessarily to have a relationship with them. A sense of relatedness is more often the result of circumstances, such as physical proximity, the sharing of a problem or a task. A relationship may grow out of this sense of relatedness; its development demands conscious participation from the persons involved.

To describe the feminine principle as eros is not to equate it with the feelings of love attributed to Eros, the god of love.

21. Jung, "Woman in Europe," p. 123.

Yet Esther Harding, a leading American disciple of Jung, points out that the arrows of passion that the god Eros lets fly are indeed connected to the feminine principle of eros because when we feel attracted to someone we want to get involved with them, to get connected to them, and place ourselves in the midst of their lives.[22] From this blind urge that brings us in touch with another person we may develop a conscious relationship.

The feminine principle is also described as a modality, as a style or manner of doing something, as an expression or arrangement of being, as the particular appearance on the surface of a deep underlying substance. Mario Moreno writes:

> . . . femininity and masculinity are conceived as two modalities of the process of separating the ego from the original self, from the unconscious matrix—giving oneself to the world and making the world for oneself.
>
> Implicit in these two modes of being are the necessity for reciprocal integration, the annuling of negative otherness, and the aim of reconstructing the self.[23]

Hilde Binswanger uses the concept of polarity to make a similar point:

> . . . masculine can only be defined . . . as a specific way of being related to, or directed towards, the feminine, and the feminine can only be understood as a specific way of being related to, or directed towards the masculine . . . Each exists only through the other, like poles in a dynamic structure, a pre-existing entity which both poles serve in being linked one to the other.[24]

For those who take the symbolic approach, then, the feminine is half of human wholeness, an essential part of it, with-

22. See Harding, *Woman's Mysteries*, p. 83 n. See also below, Appendix, "A Note on Eros and Logos," pp. 335–41.

23. Mario Moreno, "Archetypal Foundations in the Analysis of Women," *The Journal of Analytical Psychology*, X, no. 2 (July, 1965), 183–84.

24. Hilde Binswanger, "Ego, Animus and Persona in the Feminine Psyche," *Harvest* (London: The Analytical Psychology Club, 1965), II, 2.

out which wholeness is impossible. Wholeness means both poles, both modes, and wholeness is not simply identification and fusion but polarity and union. We need both poles to understand either one because each is involved in the development and completion of the other. These complementary poles mean maleness and femaleness, not as directly characterizing men or women but as sets of qualities which describe the two sexes symbolically. Symbolic description is necessary because we are describing archetypal aspects of the psyche which can never be known directly in themselves but only as we encounter them in images, patterns of behavior, and emotional response. The purpose and value of this type of description will become clear as we discuss the feminine principle in greater detail.

Two Aspects of the Feminine Principle

The feminine principle has two aspects: an elementary or static aspect and a transformative or dynamic aspect.[25] The elementary, static aspect of the feminine principle is represented as a receptive, dark, ingoing, moist, enclosing, and containing world of formation that surrounds and holds fast to everything that is created within it. Like the vibrant and fertile darkness of nature that ever renews organisms with new life, this elementary aspect of the feminine gestates new drives, images, fantasies, and intuitions and is thus associated with the unconscious and with the dark mysteries of God. Like nature also, the elementary feminine has an inert and indifferent quality, presenting itself as impersonal and nonin-

25. See Jung, "Psychological Aspects of the Mother Archetype," *The Archetypes and the Collective Unconscious* (CW, IX, Part I, 1959), pp. 81–82. The masculine pole also has a static and a dynamic aspect which E. C. Whitmont describes by making use of the ancient Chinese concept of Yang. See *The Symbolic Quest* (New York: C. G. Jung Foundation, 1969), pp. 171, 174.

dividual.[26] The very static quality of this aspect of the feminine is the basis of the conservative, unchanging, and stable quality of the feminine which predominates in motherhood.

In its positive expression, this elementary aspect of the feminine is symbolized in images of the good mother who bears, protects, and releases, leading from darkness to light. Frequent symbols are the depths, fruit with an abundance of seeds, the teeming cornucopia, the belly as a containing vessel. Representative animal symbols include the pig, because of its fertility, the shellfish with its womb shape, the owl with its uterine-shaped body. Other symbolic metaphors are the casket, nest, cradle, ship, coffin, and the mountain as meaning safety (in German, derived from *sich bergen*, to take refuge). The positive effect of this elemental aspect of the feminine makes itself felt in such emotional responses as feeling secure, protected, fundamentally accepted and acceptable, with a reservoir of hope and possibility. This positive effect of the elementary feminine is communicated in behavior that expresses a sense of confidence, security, and optimism, or that expresses protective and solicitous concern toward others, conveying trust in their essential acceptability and rightness.

In its negative expression, the elementary aspect of the feminine is described symbolically as ensnaring, fixating, holding fast, leading from light to darkness, depriving, rejecting, acting as a regressive undertow of unconsciousness that drags one beyond one's depths to be swallowed up. The elementary side of the feminine in its negative expression appears as undifferentiated and collective, as devouring, castrating, and indifferent to individual consciousness and development. This negative quality is depicted in such images as the terrible mother who eats her children alive, or the Gorgon's head that paralyzes anyone who gazes upon it.

26. See Jung, *Symbols of Transformation*, trans. R. F. C. Hull, 2 vols. (New York: Harper & Brothers, 1956), I, 218–19. See also Erich Neumann, *The Great Mother*, trans. Ralph Manheim (New York: Pantheon, 1955), pp. 26–29, 45–46, 66–71.

Other negative animal images that are typical are the octopus and the spider with their ensnaring legs, and the bear with its suffocating hug. An example of the emotional effect of such a negative image is the following description of a young male patient struggling to free himself from his ensnaring dependence on his mother: "When I am around my mother everything in me wants to break and run, but instead I feel my nerve failing and I become almost hypnotized. It is as if she is some primeval ooze slowly coming toward me to swallow me up into herself."

Typical emotional responses to the negative expression of the elementary aspect of the feminine are a feeling of inertia bordering on paralysis, a feeling of being dragged down into a depression from which one cannot escape, a sense of drifting into unconsciousness. Typical patterns of behavior that express the influence of the negative are an inability to make decisions, a feeling of being fixed in place, and a regression to more primitive behavior. One may also behave in a devouring way toward others or feel devoured by them. One may act out impulses unconsciously, without thinking the action through, or express various states of unconsciousness by addiction to drink or drugs.

The transformative, active side of the feminine principle accents the dynamic elements of the psyche that urge change and transformation. This active side of the feminine is similar to that divine madness of the soul described in Plato's *Phaedrus,* which invokes primeval forces that take us out of the limitations and conventions of social norms and the reasonable life. Eros in this sense produces ecstasy, a liberation from the conventions of the group and from one's usual public self through an expression of the irrational elements in one's personality. Ecstasy may range from a momentary being taken out of oneself to a profound enlargement of personality. Eros as the moving out of oneself to merge with another, though not identical with I-Thou relatedness, is nonetheless an indispensable part of it, because it leads to full emotional involvement.

In its positive expression, the transformative aspect of the feminine shows itself in images of birth and rebirth: a child emerging from the dark womb, a muse who inspires one to new feats of creativity, or an inspiring person who stirs one to greater intensity of participation. Among many other symbols of transformation are the growing fruit, a seed becoming an ear of corn, a caterpillar becoming a butterfly, a woman's belly as a chemical retort or transforming kiln. The analytical relationship between analyst and analysand is often likened to a vessel in which psychological transformation takes place. A related symbol is a woman's breast seen as a goblet, grail, or chalice.

The positive emotional effects of transformation are feelings of being caught up in a creative process, feelings of excitement, zest, vitality, or of being inspired and called out of oneself by something of compelling, life-giving value. The positive quality of the transformative side of the feminine may be expressed by an opening to new insights, or a changing of the shape and texture of one's life or relationships. One may lure or inspire others to new feats or new insight. One may enjoy a sense of the playful and the unexpected. One may find that one can risk exposure to forces beyond one's control with a sense of expectation rather than of fear.

The negative transformations that result from this dynamic aspect of the feminine lead from clarity to opaqueness instead of to inspiration, to lunacy and madness instead of to growth, to drunkenness and dissolution, into dark recesses of the unconscious where one's identity is seriously endangered. Symbols associated with negative transformations are the spells of evil witches that change men into animals or things, the evil succubus who steals into a man's soul and sucks it dry, the devilish temptress who brings on states of possession where one is at the mercy of uncontrollable rage or resentment or is drawn irresistibly to someone destructive.

An example of negative transformation may be seen in the dream of a young wife. In our first session she reported the dream as one that she had not been able to forget since its occurrence six months earlier. In it, a feminine figure confronts the dreamer menacingly, gradually changing into a shape that is less and less human, regressing further and further until finally she displays openly the negative side of the elementary static feminine and threatens to destroy the dreamer. The young woman reported that this dream expressed her own feelings of diffuseness and her inability to get hold of herself. No matter how hard she tried, her efforts always seemed to collapse and unravel in front of her, like Penelope's weaving. She dreamt: "As I weave the tapestry of my life, I notice a Negro woman unraveling it from the other end. I tell her to stop it, but it seems she doesn't hear me or see me. I then tell her I will hit her if she doesn't stop unweaving my tapestry. Then she fixes on me and gradually changes shape and age. At the beginning she is lovely, like a model in her thirties. Then she becomes a younger girl and tougher looking. Her face coarsens and her skin thickens. Then she has fangs and her face is like an animal's; her mouth drips blood and her body is covered with fur. She grabs at a pair of scissors and is coming for me to poke out my eyes."

The emotional difficulties that indicate negative transformation are a sense of losing consciousness, trouble in focusing on a thought or idea, or a sense of being dragged down into a confused state one is powerless to control. One may feel helplessly in the grip of an obsessive jealousy that transforms one into a suspicious unattractive person. Patterns of behavior that express this negative transformation are a regression to less adapted, more primitive modes of being that reduce consciousness rather than enhance it. For example, one may sink into a nasty passivity that spoils the situation for everybody because one sullenly expects everyone else to make life easier for oneself and is no longer willing to meet others halfway. One may retreat into silent opposition and withdraw from communicating, thinking, or feeling. Warmth may change into maudlin sentimentality, irritation into rage, jealousy into paranoid obsession. One may feel driven to actions one knows are self-destructive or destructive to others. One is possessed, and the vengeance of the possession disregards the presence or reality of other people and their feelings, and even the effects on oneself. One loses consciousness and severs relationship; it is as if everything were swallowed up in the dark.

CONTRASEXUALITY

THE FIRST WAY in which Jung's symbolic view differs from the biological and cultural views of the feminine is that Jung sees the feminine not as exclusively anatomy or a product of culture, but also as a psychic element. The second difference is seen in Jung's description of the feminine, which for him can be known only indirectly, through the symbolic concept of the feminine principle as eros and through the elementary and transformative aspects of the feminine.

The third way is the most important: it is the way of contrasexuality. The feminine, according to Jung, is not the exclusive concern of females but is a central shaping factor in both sexes, just as the masculine principle is. Because we have so neglected the feminine and its psychology, we are incompetent to deal adequately with the male personality or the male psychology that has so dominated our world, shaping our style of business practice, politics, our conceptions of value, and of civilization itself. We are unable to deal with masculine psychology unless we give vigorous and searching attention to the feminine, because we cannot fully understand the male unless we understand the feminine elements within the male—in Jung's terms, the anima. The converse is true for the female. We cannot fully understand her unless we understand the masculine elements within her personality— the animus.

The symbolic complementarity of the two sexes is seen concretely in the biological polarity of male and female and in the inner sexual polarity of each person, his anima or her animus.[27] Biology has demonstrated that woman has recessive male characteristics—male sex hormones in the blood stream and in rudimentary male sex organs—and that man has recessive female characteristics. Maleness and femaleness are determined, therefore, "not by an absolute but by a relative predominance of one set of characteristics over the other; the recessive set . . . merely operates out of sight, from a relative background position." [28]

Because the degrees of predominant and recessive functioning vary in people, we constantly observe masculine-motivated women and feminine-motivated men. Sometimes, the predominant element may not be fully conscious, which results in women who are unaware of the full range of their femininity and in men who have not fully claimed their masculinity. This unclaimed sexual identity may as a result influence the character of the unconscious contrasexual element. For example the mannish woman may have an effeminate animus, leading her to be attracted in conscious life, as we often see, to homosexual men. An effeminate man is often compensated by a warriorlike anima, which he projects onto women, thus justifying and reinforcing his avoidance of women. Both sexes often try, too, to make up in learned responses what they lack in genuine development, so that we frequently meet with sentimentality in a woman rather than feeling, and with rigidity or ruthlessness in a man instead of strength.

The whole person for Jung is the contrasexual person, who is consciously related to internal male and female elements

27. The relationship of these two primal elements is characterized in the Chinese concepts of Yin (feminine) and Yang (masculine). Richard Wilhelm writes of their interrelationship: "The receptive primal power of yin . . . is the perfect complement of THE CREATIVE— the complement, not the opposite, for the Receptive does not combat the Creative but completes it" (Richard Wilhelm, *The I Ching or Book of Changes,* trans. Cary F. Barnes [New York: Pantheon, 1950], p. 9).

28. Whitmont, *Symbolic Quest,* p. 177. See also Jung, "Archetypes of the Collective Unconscious," *Archetypes and the Collective Unconscious,* pp. 27–28.

which operate in polarity to each other. Masculinity and femininity can only be described in relation to each other as two modalities of separating the ego out of the original unconscious matrix, of giving oneself to the world and others, and of making the world for oneself. Masculine and feminine elements exist only in relation to each other and complement rather than fight each other. Feminine and masculine, then, are archetypal principles of the human psyche whose polarity and complementarity are to be found in the interaction of both sexes and in the interaction within a single person of the ego with the anima or animus.

The wholeness of every individual revolves around the axis of a fully developed polarity of maleness and femaleness, both in concrete psychobiological terms and in symbolic terms, where it encompasses all the polarities of the psyche. The polar structure of the psyche is the source of its energy and the matrix for its fulfillment. Libido, the life energy which is generated from the tension of the polarities, flows from one pole to the other, thereby differentiating the ego from its nascent unconscious state and effecting the emergence of those distinct elements whose reconciliation makes wholeness possible. Wholeness is a demand, a potential, which we experience while we are still partial and limited. Wholeness does not mean abrogation of polarity. That would be the abrogation of the source of life energy and hence of life itself, as illustrated in such dramatic events as those which accompany regression to the initial unconscious state—suicide, or the loss of discrete psychic functions (psychosis), or the splitting-off of one pole from the other (neurosis). Wholeness is effected in the fullest functioning of the polarities, which do not become fixed in opposition to each other but are rather completed in mutuality. Wholeness is an enlarged state where there is not just the masculine or the feminine but both, where there is vitality and enrichment because the two become one, and where there is engagement and fulfillment as well. Thus, in becoming whole we must grow into a conscious relationship to the masculine-feminine polarity within us. And we must do so in both the static and dynamic aspects of each pole, because through this polarity we are put in touch with all the other psychic polarities.

The development of an inner male-female polarity, however, cannot be effected without relation to the opposite sex. Just as we cannot fully relate to another being without encountering our own deepest self, we cannot meet our deepest self without fully meeting another self. Individuation is not accomplished by introversion alone. Therefore, to the other polarities must be added this one of relatedness of one's self to another. Awareness of this may be illustrated culturally in modern concerns with "marriage problems" which are reflected in the creation of new professions and disciplines to deal with them, church departments of marriage and family life, and educational degrees and state licenses in marriage counseling. The past ideal of a marriage relationship guided by duties and carefully defined collective social standards is no longer central to our culture. We have come to insist on the need to shape marriage into a personal relationship in which each partner fully accepts the individuality of the other and in which each feels the full weight of his or her own personality, in both its negative and positive aspects, in relation to the other.

THE FEMININE IN CULTURE

THE FEMININE PRINCIPLE which symbolizes aspects of being and styles of relating also feeds into our culture as a shaping force that is identified in the history of culture as a specifically feminine element. The relatively recent concern with women's rights and the fight against any kind of discrimination on the basis of sex may be a concrete expression of what Jung would call a deep urge constellated by the objective psyche to differentiate the feminine as a modality of being that influences the two sexes and their culture. Here is the precise point at which Jung's symbolic approach adds something new to other approaches. In contrast to the biological approach that sees the feminine as belonging only to woman, Jung insists again and again that we recognize the feminine as part of male psychology also, particularly in man's relation to his own unconscious. If a man fails to develop his relation to this feminine element in himself, he suffers at least a partial diminution of being and at worst, a serious mental illness. In contrast to the cultural approach that emphasizes how much our concepts of the feminine, of woman's place, and of her psychology are influenced by dominant cultural trends, we see in Jung's thought that the feminine is also a factor in shaping those cultural trends. In this sense, the concern of many women with what a woman's nature is and with what a relationship with a man should be may be considered as concrete expression of the urge to recover to consciousness the neglected feminine pole of the central masculine-feminine polarity. Seen in this way the struggle for women's "rights" is not a part of a political platform for women but a human project concerned with all of us as persons. Jung writes of woman's struggle:

> It is her individual expression of something that is general and inherent in our time, namely, a cultural tendency towards a more complete human form; a longing for meaning and fulfillment; an increasing repugnance to a senseless, one-sided attitude, and a dissatisfaction with a life of pure unconscious instinctiveness and blind happenings.[29]

The cultural emancipation of women makes accessible to concrete discussion, analysis, and conscious determination the problems that develop out of and alongside the feminine side of life. In Jungian terms, man

> has been obliged to acknowledge the existence of an autonomous and independent psyche. His old-established belief in the "superiority" of the "logos" has been decisively challenged by an equally important, but diligently over-

29. Jung, "Woman in Europe," *Contributions to Analytical Psychology*, p. 185.

looked power of the "eros." Where this challenge is accepted and answered in a constructive sense, a new and creative relationship between man and woman as equal partners can be established. Here the inner process of the synthesis between the feminine and the masculine psyche, of the creation of the total personality, has found its concrete expression.[30]

This whole movement of psychology is, in a sense, an expression of the feminine, because its pursuit of ceaselessly emerging images, of nonrational wisdom, and of the gestating, healing capacities of the psyche, its wish to make tangible to us our intuitive and diffuse feeling tones, and its charting of the non-spatio-temporal and noncausal processes of the unconscious matrix are all fervent attempts to capture the feminine modality of being in relation to the more masculine conscious approach of persons. Depth psychology in general, and Jung's focus on the feminine in particular, no matter how primitive their methods, point to a new approach to the age-old conflict between the sexes.

Though men were the original agents of depth psychology, women have provided the preponderance of its clinical materials. In most psychoanalytical practice, the majority of patients are female. The bulk of Freud's initial insights (excluding "Little Hans," "The Schreber Case," and "The Rat Man") derived from work with women. Woman's "material" makes accessible the deep-seated longings and conflicts of both sexes. Woman's concern with feelings and fantasies that hover around things, and especially around personal relationships, make unconscious contents accessible, for, "in contrast to objective understanding and agreement as to facts, human relationship leads into the psychic world, that middle kingdom which reaches from the world of sense and affect to that of the spirit." [31]

30. Gerhard Adler, *Studies in Analytical Psychology* (New York: C. G. Jung Foundation, 1966), pp. 242–43.
31. Jung, "Woman in Europe," *Contributions to Analytical Psychology*, p. 178.

CHAPTER NINE

Feminine Consciousness, Feminine Spirit

T HE SYMBOLIC APPROACH of Jung challenges the stereotypes of the feminine. In contrast to the usual equation of femininity with passivity of feeling among women, the symbolic approach describes feminine forms of activity and understanding within all people, men as well as women. In contrast to the frequent identification of the feminine with the unconscious, with nonspiritual and natural processes, the symbolic approach describes the feminine kind of ego consciousness and its relation to the unconscious, as well as the feminine qualities of spirit.

FEMININE CONSCIOUSNESS

ERICH NEUMANN calls feminine consciousness "matriarchal" to indicate a phase of human development in which the Great

Mother archetype predominates. The feminine style of ego functioning he calls the "heart-ego," in order to show that it is particularly attuned to unconscious processes. He distinguishes this set of responses from masculine, "patriarchal" consciousness, a form of consciousness which separates itself from the unconscious into a discrete and independent "head-ego." [1] Historically, feminine consciousness characterizes the early eras of humanity, and in individual lives is manifest in childhood, in moments of psychological crisis, and in the creative processes. Patriarchal consciousness dominates Western culture, but both types of ego consciousness inhere in both sexes, each finding its most direct expression in its corresponding sex.

UNDERSTANDING

THE FEMININE QUALITY of understanding begins with perception and apperception, what Neumann calls *Einfall*, hunch, the thrusting of spiritual contents "into consciousness with sufficient convincing force to fascinate and control it. . . ." [2] Whether the ego sees its *Einfall* in a primitive phase as a message from the gods or later, more sophisticatedly, as emerging psychic energies, the ego receives its spiritual contents into itself. The ego does not so much create these spiritual contents as it is created by them.

> For matriarchal consciousness, understanding is not an act of intellect, functioning as an organ for swift registration, development and organization; rather it has the meaning of a "conception." Whatever is to be understood must first

1. See Erich Neumann, "On the Moon and Matriarchal Consciousness," *Dynamic Aspects of the Psyche*, trans. Hildegard Nagel (New York: The Analytical Psychology Club, 1956), p. 51.
2. *Ibid.*, p. 53. See also Jung, "A Study in the Process of Individuation," *Archetypes and the Collective Unconscious* (CW, IX, Part I, 1959), p. 302.

"enter" matriarchal consciousness in the full, sexual, symbolic meaning of a fructification.[3]

Ideas "seize" consciousness or "arise"; they are not willed or thought out. In the process of conceiving ideas, we see operating the static elementary containing mode of the feminine. The act of understanding is an encirclement, a circumambulation of a content which has emerged. The attitude of the ego toward this is to consider and to ponder it, to have an awareness of the content rather than a directed thought or judgment about it. This kind of understanding recalls Jung's recovery of the so-called "autistic" way of thinking. This kind of understanding is concerned with what generally gives meaning rather than with facts or ideas, with organic growth rather than with mechanical processes or chains of causation. In contrast to the distant, abstract quality of thought demanded by the objectivity of the head ego, the feminine quality of understanding, according to Neumann, brings with it "an act of inclusive feeling and very often this act—as, for instance, in creative work—has to be accompanied by the most intense affect-participation, if anything is to shine forth and illuminate." [4] Here we see the dynamic, transformative aspect—the urge of feminine "relatedness" to get into the midst of things and to merge with them.

The moment of conception of an idea is veiled, often taking both the heart ego and the head ego unaware. An example is the experience of suddenly being presented with a complete thought or course of action that we have no sense of having developed for ourselves. We say, for example, "It suddenly hit me," "It suddenly came to me." Investigation of fantasies, dreams, and related images, however, usually shows that the moment of conception had already been registered unconsciously and participated in for a long time.

The circumambulation of the conceiving processes usually

3. Neumann, "On the Moon and Matriarchal Consciousness," pp. 57–58.
4. Ibid., p. 59.

takes place in stillness and darkness; hence the feminine is associated with symbols of the moon's cool reflected light, shining in the darkness and reigning over fertility and growth on earth. Darkness, as opposed to the burning rays of the sun, characterizes the world of the unseen, and the mysterious processes of the unconscious where creative activity starts, and the soul's wounds may begin to heal themselves. Nighttime is the time of sleep and of recovery, of regeneration and of healing.

> It is the regenerating power of the unconscious that in nocturnal darkness or by the light of the moon performs its task, a *mysterium* in a *mysterium*, working from out of itself, out of nature, with no aid from the head-ego.
>
> . . . the darkness where recovery takes place, and also those events in the soul which, in obscurity, by processes only the heart can know, allow men to "outgrow" their insoluble crises.[5]

The act of understanding is not only an act of conception, but also a bringing forth of the perception into something concrete and fully realized. This bringing forth is the transformative, dynamic work of the feminine. Its active eros element reaches out to complete a process begun in the unconscious. Unlike an act of intellect that can swiftly register facts, analyze, or classify them, the feminine quality of understanding conceives a content, walks around it, participates affectively in it, and then brings it forth into the world.

In the act of understanding, a personality change is brought about. A new content has seized a whole being, and that being is now both expressed in and has become part of the full-grown perception that is emerging into the world of everyday life. An obvious example of this is an artist's relation to a new painting, or a person's relation to a new insight.

The knowledge that results from this kind of growth process is comprehension rather than intellection or information about something. Because this kind of knowing in-

5. *Ibid.*, p. 61.

volves participation of the whole personality and effects concrete changes in it, the comprehension has a concrete rather than an abstract quality. Such knowledge cannot be imparted, proved, or even accounted for. The inner experience behind it is scarcely able to be communicated verbally. We have all found ourselves saying about such understanding, "If you haven't had the experience, I can't explain it to you." These are comprehensions conditioned by the personality which has them. They are not to be de-emotionalized, abstracted, or turned into isolated contents claiming universal validity. This fact often encourages nonverbal or image-laden forms of communication, such as what we call "sensory awareness," or fairy tales, or parables, or the efforts to articulate somehow, no matter how incompletely, the darkness of personal experience. This is what Jungians call feminine comprehension, a comprehension that grows quietly over a period of time and transforms the person who has it.[6] The symbolism of the feminine is mysterious, and its secrets are imparted in mysterious ways reaching back to ancient mythological rites and ecstasies associated with music and the dance, such as the Orphic and Eleusinian mysteries. Thus it is the feminine muses who preside over rhythm, over soothsaying and artistic creativity.[7] The style of feminine comprehension and communication is similar to that of the oral tradition in Christianity. The written word tells one story. The spoken word, accompanied by the gestures and tonalities of the speaker, tells another.

Activity

The quality of feminine ego activity is to accept a conception, to carry knowledge, to assimilate it, and to allow it to

6. *Ibid.*, p. 62.
7. See C. Kerényi, "Die Orphische Kosmogonie und der Ursprung der Orphik," *Eranos-Jahrbuch* (Zurich: Rascher Verlag, 1949), vol. XVII, as quoted in Neumann, "On the Moon and Matriarchal Consciousness," p. 55.

ripen. It is a way of submitting to a process, which is seen as simply happening and is not to be forced or achieved by an effort of the will. The quality of feminine activity is a mixture of attentiveness and contemplation. Like the moon reflecting the light of the sun, the feminine style of ego consciousness turns to and reflects unconscious processes, guiding itself by them, and gathering them up into itself. In this kind of activity, the ego elicits the participation of the whole psyche by "turning the libido toward a particular psychic event and intensifying its effect, rather than using the experience as a basis for abstract conclusions and an expansion of consciousness." [8]

In directing energies to an emotionally charged content, an ego allows itself to be filled and guided in its own orientation by the feelings and intuitions that cluster around half-conscious emotionally charged contents. The ego never withdraws or abstracts from this intensely personal relationship to the objects of its attention, but rather allows itself to be drawn to the contents and then circles around them. This kind of attention is inherent in psychoanalytical work in the exploration of dreams, hopes, fantasies, and all other expressions of feelings. The attentions of both analyst and patient are engaged by dream contents and both open to them, almost "dreaming along" with dreams, in order to find their message. The whole depth-psychology movement can in a sense be seen as a cultural expression of this feminine style of activity. In the process of depth psychology, consciousness is drawn to the contents of the unconscious and allows itself to be impressed with them. It is also this feminine quality of activity, with its readiness to receive and respond with the whole being, that is essential in religious experience. Our neglect of the feminine, therefore, stunts our capacity for both psychological and religious vision.

The feminine mode of ego activity is to wait and attend to things, to keep still until a dream-promise is clearly fulfilled

---

8. Neumann, "On the Moon and Matriarchal Consciousness," p. 64.

and transforming insight has come. That is why the feminine is so often symbolized by the processes of cooking, baking, boiling—all the processes involved in preparing food to be eaten. This psychological activity is manifest in the physical activities surrounding pregnancy and birth, where a woman has no control over the health, sex, or general fate of her child. Openness to a world outside her own control is the key attitude here. Similarly, a woman's openness to the overwhelming power of a love relationship illustrates this feminine style of ego consciousness.

A woman may also have her own style of patriarchal consciousness in which her head ego exercises will power, freedom of choice, and pursues actions based on clear judgments about mental contents. The head ego's stress on consciousness is in marked contrast to the usual matriarchal respect for the potencies of the unconscious and of God, on which the heart ego waits, and on which it loves to dwell.

The contrasting tones of these two ego attitudes may be a source of deep conflict and confusion for a woman if she does not sufficiently recognize their respective values. Contemplative attention to unconscious processes may be confused with passive drifting and submission, if it is viewed only from the vantage point of the value-system of patriarchal consciousness. From this one-sided view, I believe, comes the scorn felt by intellectual women—whose education is suffused with what Jungians call patriarchal consciousness—scorn for their uneducated sisters who "never think an independent thought." Female protests about male dominance, and women's exhortations to other women to free themselves from men's images of them, contain large elements of projection onto men of women's own feelings of subjective dependence on patriarchal consciousness. These protests voice hope for a different, more feminine quality of ego activity, and the desire at the same time of many other women to suppress the differences altogether because of the mistaken notion that in that way they will guarantee women's freedom, because then "we will all be alike."

Differences between the sexes have frequently been linked with discrimination against women, so that some see the only solution to that injustice in the abolition of sexual differences entirely, which would simply add psychological injustice to social injustice. Discrimination against women must of course be ended, but repression of sexual differences will not achieve that end. To repress sexual differences is only to blot them out of consciousness; they continue to exist but unconsciously, now, out of our reach and out of our control, and therefore in more dangerous form than ever. The differences between the sexes offer the most striking instances of the dark mystery of otherness. Our inability to receive this fact of otherness and respond to it appropriately leads to our repression of it. But when we repress something, our ego loses touch with it and comes to fear it because it is outside control by the ego. Then the ego must discriminate against that "other" and dominate it in order to keep it under control—whether it is the "other" of color, of race, of sex, or of country. All prejudices are, I think, traceable to this fearful response to otherness.

TIME

FOR THE FEMININE STYLE of consciousness, time is qualitative rather than quantitative. We feel time as periodic and rhythmic, as waxing and waning, as favorable or unfavorable. The moon symbolizes this qualitative time in its measuring of months by its own cycle of fullness and leanness. The moon cycle also represents the mysterious—and unconscious—and, in Jungian terms, feminine—rhythms of fertility, of growth, of birth, of withdrawal, of decline, and death. In this sense, time is cyclical. It ebbs and flows according to an inner rhythm. Each woman experiences this in the blood tides of her menstrual cycle and its attendant psychological effects.[9]

9. See Harding, *Woman's Mysteries* (London: Longmans, Green & Co., 1935), pp. 234-35, 241-43.

At ovulation, a woman's body is receptive and fertile. She may feel then an emotional expansiveness, an abundance of sexual energy, a new potency in her creative ideas and insights. If her ego is not in touch with this phase of the cycle, she often squanders her energy in increased busyness or talkativeness, or perhaps in nervous flirtations. If she is related to what is happening to her body and psyche, this time of the month can give her increased confidence and new certainty in her own capacities. Because this sense of herself is rooted in psychosomatic reality, it does not lead to inflation or a drive for power but to stabilization, and a real sense of her own strength. At menstruation, when the body passes its blood-food, a woman often feels an ingathering of her energy and feelings to a deeper center below the threshold of consciousness. If estranged from that center, a woman experiences this phase as a "curse," as moodiness, as oversensitivity and pain and irritability. If she is in accord with herself, this phase can be a time of developing fertile insights, new relationships, or creative possibilities suddenly opened to her during ovulation.

The inner and outer qualities of life are symbolized in this cyclical rhythm. What happens externally depends on what happens internally. Will power and reasoning avail not at all; the ego must watch and wait and attune itself to the favorable or unfavorable qualities of the moment. The effectiveness of feminine consciousness depends on its harmony with the unconscious. We see this illustrated in women who are productive when they relate their talents to their whole being, but become intrusive or even destructive when their gifts remain unintegrated with the rest of them. A keen intellect then becomes strident, a warmth of heart becomes cloying, a capacity to feel turns maudlin. If a woman is not sufficiently related to her unconscious roots, the tempo of her actions is capricious and erratic. When a woman's ego is in harmony with the rhythms of the unconscious, all her levels of life move in counterpoint, imbuing her consciousness with a special and positive character.[10] The accented rhythms of music and dance often play an important part in activating the feminine style of consciousness and establishing a consonance between it and the unconscious. We read, for example, of the intoxicating power of music in ancient mystery rites and orgiastic rituals associated with feminine deities. We know that music puts us in touch with our own body rhythms. We have seen what a large role music has had in the lives of young people in the twentieth century; it has been at the center of protest movements of all kinds and especially where there has been some drive toward ecstatic dissolution of problems and a simultaneous attempt to achieve a non-rational harmony.

The feminine sense of time is time felt as individual, time experienced as a series of unique occurrences—a conception or pregnancy of the moment, a sudden birth of feeling. This is very different from the sense of time as a series of equal or similar moments. It is time as *kairos* rather than as *chronos*. Thus this feminine sense of time is closely associated with all religious experience, for in the feminine consciousness of time one feels the authority of the present moment, feels its fullness and its decisiveness, feels freed from anxiety over the past or over future expectations. The ecstasy of LSD users who claim to be liberated from time and to be focused on moments of immediate perception, can be understood as the result of a reckless plunge into this feminine sense of time.

DUALITY

BECAUSE THE EGO of matriarchal consciousness is guided by cyclical processes which reflect both the static and dynamic, both the elementary and transformative qualities of the feminine modality, the feminine is characterized by duality. Like

10. Neumann, "On the Moon and Matriarchal Consciousness," p. 55.

the moon, the feminine style of ego consciousness moves between waxing and waning, appearance and disappearance, fullness and leanness. The inner rhythm of the feminine is cyclical change. When a woman is not in tune with the rhythm it shows itself in sharp alternations rather than a steady cyclical unfolding. The duality of the moon-goddess symbolism illustrates this:

> The Moon Goddess was thus believed to be giver of life and of all that promotes fertility and productiveness and yet at the same time she was the wielder of the destructive powers of nature. . . . In the upper-world phase, corresponding to the bright moon, the goddess is good, kind and beneficent. . . . When the moon is dark, she is cruel, destructive and evil.[11]

This dual nature is depicted in some religious art in the form of a moon goddess who is half dark and half light, and again in the black virgins of medieval Montserrat and Einsiedeln, where Mary is called "Moon of the Church."

Neumann notes the duality of the etymological root of that traditional symbol of the feminine, the "moon." The Sanskrit root *mas* yields *ma*, meaning to measure, which leads to *metis*, cleverness and wisdom, *metiesthai*, to mediate or to dream or have in mind, and *mati-h*, knowing. The Sanskrit root *manas* means spirit, and *mati-h* means thought or intention, which lead in turn to

> *menos*, spirit, heart, soul, courage, ardency; *menoinan*, to consider, mediate, wish; *memona*, to have in mind, to intend; *mainomai* to think, . . . to rave, . . . *mania*, madness, possession, and also *manteia*, prophecy. . . . *menis*, *menos*, anger; *menūo*, indicate, reveal; *menō*, remain, linger; *manthanō*, to learn; *memini*, to remember; and *mentiri*, to lie.[12]

Neumann sums up the duality of the feminine moon spirit in terms of emotional changes related to the activity of the unconscious:

11. Harding, *Woman's Mysteries*, p. 92.
12. Neumann, "On the Moon and Matriarchal Consciousness," p. 52.

In active eruption it is a fiery spirit, it is courage, anger, possession, and rage; its self-revelation leads to prophecy, cogitation, and lying, but also to poetry. Along with this fiery productivity, however, goes another, more "measured" attitude which meditates, dreams, waits and wishes, hesitates and lingers; which is related to memory and learning, and whose outcome is moderation, wisdom, and meaning.[13]

Dangers

THE DANGER of the matriarchal quality of consciousness, Neumann points out, is a constant possibility of a kind of aimless "mooning" and drifting along with one's streams of intuitions, with one's feelings, and images, instead of actively relating to them and making them concrete.[14] Instead of developing a hunch or momentary "conception" into a new psychological attitude or creative contribution, a woman may project the totality of her capacity to realize a conception into actual pregnancy and motherhood. She will then live out her sexual penetration, impregnation, and nurturing only on a literal plane. Then her femininity is lived outwardly, not inwardly, lived only physically, not at all psychologically. Such a woman often feels disillusioned, lost, and useless after her children have grown up. Unfortunately, the criticism of children that their mother has not become a person in her own right is often justified.

Another danger that occurs if a woman is inadequately related to this feminine style of consciousness is that she wastes her time, becoming moody and melancholy, "dreaming, imagining, wishing and fearing (i.e., negative wishing)."[15] Instead of thinking, a woman then falls into making compulsive causal connections that she dogmatically asserts as

13. *Ibid.*, pp. 52-53.
14. *Ibid.*, p. 69.
15. Emma Jung, *The Animus and Anima*, trans. Cary F. Baynes and Hildegard Nagel (New York: The Analytical Psychology Club, 1957), p. 19.

truth because she fails to distinguish between what is real and what is merely thought or imagined. She indulges in senseless mooning over what might have been, or what could have happened, or what ought to have been done. A related misfortune is a woman's tendency to avoid conflict by identifying with her own undifferentiated streams of life.[16] Instead of developing specific points of view that honestly clash with those of others, she keeps her opinions undefined so that they will never differ from anyone else's. Arguments are thereby avoided, but so are discussions. She suffers inundations of her unconscious that may lead to feeling possessed, to hysterical outbursts, to serious withdrawal and depression. Matriarchal consciousness can operate as a regressive undertow against the development of a patriarchal head ego that demands separation from the unconscious and the development of clear and precise discriminations. Regression occurs instead of creation, madness instead of healing, a feeling of senseless drifting instead of contemplation. The moon spirit can show its negative side; it may represent the devouring unconscious in the form of a bloodsucker or eater of human flesh: it may act as a bringer of madness.[17] A young woman's dream illustrates a conflict between the patriarchal ego of clarity, force, and assertion as symbolized by the sun, and the matriarchal ego as symbolized by the moon.

> I stood at the window of an empty room gazing at the sky. The sun and moon were bigger than life and swung back and forth, through the heavens. I thought to myself as they grew larger and larger, "I love the moon more than the sun." At this, the moon seemed to swallow up the sun. Then I was sitting opposite my childhood girl friend who was trying to talk to me. She said she had trouble getting

16. See Amy Allenby, "Psychological Aspects of the Father Archetype in Feminine Psychology," *Journal of Analytical Psychology*, I (1955–56), 79–80.

17. See Robert Briffault, *The Mothers*, 3 vols. (New York: Macmillan, 1927), vol. II, chap. XIX, as quoted in Erich Neumann, *The Great Mother*, trans. Ralph Manheim (New York: Pantheon, 1955), p. 70.

through to me and was worried when I said I felt the sun burning in my head.

This dream signals danger. The space the dreamer lives in is empty: ego contents are lacking. Her focus is a gazing rapture on archetypal forces which are not only bigger than those in real life but become even more powerful as her libido is fed into them. The dreamer associated herself with the moon: elements of darkness, her own feelings and moods, the poetry she was writing, and her pressing need "to be in touch with life." With the sun, she associated overbrightness and her experience of headaches as a child when she was in the sun. The sun and moon couple reminded her of her own relationship with a man; he was blond and sun-like, she was dark and moon-like. The childhood girl friend met in the dream was a pedestrian person who represented the dreamer's own inadequately developed reality function. She could not communicate with the girl. The dream said that the dreamer was in touch with powerful, life-giving forces to which she had not properly related because she was empty and without an ego position; as a result they had become inflated and powerful. The matriarchal moon consciousness—the dreamer's identification with her passions, imaginings, moods—swallowed up the sun, which could have brought light, discernment, and perspective into her life. Instead of bringing light, the undeveloped power of patriarchal consciousness burned in her head and disturbed her adaptation to reality. The dreamer's actual personal relationship with her boy friend was mixed up in a transpersonal cosmos. She dreamt of planets, not of persons; thus her feelings were contaminated by unconscious contents. Indirectly, the dream hinted that if she were better related to those archetypal forces through a firm ego consciousness, and able to channel them creatively, she could be positively in touch with a transpersonal dimension. Some of her poetry already showed an unusual if undeveloped talent. The dream pointed out some ways in which it might be nurtured.

Freud's attribution of masochism to women is related to

the dangers of matriarchal consciousness. Masochism is the extreme form of sufferance, just letting things happen, submitting and subjecting the ego to processes beyond its control, directing aggressive energy against oneself. If these tendencies are exaggerated and not balanced by contemplative and orienting activities in which a woman brings forth and asserts her own point of view, she becomes "masochistic." From the view of patriarchal activity—initiating, erecting, and developing what look like objective formulations— the activities of matriarchal consciousness can be confused with morbid subjectiveness, an attitude for which a woman may often punish herself severely. A woman may also fall into masochism if her efforts to find her feminine orientation stop at merely protesting that she is not like men, but rather the opposite of them. She defines herself only negatively, then, and does not go to a position that is clearly self-affirming. The brooding tempo of matriarchal thinking can also degenerate into mooning over past hurts. The circumambulation of a content may become a feeling of being stuck in a rut. The participations of affect and personal reaction may deteriorate into that kind of subjective pettiness which is so often characteristic of a masochistic posture.

THE FEMININE SPIRIT

THE FEMININE STYLE of psychic or spiritual transformation is a downward-going procedure through the transfiguration of the things that are lowest in one's life. Esther Harding describes the process as a searching out and accepting of the manifestations of the spirit that have taken refuge in the despised and rejected parts of one's psyche. This is a way that means exploring with a religious attitude—with careful observation, consideration, and $\pi\iota\sigma\tau\iota\varsigma$—those places in one's own experience where intensity blazes up. It is there one may find the figure of Christ in one's life. The words attributed to Jesus in the Oxyrhynchus papyri are apt: "Whoever is

near to me is near to the fire." [18] The feminine style of transformation is to seek the spirit in the hidden meaning of concrete happenings, to go down deep into personal events and
into the dark, unknown places of our own emotions, where
we find abundance of life in an intensity of our inward responses. To follow this intensity, even if its form conflicts
with accepted values, demands a devotion to the spirit as it is
manifest in one's own person and in the persons of others.
A major symbol here, the moon crescent, points downward
and then shines in the darkness: Jung writes,

> The female element in the deity is kept very dark, the in-
> terpretation of the Holy Ghost as Sophia being considered
> heretical. Hence the Christian metaphysical drama, the
> "Prologue in Heaven," has only masculine actors. . . . But
> the female element must obviously be somewhere—so it is
> presumably to be found in the dark.[19]

Because a quality of feminine ego activity is to let things
happen as they will, transformation of the ego is often seen
as achieved through sufferance, through accord of the self to
a greater will, even to the point of death of one's own ego
orientation. The deeper symbolism of the feminine transformations (of menstruation, pregnancy, and birth) becomes
clear: a woman orients herself to the changes which happen
to her rather than initiating those changes: "the spiritual aspect of the feminine transformative character . . . leads
through suffering and death, sacrifice and annihilation, to renewal, rebirth and immortality." [20] Failure to grasp the character of such a spiritual transformation results in women
seeming to have no independent will or judgment, and seeming always to be seeking pain. Women, in response to this

18. See Harding, *Woman's Mysteries*, p. 313; and Esther Harding,
"The Spiritual Problem of Woman" (unpublished manuscript, property of The Kristine Mann Library, The Analytical Psychology Club
of New York, 1935), *passim*.
19. Jung, *Psychology and Alchemy* (CW, XII, 1967), p. 144. See
also Jung, "The Structure of the Psyche," *The Structure and Dynamics
of the Psyche* (CW, VIII, 1960), p. 154.
20. Neumann, *Great Mother*, p. 291.

interpretation of their natures, become fearful of male dominance to the point of destroying every impulse to yield, either to a man or even to a psychic content that has masculine characteristics.

THE UNION OF OPPOSITES

THE SIGNAL MYSTERY of this downward-going path of the feminine is the indissoluble union of opposites it brings about, of the spiritual and the material, of the religious and the sensual, of the eternal and the historical, of the abstract and the personal, of the elemental and the transformative aspects of feminine being and of life itself.

For the feminine ego, impulses of the spirit make themselves known through material things, whether it is the material of unconscious processes, of the transformations of the body such as menstruation, conception, the climacteric, or of individual moments of concrete experience of other kinds. The personal interiority of a woman is the vessel in which she touches the spirit and is touched by it, just as her body is the vessel of her physical transformation and all its openings places of exchange between inner and outer experience. The body symbolism associated to the female represents her spiritual capacity as well as her material; the vessel, which contains something for herself and for the male, "is the 'life-vessel as such' in which life forms, and which bears all living things and discharges them out of itself and into the world." [21] The spirit is born out of the flesh and always remains incorporated with matter.

The feminine by nature is unable to cast off materiality because its spiritual exercises are conjugated in the flesh. The Annunciation of the Holy Spirit to Mary pierces her flesh, implanting it with seeds of new life. The Annunciation to Mary is paradigmatic of all annunciations to the heart ego,

21. *Ibid.*, p. 42.

such as the saving reality of love, of a new insight, or of any sense of a new relationship to come. The Spirit fecundates a woman's whole being, and she experiences herself both as subject and object in the mysterious process.[22] The religious penetration is like a sexual penetration, seeding the flesh, changing its shape both psychologically (as with Mary, from Virgin to Mother) and physically. The ego does not create the new attitude or reality but rather receives it, waiting for the impulse of spirit to be carried toward it by the unconscious. This feminine spiritual activity is determined by the unconscious which is symbolized by the moon because, like the moon, the unconscious "turns toward the ego and reveals itself, or turns away, darkens, and disappears." [23]

Pregnancy is the carrying, containing, and making of interior space in which impulses of spirit can ripen and fulfill their destinies. A woman's concrete being, her flesh, is the organ and instrument of the transformation of her own structures and those of her child. New spiritual contents grow within a woman like a child, and she feels personally related to them as to a child. For the feminine, the spirit is always an "other," and relationship to it is always intimate and concrete, never abstract and impersonal.

> In all decisive life situations, the feminine, in a far greater degree than the nothing-but masculine, is subjected to the numinous elements in nature . . . has these "brought home" to it. Therefore, its relation to God is more familiar and intimate, and its tie to an anonymous transpersonal allegiance forms earlier and goes deeper than its personal tie to man.[24]

Birth is the bringing forth out of one's prime matter of a new reality, a new attitude or feeling or intimation of the divine. Birth transforms the bearer, the borne, and all those who are in some way touched by this new being. The relation of bearer to borne is not conceptual but sexual; it is flesh of

22. *Ibid.*, pp. 285–87.
23. Neumann, "On the Moon and Matriarchal Consciousness," p. 54.
24. *Ibid.*, p. 62.

one's flesh. The relation endures after the inner being becomes outer and continues to affect and change the bearer's
life.

> With the birth of her son, the woman accomplishes the
> miracle of nature, which gives birth to something different
> from itself and antithetical to itself. Moreover, the divine
> son is totally new, not only as to sex but also in quality. Not
> only does he engender, while she conceives and bears; he is
> also light in contrast to her natural darkness, motion in con-
> trast to her static character. . . .
>
> Her delight at being able to bear a living creature, a son
> who complements her by his otherness, is increased by the
> greater delight of creating spirit, light, and immortality,
> the divine son through the transformation of her own
> nature. . . .
>
> The woman gives birth to this divine son, this unconscious
> spiritual aspect of herself; she thrusts it out of herself not in
> order that she herself may become spirit or go the way of
> this spirit, but in order that she herself may be fructified by
> it, may receive it and let it grow within her, and then send
> it forth once more in a new birth, never totally transform-
> ing herself into it.[25]

The symbolism of penetration, fructification, and birth in
the physical dimension represents the quality of the feminine
spirit in the psychological sphere. Psychologically, this is the
experience of being entered by a new content, attitude, or
numinous element and being taken over by it. One's psychological space is filled and one's psychological shape
changed. In all of this, the numinous element is not simply
an idea or intuition which one "has"; it is something that
resides in one's concrete person and grows within, housed
by one's psychological being, feeding on it, circulating
through it. Gradually, out of this material it assumes concrete form and autonomous activity which are manifest now

---

25. Neumann, *Great Mother*, p. 320. Neumann's narrative deals
with the sense of otherness elicited by the birth of a son. The birth of
a daughter produces its own kind of moving and marked sense of
otherness.

in the way one adapts to the world and to others. The feminine modality of relating to the numinous establishes a continuity, a blending, and a new unity of flesh and spirit.

The symbolism of the mixture of the numinous with the feminine is sexual. It suggests that for the feminine the heights of the spiritual passion are never divorced from sexual passion. Religion, then, is not different from ordinary life but is rather an intensification and deepening of it. Perhaps the reason that "woman" and "feminine" have traditionally connoted nature, earth, and sexuality, as if divorced from spirit, is because they have been seen from the viewpoint of the patriarchal head ego which introduces a separating duality between the flesh and the spirit.

The patriarchal consciousness which has predominated in the modern world emphasizes the reasoning, manipulative, and formulating capacities of consciousness. This head ego achieves its clarity through independence from and even opposition to unconscious processes and the genetic principle of the matriarchal world. Mythologically, this is symbolized by the slaying of the mother and the identification of the ego with the father. By that act, the ego makes itself the source of the feminine as it is symbolized, for example, by Eve's spiritual and antinatural birth from Adam's rib.[26] From this point of view, the masculine creates a new duality, seeing the feminine as

> "merely the soul," "merely" the highest form of an earthly and material development that stands in opposition to the "pure spirit" that in its Apollonian-Platonic and Jewish-Christian form has led to the abstract conceptuality of modern consciousness.[27]

In contrast, the feminine begins with the duality of its own elementary and transformative aspects, and with the heart ego's reception of the numinous as a penetrating "other" that it brings forth as something fundamentally dif-

26. *Ibid.,* p. 58.
27. Johann Jacob Bachofen, *Das Mutterecht*, 3 vols. (Basel, 1954), I, 412, as quoted in Neumann, *Great Mother*, p. 57.

ferent from itself. The feminine creates unity through yielding to, embracing, and concretizing the numinous within itself and through incorporating the effect of the numinous into conscious adaptation. The feminine urge to create unity from duality is shown again and again—in the inability of women to divorce their sexuality from the rest of their personalities, in their constant need to make a full and open commitment to relationships, in the way their sexual instinct is reached through their feelings—as against men, whose sexuality can often function autonomously and separately from emotional needs—and in the intensely numinous quality of feminine orgiastic experience. Sensual desire and religious emotion are indissolubly united for women:

> The intensity of the orgiastic passion compounded of religion and sensuality shows how the woman, though weaker than the man, is able at times to rise to greater heights than he. Through his mystery, Dionysus captured the woman's soul with its penchant for everything that is supernatural, everything that defies natural law; by his blinding sensuous epiphany, he works on the imagination that for the woman is the starting point of all inner emotion, and on her erotic feeling without which she can do nothing, but to which under the protection of religion she gives an expression that surpasses all barriers.[28]

The experience of the numinous for the feminine is historical and individual. This can be seen symbolized in the myriad concrete details of place, person, and time associated with the Annunciation of the Angel to Mary and with the birth of Jesus. Central to Christian doctrine is the celebration of historicity, of the transfiguration of the daily flesh of life by the Spirit. Because the transformation process for the feminine is so clearly made of physical materials and the symbolism is so strongly sexual, the relation of the feminine to

28. Bachofen, *Das Mutterecht*, as quoted in Neumann, *Great Mother*, pp. 293–94. For the role of imagination in female sexuality, see also Edrita Fried, *Active/Passive* (New York: Grune & Stratton, 1970), p. 27.

revelation is inexorably historical. Psychologically, this means that the spirit apprehends itself as historically generated, as a creature that, like a son, does not break its bond with its maternal source or matrix. This is the effect of a numinous content on a receiver: not only does it penetrate one's history, it changes that history, informing the past with an intentionality where the random bits of events and of people, of sadnesses and of delights, are gathered into one forward-moving purpose that is seen to be fulfilled in a present revelation. The Old Testament *Heilsgeschicte*—the telling of the history of the holy events—is an example of this, as is the penchant of all lovers to create their own "salvation history," the narrative of their first meeting, of the first moment of their awareness of their love, etc.

Because a numinous experience is historical for the feminine, it is also individual and personal. It is in *this* moment, to *this* person, that *this* event has occurred, and the carrying and transforming of the spirit is then done in *this* person's heart. The relation to the numinous is intimate and concrete, rather than abstract and nonindividualized. The apperception of God grows out of the concrete experience of a person's life. God is described in personal terms rather than by such abstractions as "pure being." Relationship to God is intimate: it is a relationship of touching and being touched in specific times and ways and places.

In the highest expression of the feminine spirit both heaviness and materiality are transcended, not to vanish into abstraction but to be transformed. It is a process often symbolized by a flower. The feminine spirit, like a blossom's scent, always remains attached to earthly foundations as to something concrete and individual but also exquisite in beauty and grace. The downward-going road of the feminine spirit is a road of the lowest dung, of the commonest air and water, of the everyday soil of experience in which one receives and achieves transformation. The flower is the supreme visible form of Sophia, the personification of wisdom; it is the symbol of Mary, and of the unity of Demeter reunited with

Kore; it is the sacred white rose seen as the ultimate flower of light, Dante's ultimate metaphor for the Communion of Saints.[29]

The feminine symbolism of the vessel at its highest level is the vessel of spiritual transformation—the Grail, the cup of the Last Supper, representing not only "the earth and heaven of the retort that we call life, and . . . the whirling wheel revolving within it, but . . . also the supreme essence and distillation to which life in this world can be transformed." [30]

FEMININE WISDOM

THE FEMININE SYMBOLISM of the mother at the highest spiritual stage is the heartspring of Sophia from which flows "the spirit-nourishing 'central' wisdom of feeling, not the 'upper' wisdom of the head." [31] This is represented for Neumann by the symbol of "Vièrge Ouvrante," which on the outside is an unassuming mother with child, but when opened, is "God the Father and God the Son, usually represented as heavenly lords who in the act of pure grace raise up the humble, earthbound mother to abide with them, prove to be contained in her; prove to be 'contents' of her all-sheltering body." [32] This is also represented in paintings where Mary, as a child, sits with Christ in the lap of St. Anne, who can be seen in this instance as a symbol of the Great Mother.

Psychologically, Neumann points out, this symbolism indicates a specific kind of spiritual wisdom which is the highest expression of the feminine modality of being. It is the wisdom of the heart which lacks that universal, nonindividual, and absolute character that patriarchal consciousness asserts

29. See Neumann, *Great Mother*, pp. 325–26.
30. *Ibid.*, p. 325.
31. *Ibid.*, p. 330.
32. *Ibid.*, p. 331.

as the highest spirituality. It is not abstract nor disinterested knowledge, but a responsive wisdom that comes from loving participation in a relationship. Just as the unconscious is always reacting, "so Sophia is living and present and near, a godhead that can always be summoned and is always ready to intervene, and not a deity living inaccessible to man in numinous remoteness and alienated seclusion." [33]

Feminine wisdom is bound to the earth, to organic and psychological growth, to living reality. It issues from one's instincts, from one's unconscious, from one's history and relationships. It is nonspeculative wisdom without illusions, and it is not idealistic in its approach to reality but prefers what actually is to what should or might be. Feminine wisdom nourishes, supports, and develops the strongest possible ties to reality. It is the wisdom of feeling and compassion, coordinated to the qualitative moment and the specific instance rather than to an unrelated code of law. Feminine wisdom is personal, never impersonal. It always evolves out of relationship to an "other," whether it is the other of unconscious processes, or numinous contents, or another human being. It is a paradoxical wisdom which never juxtaposes opposites into "either-or" pairs but gathers them into "both-and" relationships, into "the indissoluble and paradoxical unity of life and death, of nature and spirit, to the laws of time and fate, of growth, of death and death's overcoming." [34]

Such wisdom brings ecstasy and illumination rather than knowledge. The heart and soul of consciousness are carried beyond themselves into intimations of the deepest mysteries. The darkness of the feminine is brightened with light, made luminous and shining, resplendent, illustrious. It is a wisdom which sets things right and elucidates them. The wisdom of the feminine sanctifies what it touches, making pure and efficient one's deepest roots in the earth, making sacred one's

33. *Ibid.*
34. Neumann, "On the Moon and Matriarchal Consciousness," p. 67.

most awkward gestures and clumsy performances, one's stut-
tering passions and stammering aspirations, unashamedly
gathering all this into a wholeness and holiness where the
commonest events of the flesh become a treasury of graces.

> Thus the spiritual power of Sophia is living and saving;
> her overflowing heart is wisdom and food at once. The
> nourishing life that she communicates is a life of the spirit
> and of transformation, not one of earthbound materiality.
> As spirit mother, she is not, like the Great Mother of the
> lower phase, interested primarily in the infant, the child, and
> the immature man, who clung to her in these stages. She is
> rather a goddess of the Whole, who governs the transforma-
> tion from the elementary to the spiritual level; who desires
> whole men knowing life in all its breadth, from the ele-
> mentary phase to the phase of spiritual transformation.[35]

Neumann sums up such wisdom in terms some may think
too glowing, but the kind of wisdom the feminine contributes to men as well as to women can really reach such
heights and depths.

35. Neumann, *Great Mother*, p. 331. See also Jung, "Answer to Job,"
Psychology and Religion: West and East (*CW*, XI, 1958), pp. 388–89.

CHAPTER TEN

Archetypes of
the Feminine

THE FEMININE MODALITY of being makes itself known in human history in various archetypal forms, that is, in recurrent clusters of images and patterns of behavior that are associated with certain dominant types of the feminine. The fundamental archetypal forms of the feminine come from various combinations of our basic instinctual traits, from the influence of environment and culture, and from our adaptation to these factors. Each form of the feminine has at its center a specific archetype which can be described only indirectly in terms of its accompanying images, value system, and behavioral patterns.

These fundamental archetypal forms of the feminine are described in the myths and legends of all cultures throughout history, as for example in the recurrent tales of the princess, the maiden, the wise woman, the witch, etc. In our everyday speech, when we describe women we know or know about, we often resort to typing them, unconsciously using archetypal imagery. Common examples are the references to a woman as "a witch," "a man-eater," "a man's woman," "a mother's daughter," "a daddy's girl," and so forth. The archetypal forms of the feminine describe certain basic ways of channeling one's feminine instincts and one's orientation to cultural factors. They also indicate the type of woman one is or the type of anima personality a man is likely to develop. These archetypal forms of the feminine are descriptive only; they are never definitive. For example, if one were to say that a woman was a "mother type," one would be describing her general and habitual orientation to the maternal; one is not summing up her entire personality. Mothering and all that that would imply would be the main source and force of her identity, but that would not necessarily mean that she had no other capacities.

Toni Wolff, an early disciple of Jung's, sketches four structural forms of the feminine which she calls the Mother, the Hetaira, the Amazon, and the Medium, forms that, once again, may refer to the masculine anima as well as to the archetypal bases of female identity. Like the four psychological functions discussed in Chapter Three, each pair of the forms of the feminine is a set of opposites: the Mother and the Hetaira are the collective and individual forms of relatedness to persons; the Amazon and the Medium are the collective and individual forms of relatedness to nonpersonal values. As with the psychological functions, one of the four feminine forms is "superior" to all the others. A second appears as "auxiliary" to it. The opposing third and fourth forms are initially unconscious and can be made conscious and integrated only with difficulty.[1] In other words, every woman potentially has all four structural forms, although one or two are more readily accessible to her than the others and become her pattern of functional adaptation.

1. See above, Part I, Chapter Three, pp. 78–79.

Her wholeness requires the fullest integration and exercise of all four modalities: "Just as the coming to terms with the fourth function is the way to psychic totality, the integration of the fourth structural form of the woman is an approach to the Self." [2] That is a lifetime task, of course. In a sense, the four structural types form the stage on which a woman may live out her personal drama. The gestating static aspects of the feminine are manifested in the Mother type as directed to persons, and in the Medium type as directed to the nonpersonal collective unconscious. The dynamic outgoing eros aspects of the feminine are manifested in the Amazon type as directed to nonpersonal goals, and in the Hetaira type as directed to personal involvements (see below, Diagram A). [3]

I will combine the contributions of Wolff and Mario Moreno, a Jungian analyst in Italy, in reviewing these types. [4] Each archetypal form involves (1) a personality type, which is shaped by (2) a dominant archetype, which manifests itself (3) positively and negatively, and has (4) a positive and negative expression in the woman's identity, (5) shaping her attitude to actual men and (6) to the inner masculine animus figure. For a summary of the schema, see Diagram B.

2. Toni Wolff, *Structural Forms of the Feminine Psyche*, trans. Paul Watzlawik (privately printed for the C. G. Jung Institute, Zurich, July, 1956), p. 12. Obviously, what one learns about the structural forms of the feminine as they may turn up in a man's anima is of vital importance in any attempt to understand the masculine self. But Toni Wolff is concerned, as her title makes clear, with the feminine psyche, and therefore does not deal with these forms any more than I do in this book, which is concerned with the feminine as it appears in women.

3. *Ibid.*, p. 11. See also Edward C. Whitmont, *The Symbolic Quest* (New York: C. G. Jung Foundation, 1969), p. 179.

4. See Mario Moreno, "Archetypal Foundations in the Analysis of Women," *The Journal of Analytical Psychology*, X, no. 2 (July, 1965), *passim.*

DIAGRAM A

Static Pole of the Feminine
Mother

	Relates to persons in a collective way Relates to persona in man

Static Pole of the Feminine	Dynamic Pole of the Feminine
Medial Woman————————*Amazon*	
Relates to nonpersonal goals in an individual way Relates to collective unconscious and objective anima in man	Relates to nonpersonal goals in a collective way Relates to ego in man

Hetaira
Dynamic Pole of the Feminine

	Relates to persons in an individual way Relates to personal unconscious and subjective anima in man

DIAGRAM B

Type	Dominant Archetype Positive-Negative	Woman's Identity Positive-Negative	Relation to Man	Relation to Animus Positive-Negative
Mother	Great Mother helps; or devours	Nourishes others; or evidences masochistic protest	Homemaker, mother (to persona)	*Puer aeternus*: revolutionary; or projects unrealized creative life onto son
Hetaira	Great Father relates as individual; or submerges own ego in identification with father's anima	Awakens individual psychic life; or plays role of temptress away from realistic adaptation	Daughter (to shadow, subjective anima)	Hero: frees her for equality; or ravages her
Amazon	Virgin self-contained; or remains cold and unrelated to feminine instinct	Develops own ego; or identifies with shadow of mother, and mother's animus	Comrade (to ego)	Father: as spiritual guide; or as tyrant
Medial Woman	Wise Woman prophetess, furthering culture; or witch, furthering evil	Displays firm ego with discriminatory faculties; or loss of ego in collective unconscious	Mediatrix (to objective anima)	Mediates unconscious: as Wise Man; or as Magician who tempts her to inflation

THE MOTHER

THE FEMININE structured as Mother produces a personality which is primarily maternal in its orientation and is dominated unconsciously by the Great Mother archetype. In its positive manifestation, the archetype induces in a woman maternal cherishing and concern for those things which are undeveloped, in the process of becoming, or in need of care, help, or protection. A maternal woman, in this sense, can support people and ideas without condescension, can make space for that which needs to grow, and can provide security for what is still unaccomplished and needs room for psychic development. In its positive expression a woman with this type of identity finds her fulfillment in actual motherhood or in activities that call for maternal virtues. One possible source of fulfillment for her is in charitable activities that strengthen the development of others until they can be dismissed from her care or, if this is not possible, until they have maximum security. The Mother type represents a collective orientation to people—for example, to a man as "husband" rather than to his particular individuality, or to her children as "the children" more than to their specific personalities. A woman who is of the Mother type will have an identity which tends to renounce subjectivity; she lives for others, even if unconsciously.

In its negative aspect, the Great Mother archetype induces anxious overprotectiveness in a woman and possessiveness of the "other" who has outgrown such support or never really needed it. This oversolicitous attitude communicates a lack of confidence in the other's strength and independence and may interfere with his development. It implies that the other cannot do something, and therefore dare not do it; it suggests that he has no right to exist apart from the mothering woman. Such a destructive holding on to the "other" is symbolized for Jungians in images of the devouring mother. This negative aspect of a woman's personal identity is colored by a masochistic protest, which compensates for her renunciation of subjectivity. Her ego functions only in this motherly fashion and feels empty without it. Furthermore, the unlived and unaccepted aspects of her own personality may "infiltrate into the protégés and may tend to realize themselves through them—consciously in the way of guidance or, which is worse, unconsciously by infecting the objects and thus filling them with a life which is not theirs." [5] An example is the martyr who is hurt that her child, after all her work and encouragement, has not fulfilled her expectations.

The delineation of this Mother type may give us a more precise understanding of masochism in women. The Mother type, meaning either, literally, a mother with children or, figuratively, a maternal woman with strong helping, nourishing, need-answering attitudes, has been the predominant cultural definition of femininity in Western culture. A random sampling of descriptions of the highly feminine female will usually indicate a maternal orientation. A logical inference from this is that genuine feminine identity for a woman is based on identification of her whole self with her maternal instinct. In psychoanalytic literature, for example, it is generally agreed that abortion results in such enduring guilt for a woman because she has turned against her fundamental maternal instinct, which is her root identity. In asserting herself against her maternal instinct, she has ceased to be feminine. An abortion may be tantamount to a schizoid episode for a woman. Conscious self-assertions against other instincts, however, such as sexuality or the power drive, are not associated with such a splitting in two. This is evidence, even if indirectly, that the conception of the feminine is not as differentiated from the maternal instinct as it is from the aggressive and sexual instincts. The traditional identifi-

5. Wolff, *Structural Forms of the Feminine Psyche*, p. 5.

cation of the feminine with the maternal also may be a factor in the Catholic objection to birth control, which, if it is to be sustained, demands a psychological differentiation of a woman's ego from her maternal instinct so that she may choose when and if she wishes a child.

The results of masochism are an inability to say no to pain and the turning of one's aggression against oneself rather than channeling it into self-assertion and balanced relation to the world. It is an exaggerated acceptance of the other at the expense of oneself. The mothering instinct in its static aspects tends to renounce subjective wishes in order to be inert, to be present to the other. In its dynamic aspects, it reaches out in caring and responding to the needs of others, even if this involves great inconvenience or pain to oneself. These containing aspects of the maternal imply a brooding quality of feminine thought and memory, conducive to a masochistic rumination over old hurts, carefully stored and brought out now and again to be reinspected and relived. This is illustrated in the familiar astonishment of a man at a woman's capacity to remember detailed instances of when he said an unkind word or made a nasty remark. The prevalence of attitudes of martyrdom among women and their easy ability to lapse into hurt silence are other examples of the same sort of masochism.

The propensity women have toward masochistic responses is, I think, proportionate to the intensity and degree of their unconscious identification with the maternal instinct. To be able to say no to another's need, especially that of a loved one, is notoriously difficult for a woman. It is not unusual to hear a woman say, for instance, that she always complies with her husband's sexual requests even though she prefers at the moment to refuse, and that her mother, in telling her how to relate to a man, advised her to do just this. To refuse, she thinks, is to incur the accusation that she is not a woman, either from her husband or from herself because she is not giving, in response to his need, wish, or hope. For a woman whose unconscious definition of her feminine identity is maternal, to answer needs and feelings with warmth, encouragement, and supportive interest, to be able to say no, and without guilt, because it conflicts with her own faith in herself and what is appropriate for her at the moment, is to sever identification with the maternal instinct as the root of her identity and to develop a real sense of herself and her femininity which is not tied only to the maternal. If she can achieve this, she can relate to maternal attitudes and actions directly and from real choice rather than unconscious compulsion. Then the woman's maternal instinct is only one of several important modalities, rather than the sole instinct possessing her. Wolff's schema is helpful here because it sketches many modalities of feminine adaptation in addition to the maternal.

A woman who is conscious of her predominantly maternal attitude will arrange her outer life accordingly, through marriage or through a motherly profession. She will see marriage as affording the optimum conditions for the creation of a home, which will be enhanced by the social position, career, general background, or paternal qualities of her husband. But for those in the motherly professions, institutions of public care may take the place of the home as, for example, nursing did with Florence Nightingale. There are opportunities, too, for motherly activity in countless forms of human relationships that do not involve marriage or career, such as the roles of the supportive friend, the informal counselor to younger people, the understanding sister to a man.

The Mother type sees the male primarily as father of her children or as a paternal influence upon her charges. She will promote and protect for her husband all that has to do with his position in the world—his "persona," as Jung calls it. She may ignore or suppress his other qualities or interests because she sees them as threats either to herself or her home. As a result, a man may come to feel that he is merely a household fixture, or at best a son, and he will try to compensate for this attack on his virility by spending a great deal of time in male company, say at the golf course, or in his job, or will involve himself in a love affair. He may not find the necessary psychic space for his personal psychology to develop, and much of his unique individuality will remain unconscious and suppressed.[6]

The animus of the Mother type will tend to compensate for her conscious view of her husband. Consciously, she sees him as head of the household, but inwardly, psychologically, the animus reduces him to what Jungians call the *puer aeternus*, the "eternal boy." The animus images of her actual husband, or of other men, that turn up in the dreams or fantasies of a Mother type usually have a boyish quality. This boyish, youthful quality of the animus can express itself positively or negatively. In its positive expression, this son animus is a creative figure, one that is likely to evince talent, ideas, skills. The animus may appear in the role of a revolutionary, for example, who has antitraditional moral, social, or political attitudes. The animus may appear as a creative artist of some kind, or as a philosopher. The animus may appear as a sexually exciting figure who arouses the woman, in her dream, to a passion that she has not consciously experienced. In its negative expression, the son animus may appear in the role of a sulking boy whom no one understands, or as a potentially creative man who never develops his talent, who always begins projects and shows great promise, but never follows them through. This negative expression of the Mother type's animus can have serious repercussions for her children. The unlived creative animus capacity may be projected onto her actual son, to be realized later on in his life.[7] Unconsciously, the Mother type will pressure her son to realize in his life the creative animus capacities that she failed to develop in her own life.

6. See Jung, "Marriage as a Psychological Relationship," *The Development of Personality* (*CW*, XVII, 1954), pp. 192–93.
7. *Ibid.*, p. 191.

THE HETAIRA

THE FEMININE STRUCTURED AS Hetaira or companion is the opposite of the motherly type. She is instinctively oriented to the personal rather than to the collective psychology of the male, and to her children as individuals rather than as a group. The Hetaira structure produces the personality type that Jung calls the *puella aeterna,* the "father's daughter" who is identified with her father's anima. Here, the dominant archetype is the Great Father. In its positive manifestations, this type awakens and arouses the individual, subjective, psychic life in herself and others, conveying a sense of personal value quite apart from collective standards, a value that can stimulate and promote something close to a total realization of personality.[8] She finds love an end in itself rather than something subordinated to family and social forms.

In its positive aspects, this type constellates a personal identity which centers around the values of individual relationship and the fulfillment of personality, all symbolized for Jungians in the images of the priestess dedicated to the service of love, the love deities, the hierodules, and the woman who inspires men to prodigious feats. Negatively, in her concern with the fluctuations of individual feeling, the Hetaira may be unable to make any permanent commitment to her own attitudes or to an actual relationship but may instead have to lead a life full of emotional wanderings and merely tentative attachments. The personal identity in this negative aspect is symbolized by the image of the eternal daughter idolizing her father, sacrificing her own development in her dedication to the "other."[9] Her negative effects may also be manifest as she tempts herself or a man away from collective responsibilities and from realistic adaptation,

8. See Wolff, *Structural Forms of the Feminine Psyche,* p. 6.
9. See Moreno, "Archetypal Foundations in the Analysis of Women," p. 180.

as symbolized in images of nymph, seductress, harlot, or witch.

The Hetaira's relation to the male stimulates and promotes his individual interests, his inclinations, and even his problems, thus affecting his shadow side and the subjective side of his anima.[10] This can be dangerous if she has not learned what properly belongs to the relationship and what does not. She may overemphasize her individual relation to a man to the point of neglecting his need to establish his career, to make a living, to find himself in society. For example, she might insist that he follow some illusory talent and lead him to lose his sense of reality; she becomes a kind of Circe in a man's life. Another danger, if she is unmarried or without a profession herself, could be her failure to find or to provide for herself the security afforded by such things as home and job and career, a security which is a vital necessity to almost all women. These needs will then creep into the Hetaira relationship and disturb it at its center. If she is married and unaware of her Hetaira nature, she will bind her children to her in just as destructive a way as the Mother type who is unconscious of her maternal nature, by becoming a girl friend to her sons and a "best friend" and confidante to her daughters. The abolition of sexual taboos is also something the Hetaira must carefully consider. For her, according to the law of individual relationship, sexuality may be inappropriate altogether; most often sexuality does not begin a relationship for the Hetaira but may shape and express it eventually when it "has reached a certain depth and psychic consolidation and may . . . represent a psychic equivalent to the security offered in marriage." [11]

The animus of the Hetaira tends to compensate for her outer orientation as *puella aeterna* and for the inner dominance of the Great Father, by assuming the form of a hero. In its positive expression, a hero saves a girl from her eternal

10. See Wolff, *Structural Forms of the Feminine Psyche*, p. 6.
11. *Ibid.*, pp. 6–7.

dedication to the father, as expressed in her relationship with a man, and suggests instead a more equal relation between the male and female partners. A hero makes a woman out of a maiden and incites her to integrate within herself her own spiritual qualities. Negatively, the hero animus becomes unrelated aggression, ravaging her, severing ties both within herself and outside her in destructive ways. The maidenly softness of the Hetaira often alternates with willfulness and power drives.

THE AMAZON

THE FEMININE structured as Amazon produces a personality which is self-contained and independent, one which Moreno calls the personality of a "mother's daughter." The dominant archetype is that of the Virgin, and the daughter usually identifies, at least in part, with her mother and thus is easily influenced by her mother's animus. Insofar as she is identified with the mother, many of her own feminine qualities are inhibited; she lives in her parent's shadow and feels inferior to her, even though her own rather passive and undefined feminine quality may be attractive to men. Insofar as the mother's animus influences her, she "acquires a certain independence of man through a relation with objective cultural values." [12]

In its positive manifestation, the Virgin archetype constellates an independence based on fidelity to the feminine principle, one which yields an identity where the woman feels she is a person in her own right and not simply a counterpart to the male. Her sovereign allegiance is to something feminine—the expression and fulfillment of her own feminine goals and purposes—rather than the fulfillment of a male person. Her psychological development is not at all based

12. Moreno, "Archetypal Foundations in the Analysis of Women," p. 179.

on relationship to the male; she is quite independent of him. The conscious values he represents are also her values.[13] She devotes herself independently, in a feminine way, to cultural values. This is symbolized in such images as that of the chaste huntress Artemis, or Pallas Athene. Modern women who might exemplify the Amazon type would be women scientists such as Marie Curie, distinguished business women such as Elizabeth Arden, or women who, though married, do not feel sufficiently taken up by their families and so devote themselves to useful enterprises outside themselves.

In its negative expression, domination by the Virgin archetype may constellate a premasculine orientation, where a woman remains contained in her original mother-daughter relationship and is never penetrated nor awakened to her deepest feminine self. This can produce an identity where a woman takes over collective masculine values, reinforcing her persona as a "virile woman" while avoiding relationship with the animus and its spiritual elements.[14] While being outwardly energetic and dedicated to a cause, such a woman remains inwardly passive and without ideas or initiatives of her own. Another type of negative identity may be that of the cold woman whose sexuality is repressed, or is pressed into the service of her ego. Sexuality then manifests itself as power, either in autonomous outbursts which are devoid of personal relatedness to a partner, or in manipulations of a partner simply to further her own ambitions. Her feeling remains undeveloped, and she herself remains untouched and basically uninvolved, a person in her own right, but isolated, quite alone in the world. Like the mermaid who lures men to their death, she is unrelated to her own instincts and hence is not fully human.

The Amazon type relates to a male positively as to a comrade, a colleague, or a competitor, devoted to the same conscious ideals as he is. She makes no personal demands, but

13. See Wolff, *Structural Forms of the Feminine Psyche*, p. 7.
14. See Moreno, "Archetypal Foundations in the Analysis of Women," p. 180.

she deserves to be taken seriously, for she inspires his ambitions and his largest achievements as a male. The Amazon relates to a male negatively as a kind of rival sister who, driven by envy, wants equality with her brother—or more —and will not recognize any male authority and certainly will not accept the possibility of male superiority. She fights violently and becomes paranoid in her defense of female "rights," at the same time knowing very little about her own feminine resources. Relationship and marriage are appraised in terms of public accomplishment and may easily be sacrificed for the sake of personal ambition. Efficiency and success are her values. Personal issues are suppressed or dealt with in a brusque "masculine" way. Patience or comprehension for anything still undeveloped or in the process of developing is lacking, both in respect to herself and others. Typical is the very bright mother of a college girl, who often said to her daughter, "When are you going to grow up so I can talk to you?" Perhaps it is this negative Amazonian type upon whom Freud based his penis envy theory and Adler his concept of "masculine protest." Our present culture offers the widest possible range to the Amazon and Mother types. The Hetaira and Medial types, on the other hand, found their cultural support in antiquity, in the Middle Ages, and in the Renaissance.

The animus for the Amazon type is personified as the father, who in his positive aspects represents the spiritual guide, counselor, and even priest, initiating the Amazon into a genuine and often original spiritual development. Negatively, the animus is like a tyrannous old king who tears his daughter from her mother, thus severing her connection with her feminine roots, after which she becomes lost in cold exploitation of people or in power plays.

THE MEDIUM

THE FEMININE structured as Medium relates to the nonpersonal objective psyche upon which consciousness rests and out of which grow objective cultural values. "Medium" means neutral, neither precisely one thing nor another; it is something in-between, intermediate, an agent, a mediator, a means, not an end. "The medial woman is immersed in the psychic atmosphere of her environment and the spirit of her period, but above all in the collective (impersonal) unconscious." [15] When the unconscious becomes constellated and reaches consciousness, it exerts an effect. The medial woman is deeply moved and shaped by this effect; she finds herself engrossed in it and may embody it in her own person. She mediates the deep abysses of the feminine, in an individual, subjective way, to those around her.

The dominant archetype for the Medium is that of the Wise Woman, who positively constellates what is in the atmosphere and is just beginning to find expression. The positive identity of a medial type of woman is to inspire others to become conscious of their own psychic contents and those of others. She abandons identification with the mother figure, the mother figure's animus, or the father figure's anima and develops an ego of her own which truly mediates the powerful world of the objective psyche for herself and for others. Necessary to establish a positive identity for her are a firm ego and a well-developed capacity to discriminate what belongs to the ego from what belongs to the environment, what is personal from what is impersonal, the values and limits of consciousness from those of the unconscious. Her capacity to let herself be molded by objective psychic contents can thus effect a positive influence. The Wise Woman is symbolized mythologically by the figure Sophia or by the Cumaean Sibyl, and is represented historically by those women who devote themselves to what they see as the new spirit of their age, as did the Christian martyrs and mystics, or to the work of a man they see as a great leader.

The negative aspect of the Wise Woman archetype is expressed in the swamping effect of objective psychic contents

15. Wolff, *Structural Forms of the Feminine Psyche,* p. 9.

on an individual ego that is weak or even entirely lacking. Then, instead of being a Medium, a woman's personal identity becomes simply a means of articulation for the objective psyche and can turn into an agent of confusion or destruction. This is symbolized by the witch, or by fortune tellers, who assume the power of the unconscious as their own and "become the playthings of potentially destructive psychic influences and thereby sources of psychic infection and decadence."[16] Most frequently what an environment will not or cannot permit to come into consciousness is the negative aspect of an idea or situation, and thus the Medium, if her ego is weak and unable to differentiate, activates and develops what is negative.[17] Medieval witches in large part represented the unacceptable heresies and evils of their times. If objective contents in herself or others are taken personally or misunderstood, the medial woman may feel driven by a destiny that is not her own, or driven to experience as a personal fate something that does not really belong to her.

We have seen that the Mother type relates to a man's persona, the Hetaira to his personal unconscious in the form of the shadow or the subjective side of his anima, the Amazon to his ego. The Medium relates to the collective unconscious of a man, activating its archetypal contents and especially the nonpersonal side of a man's anima. This can be extremely helpful, because the contents which the Medium senses and seeks out do not belong to the ego but really should become conscious, enlarging and enriching a man's conscious adaptation and furthering his cultural development. She gives shape to what is beneath the surface. This requires proper preparation and timing. Without either, her effect on a man may be bewitching and destructive.

The medial type can cause serious problems. She may stifle in others—her children, her friends, her lovers—the development of potentialities of which they are as yet unaware.

16. Edward C. Whitmont, *The Symbolic Quest* (New York: C. G. Jung Foundation, 1969), p. 180.
17. See Wolff, *Structural Forms of the Feminine Psyche*, p. 9.

The medial type of woman often sees in others talents that still reside in the unconscious, and she often foresees what shape these talents might assume. She intuitively senses and lives out the development of potentialities that belong to others. This can have the result—particularly for children whose egos are still unformed and incapable of effective resistance—of robbing others of experiences that belong to them.

The animus of the medial woman is in large part projected onto objective psychic contents. In its positive expression, the animus focuses on the meaning of cultural events that indicate that some new form of life is emerging. The animus in its positive function may appear in a dream or fantasy as a Wise Man, or teacher, or leader, conveying emergent meanings to the dreamer. In its negative expression the animus may appear as a devil or magician seducing a woman into inflated states of power, tempting her to take as her personal possession potentialities that belong to others, or to take as her personal meaning the meaning of emergent cultural movements simply because she perceives them. To succumb to this temptation will result in an inflated sense of guilt, because the medial woman may take as her personal responsibility that which is the responsibility of others or of groups of people. At the same time she will ignore what is her own proper responsibility.

The four types of women encompass almost every aspect of the feminine. What makes this a particularly useful typology is its close attention to the cultural contexts in which the Mother, the Hetaira, the Amazon, and the Medium appear and the mythological symbolism, always fundamental to Jungian theory, which best expresses both the types and their various environments.

If a woman is aware of the archetypal dynamism underlying her own femininity, she knows more of herself. If she knows herself, she can avoid developing her own stereotypes of women and avoid having those of others foisted upon her. She falls neither into the trap of thinking and act-

ing as "just a housewife," or "only a career woman," etc.,
nor into the opposite horror of being unable to accept the
pluralism of the contending forces within her that might
lead her to be more than one kind of woman. If she responds
to the archetypes underlying her nature, then she can respond to the deep motivations that the archetypes provide,
which can only enrich her life, her relation to others, and
her contributions to her society.

CHAPTER ELEVEN

Stages of Anima Development

THE QUALITIES OF FEMININE CONSCIOUSNESS and spirit find concrete application in the lives of men and women. This chapter focuses on the anima—the feminine within the masculine—and its stages of transformation, which effect the fulfillment not only of feminine elements but also of a dominant masculinity. It is important to remember that the anima in its subjective aspect is the stuff of man's inner experience and of his perception of the feminine as he has met it among the actual women he has known. The images of these experiences, inner and outer, shape his relationships to the opposite sex and thus have everything to do with their success or failure. In its objective aspect, the anima brings to the ego the contents of the objective psyche, whose "otherness" is conveyed through the contrasexual personification which the anima is. For a man, the anima is the gateway to the experience of the self, which he experiences in an essentially masculine way. It must be confusing to many when

Jungians conceptualize the unconscious of a man as feminine and the soul of a woman as masculine. It is better, I think, to say that the mediator to these deep psychic layers is personified in "contrasexual terms," a set of words which fittingly captures both the foreignness and easy accessibility of the objective psyche.

SEXUAL POLARITY

IT IS VITAL to incorporate the contrasexual element into any psychology, for it grounds sexuality as a *sina qua non* of being human. Contrasexuality represents the polarity of human life, symbolizing all the opposing forces which are woven into our individual persons and which structure our relationships with each other—especially with the opposite sex and with the divine.

The significance of contrasexuality is pointed up in Jung's conviction that the movement toward wholeness, the entrance to the self, is through the opposite sex each one of us contains within ourselves. The mysterious otherness that a man and a woman experience when they meet fully is echoed again in the encounter of the ego and the anima, or of the ego and the animus.

However, otherness arouses fear, and we defend against it by repressing it, by saying it isn't there ("Women are no different from men"), by killing it, saying it is a mere relic of the past ("God is dead"), by controlling it through political oppression, or, on the personal level, by stereotyping ("the establishment" versus "the rebels"). The only adequate response to otherness is to relate to it clearly and openly, to consent to I-Other polarity, for from it comes new life. Although one may see the I-Other polarity as crucifying, one should recognize that, like the cross of Christianity, it may lead to resurrection. The power of the meeting between a man and a woman, or of ego and animus or anima, gathers some of its force from this symbolic dimension. This personal experience of the other sex represents the central fact of otherness in human life.

Because the self is understood by Jung as a psychological description of the integrity of religious figures, and because the experience of opposites is necessary to the development of wholeness, the symbolism of the sexual conjunction, representing the reunion of all the opposing forces of human life, is intrinsic to our relation to God. Sexual imagery has been used to describe the marvels of interiority, to describe life's deepest mysteries as revealed in the meetings between a man and a woman, to describe the cleansing sanity of prayer. I must emphasize it again: sexuality is not only a part of a religious life, it is the primary means of creating and developing that life. This major implication of Jung's research into the feminine is a far cry from the ascetic denial of sexuality by Christians. The love which is the reality of God is generated and incarnated in the love between the sexes, whether one refers to inner or to interpersonal sexual polarities, whether one means the quick spark or the steady flame of passion, the barely warm ashes of a dying sexual love, the steady burning of parental affection, or the consuming love of one soul for another where one loves the other in God and loves God in the other. No matter the kind of love, where love is, God is, from the most literal physical expression of love to the farthest reaches of its symbolism. A rock and roll song describes this well: the narrator believes in no God, nor in love, except as something in fairy tales; then he sees "her face" and exults—"Now, I'm a believer!" The large numbers of people who have felt their creative powers by falling in love illustrate its connection to the abundant life described by Jesus.

The exploration of the feminine as anima within the masculine focuses on the sexual polarity within man as it affects and is affected by his relations with woman, in order to gain a greater understanding of human nature. Because the variations in individuals' lives are so many and not easily conducive to clarity, I have chosen a symbolic paradigm of man's relation to the feminine as a means of sketching out the basic stages of this relationship in all its archetypal dimensions.

THE STORY OF EROS AND PSYCHE

THE STORY OF EROS, or Amor, and Psyche is interpreted by Erich Neumann as a description of feminine development within a woman.[1] With appropriate modifications of interpretation, I think the story is more accurately read as the development of a man's anima. As with any myth, there are many levels of understanding. My own interpretation is based on the fact that this story is one episode in a larger narrative of a man's psychological transformation; the all-embracing context is masculine.[2] One sees, this way, that the interchange and reciprocal influence of the anima and the man's experience of actual women are inextricably united.

I will summarize the story of Eros and Psyche, and then go through it step by step to point out the salient psychological parallels between Psyche's adventures and the development of the anima within the masculine personality. Where helpful, I will add clinical material to illustrate my interpretations.

There are five parts to the story. The introduction describes Psyche's great beauty, which arouses the envious wrath of Aphrodite who then sends her son, Eros (or Amor), to cause Psyche to fall in love with a monster. Psyche has had no joy from her loveliness because all possible suitors only gaze upon her as upon an exquisite statue. Her father consults the oracle Apollo to find a husband for her, only to learn that he must leave her on a mountain crag to await the

1. See Erich Neumann, *Amor and Psyche*, trans. Ralph Manheim (New York: Pantheon, 1965).

2. Neumann interprets the tale of "Cupid and Psyche" as it is recounted in Books iv–vi of *The Golden Ass of Apuleius of Madaura*, trans. H. E. Butler (Oxford: Clarendon Press, 1910).

coming of a husband who is not mortal. Psyche, therefore, must dress for a funeral because her wedding will also be her death. In the second part of the story, Psyche goes to a lonely cliff to await her "marriage of death" to the supposed monster-god. But here Aphrodite's plan goes awry because her own son Eros falls in love with Psyche and spirits her away to a hidden palace where they live in nuptial bliss. To ensure his deception of his mother, Eros never lets Psyche see him or know who he is, but instead comes to her only at night. Further, Eros warns Psyche that if she tries to find out who he is she will lose him forever. The third part of the story begins with the arrival of Psyche's sisters, who believed her dead and are, on the surface at least, very pleased to see their sister alive and to talk with her. Beneath the surface, however, Psyche's sisters are very jealous of her palace, her jewelry, and her marital happiness. Neither of the sisters is happy with her own husband: one is little more than a daughter to an old man, the other a mother-nurse to an invalid. The two sisters scheme to wreck Psyche's happiness. They goad her to look upon her husband and see what kind of "monster" he is. Psyche takes an oil lamp and a knife to look at Eros as he sleeps, and, if necessary, to kill him. She sees his great beauty, examines his arrows of love, and pricks her thumb on one of them. She is overcome with love for him and by accident then spills a drop of oil on the sleeping god. He awakes, is angry with Psyche's disobedience, and flies away, spending much of the remaining part of the story, until the last part, sulking in his mother's, Aphrodite's, house. Psyche is desolate over the loss of her lover and husband and wanders the earth in search of him. To add to her burdens, Psyche is also pregnant. In the fourth part of the story, Aphrodite sends for Psyche and treats her vilely, but also gives her a chance to rewin Eros. She sets Psyche four impossible tasks. By completing these tasks, Psyche may reunite with her husband. The tasks are too difficult for any mortal to accomplish, but Psyche is aided each time by magical helpers. Thus her recurring temptation to end her misery by killing herself is finally overcome, and she perseveres in her work of finishing the tasks. The fifth and last part of the tale describes the happy reunion of Psyche and Eros, the admittance of Psyche into the realm of the gods, and the birth of their daughter who is called Joy.

Having summarized the story, let us now take up each part in greater detail and see how it might shed light on the psychological development of the anima in the masculine personality, and how it might be illustrated in a man's relationships to the opposite sex.

Part I

IN THE INTRODUCTION, Psyche's overwhelming beauty causes men to neglect the cult of Aphrodite. In revenge, Aphrodite commands her son Eros to punish Psyche by making her fall in love with the vilest of men. Psyche, for all her beauty, is unloved and lonely. When the oracle says she must be abandoned on a crag to await her monster husband, she willingly consents.

These mythological happenings may be interpreted as a description of the emergence of the anima, Psyche, out of the collective matriarchal unconscious, Aphrodite. The conflict of the two females illustrates the inevitable struggle of the masculine ego to free itself from identification with the unconscious and eventually to build a relation to the unconscious through the anima. The initial move toward masculine independence from the maternal unconscious, comes, curiously, through the agency of the feminine anima. The anima must become differentiated from the maternal unconscious. The fact that in the story Psyche's birth means a neglect of Aphrodite's cult indicates that Psyche (an anima figure), is not simply an incarnation of the goddess (the maternal unconscious) but something new that exists in its own right. She is a more human form of the archetypal feminine and occasions the development of a more differentiated eros in man.

A male often goes through this stage of inner anima development in conjunction with the experience of falling in love with his "first girl." Heretofore, the feminine has been carried by his mother, which means he has related to it as a son. Intrapsychically, his ego has been more or less contained and supported by the maternal unconscious. His attraction to a girl constellates a different relation to the feminine: he is not a son revolving around a greater parent figure but is more autonomous and begins to establish a more individual relationship to the feminine. Inwardly, his ego begins to relate from its own conscious standpoint to the anima figure.

The problem of interpreting the symbolism of Eros psychologically is a complicated one, because Eros is himself confused in the story. He is not sure whether he is love incarnate, and thus a deity, merely a human son at the beck and call of his mother, or primarily a male who falls in love with a human female and thus must fall into space-time relationships. These confusions are acted out in the story. Eros runs errands for his mother and retreats to his mother; he defies his mother by taking Psyche for himself, but he also hides her from his mother. He excites Psyche into achieving her adult womanhood and yet is himself humanly dependent on her in order to achieve his own autonomy. These confusions typify the adolescent male who alternately thinks he is all these things: a mama's boy, love incarnate, *the* male, a god, an ordinary man. Interpretation is further complicated by the fact that, although masculine eros, the drive for relatedness, is not the same as the male ego, ego differentiation is occasioned by the arousal of eros. For a man, eros usually makes its first appearance through instinctual drives; sexual arousal forces a boy away from his mother to his own body, in masturbation for example, and to girls. The usual pattern of a boy's development is that involvement with girls, in fantasy or in fact, forces the development of feelings of greater consciousness of himself and the development of his own autonomous personality. A negative illustration of this fact is the emotional paleness, passivity, and weak personality of men who fail to become erotically aroused and involved, men who in fact often live out their lives with their mothers. In the myth, Eros, struggling to get free of Aphrodite and to be with Psyche, represents both masculine ego and masculine eros, as yet undifferentiated from each other, as with an adolescent. The tale's emphasis, however, is upon anima differentiation.

Aphrodite's rage symbolizes the regressive reaction of the elemental conservative side of the unconscious which works against differentiation and represents the ambivalence mothers often experience when their sons turn from them to find girls of their own, thus ending the Oedipal and counter-Oedipal interaction. Aphrodite's bidding to her son and her means of persuasion are significant: she kisses him "with parted lips . . . long and fervently," thus symbolizing the strong incestuous flavor of mother love in its regressive phase, and, intrapsychically, the lure of unconsciousness. This is not unlike the entreaties mothers make to their sons to give up a girl who they feel, as Aphrodite does of Psyche, is merely "dirty muck of the earth" and unworthy of such devotion.[3] Intrapsychically, this is the conflict between the elemental and transformative, between the static and dynamic aspects of the feminine. The elemental feminine opposes the emergence of the transformative anima and manifests itself as a terrible, devouring mother, preferring incestuous containment to conscious differentiation.

The punishment concocted by Aphrodite is befitting the angry mother: let the girl fall in love with "the vilest of men" and thus be degraded, showing her true nature as nothing but that of a harlot, unworthy of her precious son. If the male is thus influenced to see the anima as degenerate and promiscuous, he will repeatedly project her onto one woman after another. Such affairs, compulsive in nature, symbolize the unbroken tie of son to mother. The affairs

3. As quoted in Neumann, *Amor and Psyche*, p. 60.

never become relationships, and the anima is never differentiated from the containing mother. They also show the fierce efforts of the anima itself to break away from anything lasting in order to continue the search for the woman whose value will supersede and conquer that of the mother.

A contemporary dream illustrates much of this. The dreamer, a young married man, identified his wife with the maternal because of her association with home, children, stability. In his effort to free himself from the maternal grip and to achieve individual relationship, he fell into brief, obsessive affairs which he deplored but could not stop. He dreamt: "A woman is holding some beautiful material of precious gold or silver. I am drawn to a cross that is part of the design of the material and I touch it. As I rub it, the cross becomes my wife's genitals and I wake up actually making love to her." In his association the material was like some cloth from which his wife used to make him neckties, though the cloth in the dream was of greater value, consisting as it did of silver and gold. He liked the ties a lot and saw them as signs of his individual masculinity. The cross was a symbol of supreme value to him—representing the opposition between wanting to be with his wife and wanting to be involved in affairs; it was to him a symbol of consent and of reconciliation, a kind of cross of Christ. The transformation of the cross into his wife's sexual organs impressed him very much and seemed to say to him that the value of his masculine individuality, the neckties, was to be found in the material of the relationship with his wife, and the more far-reaching value of his conflict and its resolution, the cross of Christ, were at the root of his obsessive sex compulsion and were really fulfilled in the sexual act of love with his wife. Then began the process of clearing up the contamination of his anima and of his wife with the regressive hold of the unconscious and his mother. The precious anima values he had sought in his affairs were found in his wife, whom he began to see as a woman in her own right and not a mere incarnation of his mother.

Part II

IN THE NEXT PART of the story of Eros and Psyche, Psyche is given over in "a marriage of death," supposedly to a monster, but in fact she is carried off by the West Wind to a paradise-like palace to become the bride of Eros.[4] Eros, however, never allows Psyche to see him. He comes to her only in the dark of night.

Intrapsychically, the marriage of death symbolizes a marked change in the nature of the anima. Heretofore, the anima has been contained by the unconscious, and personified as Psyche first appears in the story, as a sweet, flower-like, untouched maiden. Just so, a young man's undeveloped feelings have a sweet, virginal quality, quiet and withdrawing, unknown to the storms of passion. His anima is held intact in his unconscious, a mere reflection of his more powerful mother. The marriage represents the death, by defloration, of this virginal anima which, like the girl, is awakened by the penetration of Eros and knows sensual passion. Psyche says, "For whoever you are, I love you and adore you passionately. I love you as I love life itself." [5]

This passion represents the awakening of the boy's erotic life which awakens in his first sexual experiences—eros arouses his anima feelings through the sexual instincts. The anima is sexual and impassioned but remains anonymous, unseen. It is projected onto his first partner, who may seem more dear than life itself to him, but who is known only through a generalized anonymous sexuality rather than through one of relationship. The first love-making takes place in the dark; it is not fully conscious or fully personal but surges with the force of instinct. This is the beginning of the differentiation of the anima from the unconscious. It is

4. *Ibid.,* p. 61.
5. *Ibid.,* p. 70.

awakened and experienced as carrying basic life energy, which is now felt as sexuality.

A man at this stage of development remains, however, in passive identification with his anima, carried by its erotic passion but not consciously related to it or having it openly at his disposal.[6] His ego identity, that is, his sense of who he is, his anima, that is, his emotionality, and his eros, his drive to involvement, are all mixed together. Hence for him, feeling is a driving urge and, because eros is undifferentiated from the sexual drive, this urge becomes sexual. The quarrels between an adolescent boy and girl often involve the girl's question whether the boy feels anything for her besides a primitive sexuality and the boy's answer that of course he does because he feels such an intense sexual attraction to her. For him, at this stage, sexuality *is* feeling. The man who thinks an argument can be settled by having sexual intercourse is arrested at that early stage of development. He feels carried along by the erotic urge, and his feeling of inflation alternates with deflation. He is powerless. Sexual feeling is not at his disposal; he is at its disposal. This is illustrated by what happens to a boy when his mother disapproves of his girl. Whether he likes it or not, the girl continues to carry his anima projection; it belongs to her rather than to himself, and he will secretly continue to see her, either in fact or in his fantasies, regardless of his mother's disapproval.

Paradoxically, the negative actions of the unconscious or of the actual mother promote this first stage of anima differentiation. The mother's strong "no" occasions the boy to think for himself and to follow the force of his own emotions which are felt to be really his own when he defies his parent's disapproval. Jung remarked that without Hera's rage and the setting of labors for Heracles the full development of his masculine heroic nature would not have been challenged and brought out. Similarly, Aphrodite's disap-

6. See Esther Harding, "The Anima and the Animus" (a paper read to The Analytical Psychology Club of New York, January 19, 1951, privately printed), p. 29.

proval of Psyche puts a stop to the adoration of Psyche as an idealized beauty, and leads Eros to take her as his sexual partner. This part of the tale may be understood to symbolize the death of fantasy idolization of the female for a boy and the beginning of his real experience of the feminine. For his psyche it means the exchange of the dreaming quality of his emotional life for concrete sexual feelings. The anima in its virginal state is sacrified so that a deeper erotic life may develop.

A man at this stage, however, is still enmeshed in a "harem psychology," seeing the woman, or his anima reactions, as there simply for his pleasure, without his having to give himself or make himself known to the girl, or even to become conscious of his own feelings. He is passively identified with his anima, a state which Esther Harding describes in some detail.

> When the space of the subjective life which should be occupied with conscious contents—feelings, thoughts, reactions of all kinds, . . . all those contents which make up consciousness and whose sum produces the ego—is left empty and the work of creating an adequate reaction is left undone, the lack is made up from the unconscious via the anima . . . instead of having a clear-cut reaction to the situation that meets him, either from the outside world or from within, the individual reacts merely by a mood of which he is the victim . . . [he] is left with a rather vague attitude of wishing, instead of knowing what it is he wants and being able to do something about it . . . he becomes the victim of the reactions which take place autonomously inside him . . . and is rendered quite helpless, not only before the unconscious . . . but, because he does not know his own reactions to the outer world, he is equally helpless before the movement of outer events. . . .[7]

An overt move to change this situation usually comes from the woman, or intrapsychically, from the anima.

7. *Ibid.*, pp. 29–30.

Part III

PSYCHE'S JEALOUS SISTERS provoke her to bring an oil lamp into the darkness to look at Eros, and perhaps to slay him if he is really a monster. At this point in the story, he is still thought to be a monster, which symbolically represents the nonhuman, nonrelated quality of the man's erotic passion in its first stages as discussed above.

The hostile sisters represent neglected and hence angry feminine elements in the woman or in the anima which press for integration and a deepening of consciousness. Like an enraged mother, this apparent negative factor may occasion good; it may be a step toward consciousness and thus into real relationship. These neglected aspects symbolize the way split-off complexes in the female unconscious press for attention and, in the male, are directed to consciousness through the anima.

The sisters further personify resentful, jealous feelings which have not been satisfied in their relationship with their own husbands. One acts as daughter to a father, the other as nurse-mother to an invalid son. They typify two inappropriate ways in which men relate to their anima and to women, with tolerant and superior attitudes toward silly, touching, or sentimental girlish feelings, or as suppliant and dependent sons looking to be supported by their mother's emotions. To relate to a woman or to the anima in these ways almost always occasions counterreactions of surliness, moping, resentful condescension, or hostile withdrawal, that is, a general dissociation of feeling from consciousness.

The sisters' urging that Psyche look at Eros in a clear light signals the summoning by the anima of unconscious complexes to full consciousness. If this does not happen, a man's emotionality usually remains in a state where he alternates moments of touching sweetness with moody resentment, hurt feelings, subterranean hostility or captiousness, as if he felt as unfulfilled and left out as Psyche's jealous sisters.

Psyche takes a lamp to look at her husband, and a knife so that she can slay him if she must. While looking at Eros, she pricks herself on one of his arrows and, suddenly overwhelmed with love, she stoops to kiss his sleeping form. A drop of oil falls from her lamp and burns him, and, because Psyche has disobeyed his commands, he flees. This shift in Psyche's behavior—from passive obedience to initiative—symbolizes the anima's emergence from the darkness of anonymous, unconscious emotion and sensuality into consciously directed love. Psyche looks at Eros, seeing him no longer as instinctive passion, as a beast, or as a godlike husband; now she sees him as a god in human form—a god incarnate in a human person who unites man's higher and lower aspects. The sexual instinct, the erotic drive, and human feeling begin to be differentiated. The beast, the god, and the man begin to be distinguished. The anima, the male ego, and eros begin to be separated. This forthright seeing is an act of love. The anima functions to differentiate as well as to integrate all these elements and, as the subsequent tasks will suggest, goes through many stages to effect this integration.

In actual experience, a woman who sees a man as a person whom she loves, not only as a sexual partner or a partner of the mind, or as a representation of some ideal, initiates him into the first pains involved in differentiating and reconciling these inner oppositions in himself. The woman and the anima humanize the man. When this humanization does not occur, a split between spirit and passion, between idealization and degradation, between feeling-security and feeling-arousal must ensue. This split is personified for the male in opposing anima images which are projected onto women. He will see a woman, for example, as either a goddess or a harlot, as likely to be a loyal but dull wife, or as an exciting but dangerous "other woman." Psyche's initiative in *seeing* her husband may be interpreted as the anima's, or a woman's, refusal to be the passive servant of a masculine ego; she demands relationship. The urgency of this demand is symbolized by Psyche's willingness to kill Eros if need be. This is not unlike the woman who will give up a relationship to a man if he refuses to meet her as an individual on mutually acceptable terms. Similarly, the anima may sever relations with the ego that is unwilling to give the anima its due.

The experiences of a young male patient illustrate this breaking of communication between the anima and the ego. The young man had a homosexual predilection which he worked hard to overcome. He had begun to develop lively contact with his feelings and, with that development, new experiences with women. He had stirring dreams of an inner woman who came to symbolize to him all the repressed passion he felt for life, for its deeper meanings, and for the unspent treasury of his emotional responses. He had refused to be drafted by the army, not because of political or religious convictions but simply because he did not want to go into the army and therefore saw no reason why he should. He summed it up—"It was inconvenient." This reasoning reflected his regression to infantile logic where any demand that contradicted his wishes was rejected. This attitude displayed the way he saw himself—as a child upon whom grownups imposed unwanted restrictions. He was willing to sacrifice anything to get his way and only afterwards realized how literal and exacting that sacrifice was to be. When interviewed by the military, he said he was homosexual and addicted to drugs, which accurately described his past but was no longer true. When pressed by the army psychiatrist, he denied his hard-won new feelings by saying he did not like women and had no wish to deal with women at all, preferring his homosexual adaptation.

The lie succeeded in freeing him from the draft, but a few nights later nightmares attacked his sleep. In one, "A woman who somehow belonged to me was trapped at the army base. I went to rescue her, but never was able to reach her. Then I found myself being interviewed by an army psychiatrist who said to me that because of the drugs I had taken my brain was permanently damaged." He himself identified the woman as his "inner woman." He described the army as "the world of stupid middle-class shoulds and should-nots" and saw the brain damage as symbolizing a decrease in his capacity to think, to feel, or to be conscious. As his sessions developed, it became clear that his denial of the anima, to avoid the inconvenience of "giving up" two years to the service, resulted in a complete loss of contact with that central part of his psyche. He became querulous and defensive in conversation and said he felt as if he were hiding in a closet. Finally, he became clear about what the whole series of events meant. Before the army incident, he felt he had nothing to prove in life; now he felt he had to prove he was a man by becoming tough, which to him meant quarrelsome. Having rejected all means by which he might learn to act as an adult, if necessary even against his own wishes and thus beyond impulse-levels of reacting, he was now presented with that need in another form. He had resisted the army for fear of losing his life; now he felt he was fighting for his identity, for his life. He had to be defensive—everything was at stake. He recognized that this kind of fighting might kill him rather than save him, because he was fighting so hard to resist consciousness of his lie and its terrible effects. He was unwilling to give up two years to fighting, but now he felt he had lost seven months of analytical work, feeling he was back at the very beginning of analysis and would have to start all over again making the first primitive contacts with his unconscious. It was a great loss of time and a major setback, but he learned that he could not manipulate his anima but must relate to it on mutually acceptable terms.

Psyche, in our story, also has a major setback when she wounds Eros with a drop of oil from her lamp, because then Eros awakens and flees. The symbolism of oil is important to our understanding of the role of the anima. Oil is used to nourish, to soothe, to illuminate, to anoint, and to kindle passion.[8] This singularly feminine symbol, which awakens the male, configures the range of the anima's gifts. She, like

8. See Neumann, *Amor and Psyche*, p. 84.

oil, is a mainstay of life, a natural substratum which supports and nourishes psychic life, giving it ease, flow, and harmony. The disappearance of the anima into the unconscious leaves life harsh, dry, and barren. The ineffability of the anima's presence and the balm of feelings with which she connects man may soothe the raw edges of experience and its undigested hurts, or, if inadequately related to, may be felt as oil poured on troubled waters, accenting the separation and immiscibility of elements in a man's psyche. Oil, especially of olives, was long thought to be an aphrodisiac. Symbolically, this depicts the arousing power of anima moods or projections, where the passions of lust or anger may surge up at any moment into violent consciousness and accompanying action. Oil also was used as a temple offering and for anointment of the chosen of God. Just so does effective relation to his anima open a man to the psychic meaning of experience and to significant intimations of the spirit. Without this sense of relation, the anima remains only a cluster of personal feelings catalogued in some small slot in the psychic economy. Oil brings light, not in harsh piercing shafts, but in a warmth and steadiness of illumination, with the connotations of inner vision and perception of mystery, all characteristic of the feminine spirit. Without such illumination there is inner darkness, relieved only by occasional fitful insights.

Awakened to consciousness by his anima, a man sees his feminine qualities very differently—not as his own possession, not to be bent to his will, but as a force aggressively initiating a new phase of relationship where the anima wants to see as well as to be seen. This parallels a frequent experience of men who want to keep a woman "just an affair," but who find themselves caught up in something that is more significant to consciousness and demands from them more involvement.

Neumann says that the anima is an instigator of change, "whose fascination drives, lures and encourages the male to all the adventures of the soul and spirit, of action and creation in the inner and outward world . . . it sets the personality in motion, produces change and ultimately transformation."[9] Thus is brought to an end the first phase of anima development where a man passively lets his feelings happen to him and sees them as strictly directed to his own use and pleasure.

A new phase begins when a man recognizes that his anima is not identifiable with the woman upon whom it is projected but rather belongs to himself and requires that his individual ego relate to it. Eros' fleeing, in the story, represents the sense of estrangement a man feels when he no longer can project his anima as before but has not yet found a new way to relate to it.

Psyche's act of wounding herself on one of Eros' arrows symbolizes a second defloration, not passively received but active and voluntary, initiated by the anima, or the actual woman, or both. Psyche loves consciously and individually. It is Eros she loves, not submergence in her own instinct. The point of contact is her feeling for him. In this act of love she knows herself in a new way, no longer feminine like the natural sexuality and fertility represented by Aphrodite, but feminine now as a human force of devoted, individually related sexuality. She is no longer just known but has become a knower herself and effects in a man a similar transformation, in which he is no longer just a knower but is known.

Psyche as anima begins to assume Amazonian proportions of self-originating and self-fulfilling intentions, effecting a mutuality between herself and the masculine ego. She initiates recognition of the sexual polarity, of the otherness that exists between them. She opposes the man who knows himself simply as a mother's son and who therefore relates only to a woman as an anonymous being, still the operative modality for Eros at this point in the story. Psyche demands

9. Erich Neumann, *The Great Mother*, trans. Ralph Manheim (New York: Pantheon, 1955), pp. 33-34.

that Eros assume comparable heroic proportions encountering and relating to the feminine on an individual rather than a collective basis, that is to say, not to woman, but to *this* woman, not to sex, but in a sexual response to *this* person, not knowing himself as male, but as *this* particular man who knows his maleness in relation to *this* woman. The masculine identity then becomes self-generating; he is no longer just a mama's boy. This is illustrated in the ordinary course of things when a husband takes his wife's part against his mother. The dangers of regression involved in this step are illustrated by Eros' return to his angry mother, where he sulks around the house like a misunderstood youth.

A dream illustrating the successful triumph over such a regression came for a young male patient of mine soon after his realization that he had related in analytical sessions as a son to a mother. Though initially necessary, the role became anathema to him. He dreamt: "I was entering the subway gate to come to our session. A woman ticket taker said I shouldn't wear the tie I had on and started telling me how I should dress. I got furious and told her I'd dress any way I damn pleased! It was my tie, my body, and my self, and my trip. When I said that, she let me pass." He felt the subway as the undergrounding of the unconscious and our sessions as the focusing point for his coming to himself. He felt his self-assertion against the motherly old ticket taker to be a declaration of independence from the containing aspect of the feminine on which he had hitherto felt dependent. He felt he could now proceed on his own terms rather than those dictated by supportive mother types. This seemingly trivial dream is a modern example of the myth of the hero slaying the mother-dragon and, with the slaying, being initiated into his own manhood, "my tie, my body, my self, etc."

Psyche's act of seeing, her wounding of Eros and her self-wounding, followed by her movement in love toward Eros are essential points in the story. As indicated above, these acts effect a transformation in the two characters' identities, which now begin to be revealed in the polarity of the sexes.

"Polarity" is used here in its conventional dictionary sense to designate the quality or condition inherent in a body that exhibits opposite or contrasted properties in opposite or contrasted directions, and a concomitant attraction toward a particular object or direction. Psyche separates herself from unconscious identification with Eros only as she consciously knows herself as herself, and, at the same time, is directed toward Eros. She knows her separate unique being only in relation to Eros, and yet she fulfills the relation only by fully claiming her own uniqueness. The union of masculine and feminine is no longer universal, collective, or anonymous as it was under the dominance of the Great Mother archetype, Aphrodite, but has now become an encounter of conscious individuals fulfilling their existence through love. As Neumann writes, "With Psyche, then, there appears a new love principle, in which the encounter between feminine and masculine is revealed as the basis of individuation." [10]

The story demonstrates that the masculine-feminine polarity reveals the secret of love, for only when Psyche sees Eros, only when she is pricked by the arrow point of their sexual difference, of their otherness, only then does she consciously fall in love with him. The obvious sexual reference of the arrow point suggests that sexual intercourse in conjunction with Psyche's conscious wish to see Eros carries this mystery of otherness. The masculine-feminine polarity fulfills the individual as an inner modality of the anima leading to the self; it fulfills two persons as an outer modality celebrating uniqueness-in-relationship and relationship-in-uniqueness; it fulfills the human in relation to the divine and the divine principle of love as it is incarnate in the human.

10. Neumann, *Amor and Psyche*, p. 90.

Part IV

APHRODITE GIVES PSYCHE four tasks which she must complete if she wants to overcome the separation she has occasioned from Eros in the course of claiming her individuality. This long separation and its various phases symbolize the dividing polarization that at first afflicts the recognition of sexual polarity, when the uniqueness of each male and female asserts itself in opposition, in driving apart, rather than in uniting and coming together in love. The failure to achieve a sense of true polarity, which occurs when polarity remains unconscious, may be felt in various ways: as a fusion with a partner which expresses itself as possessive grasping, in the dullness of taking the other for granted, or as estrangement from the partner where each goes a separate way, detached, and yet still full of a deep, if buried longing.

The tasks that are imposed by Aphrodite also symbolize the stages in which the anima frees herself from the collective maternal unconscious and secures her unique pole in the polarity of being. The danger of regressing to unconsciousness is symbolized by Psyche's despair at ever completing the tasks and her temptation, therefore, to drown herself in the river. Moreover, suicidal thoughts afflict Psyche at later stages as well, thus symbolizing that regression tempts at each new level of anima development and is never really overcome until the final emergence of the anima in full and effective relation to the ego. That climax is described in the story in terms of the reunion of Psyche and Eros.

The anima's special function is to mediate the collective unconscious to the ego. It must be strong enough to mediate and not allow itself to be swamped by the contents of the unconscious, and it must remain strong enough to communicate those contents to the conscious ego. The tasks, seen in this light, become the way and the means of transformation. It is at this point in the story that we learn that Psyche is pregnant, which raises a question. Did her act of love in seeing and kissing Eros have the deeper meaning of conception, thus again depicting the transformation of the instinctive passion of Eros and Psyche into human form and the planting of the seed of the anima as mediatrix? With each task the anima, Psyche, achieves differentiation from the static elementary aspects of the feminine, Aphrodite, and achieves a role as the transformative feminine element in a man's personality. Each of these tasks symbolizes how the anima gradually changes the man's personality.

The first of the great tasks set Psyche by Aphrodite is to sort out hundreds of different kinds of seeds into their proper categories. This Psyche accomplishes with the help of ants. The seeds may be interpreted to represent the male's promiscuous tendencies when he is still playing the son to the nonpersonal, collective, maternal unconscious and is relating to women as a "sower of wild oats." The anima, with the help of the instinctive ants (which according to Neumann represent the selectivity of the vegetative nervous system), begins to order the boundless potentialities of the masculine psyche and to prepare it to assume relatedness.[11]

Psyche's second task is to gather some wool of great radiance from the sheep of the sun that graze by the river. A reed growing by the riverside talks to Psyche. Psyche listens to the reed, who advises her not to approach the sheep in the midday sun, when their power is at its most destructive, but to wait until the sun has fallen lower in the sky before gathering the wool from the bushes they have grazed against. This task may be interpreted to represent the depotentiating of the blunt, ramming aggression of the male that destroys what it loves. Psyche's task is not to castrate this power but to make it relatable. Completion of this task may also be seen in the way in which an argument can be resolved successfully if a woman is silent until her man's storm blows

11. *Ibid.*, p. 95.

out its full force; only when things are calm again does she gather some of that precious power and tame it. The anima thus avoids the lethal invasion of the unconscious powers into the ego, choosing instead to take up their shining essence in small manageable quantities. The key point is the refusal of the woman, or the anima, to engage in a death struggle with masculine aggression, avoiding direct assault and with it the stalemate of polarization. As a result, contact and interchange between the masculine and feminine are possible. In this instance, the masculine ego is instructed by the anima in the procedures of correct timing, learning how to let things pass and how then to gather their essence. These first two tasks, then, deal with the anima in relation to the personal unconscious, first in terms of the seeds of sexuality, and then by means of the force of the power instinct. The next two tasks deal with the way the anima mediates the collective unconscious.

Psyche's third task is to fill a crystal vessel with the spring water that flows from the highest mountains to feed the rivers of the underworld, the Styx and the Cocytus. This precious water is hard to obtain because it unites the highest and lowest elements, and because it embodies eternal change and movement. Symbolically, the water represents the vital energy of the collective unconscious, that is, the generative and numinous power of the male in its highest spiritual aspects and its deepest arousing aspects. The task of the anima is to give form to this energy, to put it in a container through which it can be mediated to individual ego consciousness, and thus to provide a stable contact for the male ego to its own masculine energy. The anima must provide the ego with concrete accessibility to this flowing energy of life. Insofar as it does this, the anima becomes a vessel of individuation and a way to the self.

Zeus's eagle, which had brought him his own homosexual love, Ganymede, helps Psyche in this task by removing a cupful of water from the endlessly circulating stream of life. This may be interpreted to represent the salutary effects of male friendship, and even of homosexual love, as an ally of the masculine element in its initial struggle for liberation from dependence on the mother. The impulse of some young boys, for example, to show off their aroused masculinity to members of their sex is often a way of claiming their own sexuality.

The anima in this task enlists the support of male love in its efforts to differentiate the ego from the collective unconscious and to differentiate feeling from sexuality. It focuses, limits, and mediates the abundant unconscious resources to the ego. It is aided by masculine qualities, represented by the eagle, but does not become masculine itself. Where efforts at differentiation fail, the active identification of the ego with the anima and the continued identification of sexuality with all feeling may be expressed in overt homosexuality. When that occurs, the anima—meaning the man's emotional life—is still subservient to the mother archetype, and a man is cut off from his own sense of inner support, experiencing his masculinity not in its own right but only in terms of serving his actual or symbolic mother's purposes. In an effort to make his maleness secure he turns to men.

In her third task Psyche had to reach to the heights of masculine spirituality and give its boundless energy concrete form. In her fourth task she must go to the depths of the underworld, to the realm of death, to bring back the ointment of immortal beauty for Aphrodite. This time Psyche must go herself; there are no magical helpers who can do the task for her as in the first and third tasks, nor can she wait until danger has passed and then collect her prize, as she did with the second task. Psyche fears she cannot succeed, and in her despair she wants to kill herself by throwing herself from a tower. Psyche's suicidal wish when she has only one more task to complete symbolizes the regressive pull of the unconscious that asserts itself most strongly when the goal of finally achieving differentiation from the unconscious is almost won.

For the sake of her love, Psyche, the anima, must enter the world of the dead. The anima in this task achieves full religious stature as mediatrix of the reality of death, which must be met, accepted, and then overcome. A young man's dream captures this anima aspect well. He summed it up. "I was traveling on a road unknown to me, which seemed to be my road in life. I saw a beautiful girl on the side of the road. I went up to her and embraced her passionately. As I held her in my arms, she became old, very old, as if she had been dead for a thousand years." In the dream the anima confronts the dreamer with the realities of death, not by means of abstract explanation, but through the intimacies of a passionate embrace. The anima shows the dreamer how age shrivels the skin and changes beauty to a death mask.

Psyche is saved from killing herself by the very tower from which she wants to jump. The tower, gifted with speech, advises her to resist the supplications of a lame man driving a lame donkey, a corpse, and weaving women, all of whom she passes on the road to the underworld. This advice may be interpreted to mean that the anima must be strong enough to resist pity, to resist losing her function as media-trix by succumbing to her desire to help those she passes on the road, thus emotionally embracing all the needs of the world as if she could really cater to them all. A man may experience the threat of losing his firmness of ego in the face of a woman's tears or he may lose his relationship to a woman because he must compulsively help other women in his life—such as his dependent sister, or his ailing mother, or his neighbor, a divorcée, who cannot seem to manage with-out his advice. If the anima successfully gives up the desire to help and nurture everyone, preferring to achieve individual relation to the ego, it may finally break its identification with the maternal instinct.

Resisting the corpse in the tale means resisting possession by an ancestral spirit in order to follow instead the summons for an actual and immediate love. An instance of failing to do this is a man who stays possessed by the spirit of his mother or sister rather than trying to find a woman of his own; or a man who remains tied to a woman long dead or to a fantasy woman. In these cases the anima lives in the underworld rather than on earth. Resisting the weaving women in the tale means resisting the world of weaving fantasy, the world of wishing and dreaming, choosing rather to live in the real world. If unsuccessful in this task, the anima is tied to the world of fantasy and cannot serve reality.

In the first three tasks, the anima becomes sufficiently developed in its ability to mediate to the ego several fundamental masculine elements which can then be concretized in human relationship. First, there is the fecundating power of the male, which if unmediated may be scattered in senseless promiscuity. Second, there is the force of masculine aggression, which if unmediated turns destructive; and third there is the numinous spirit world of the male, which if unmediated remains uncontrollable and unreachable. At each stage, if its force is not dissipated, the anima becomes stronger and more adequate to channel the power of eros.

In the first three tasks Psyche wrestles to differentiate various elements of the masculine psyche; in the fourth she achieves her full femininity in relation to the masculine eros. This is depicted in Psyche's opening of a beauty box to take an ointment for herself so that she may be eternally pleasing to Eros. Aphrodite's hope is that Psyche will succumb to this temptation, fall into a deathless sleep, and so be lost to Eros forever. But the result is quite different. Psyche does not open the box until she has left the underworld, and although she falls asleep it is a sleep from which Eros can awaken her. In other words, the anima succeeds in bringing the treasure out of the unconscious depths; she opens it, not to become beautiful but to be beautiful for Eros. The anima embodies this beauty not for the purpose of unconscious narcissistic, self-idolization but in direct relation to masculine eros; it is for the sake of eros that the anima assumes this immortal beauty. Furthermore, in that act, the anima is fully differentiated from the mother archetype, because, instead of giving the immortal ointment to Aphrodite and thus consecrating the anonymous collective maternal, in the guise of Psyche she takes it for herself as a means of relation to Eros. The fascination of the feminine is now put at the disposal of masculine eros in order to build a human relationship.

Eros symbolizes both the transpersonal archetype of relatedness to a deity, that is, as a nonhuman principle, and also the human masculine ego that depends on the anima to free its eros drive from the maternal unconscious.

Part V

AT THE END OF THE STORY, Psyche, too, is received as one of the gods at Mount Olympus. The deification of Psyche and Eros may seem confusing, because the anima and the ego are clearly human elements and not divine. It is helpful, I think, to understand the deification as symbolizing the far-reaching effects of a fully developed otherness. The incarnation of this mystery in human elements is felt as an ascent into something like heavenly bliss and fulfillment and may even seem to some a partaking of the mysterious unity of divine life. The means of this ascent and participation is the full development of sexual polarity, both intrapsychically and between man and woman. For this reason, when the full union of Eros and Psyche is divinized, it represents to Jungians how powerful this polarity is, how well it captures the ascending and descending intercourse of the divine and the human.

Psyche (or the anima), who so actively achieved the first tasks, now surrenders her achievements in this last failure. By taking the beauty ointment herself, Psyche is ready to sacrifice spiritual development in order to be pleasing to the man she loves. The depth of meaning of the polarity of the sexes now reveals itself. The feminine element achieves its full stature, not to separate itself from the masculine nor to save

or perfect the masculine, nor even to exalt and remain en-
closed within the feminine, as would be the case if Psyche
were to give the ointment to Aphrodite. Rather, her full
stature is achieved in love of the masculine, and it evokes a
corresponding stature in the masculine, for Psyche is rescued
from her sleep by Eros. Just as Psyche had originally brought
light into the darkness in order to have Eros more fully,
she now brings darkness into the light she achieved and thus
evokes in Eros his full masculine stature. In full consciousness
the masculine ego, infused with eros, now willingly relates
itself to the anima, and as a result, rescues it from immersion
in the unconscious, and heroically saves it for the life of
union. In a man's relation to a woman, this richness of relationship occurs when the woman's devotion and trust
evoke his manliness and encourage the full development of
his own eros that results from direct contact with his own
ego identity, sexuality, and creative feeling.

The triumph of full sexual polarity is dramatized in the
tale when Psyche is admitted to the realm of the gods. Symbolically, the soul's individual ability to love consciously,
out of a full identity of its own in relation to a full opposite
identity, is celebrated as divine. It is a kind of paradigm of
the union of the soul and God. The union of Eros and
Psyche issues in a daughter called Joy, who is both human
and divine. Neumann writes:

> This love of Psyche for her divine lover is a central motif
> in the love mysticism of all times, and Psyche's failure, her
> final self-abandonment, and the god who approaches as a
> saviour at this very moment correspond exactly to the high-
> est phase of mystical ecstasy, in which the soul commends
> itself to the godhead. . . .
>
> "In the language of mortals" Psyche's child "is called
> Pleasure." But in the language of heaven . . . this child is
> the mystical joy which among all peoples is described as the
> fruit of the highest mystical union. It is "Joy indeed, but
> surpassing sensuality." [12]

12. *Ibid.*, p. 140.

In sum, this story stands, I think, as a remarkably accurate description of the inner sexual polarity of the male—of the feminine anima and the masculine ego, of the polarity of the sexes of Psyche and Eros, of the soul's intercourse with the divine. The transformations of the anima initiate a symbolic development of masculine personality which goes from dragon-devourer at betrothal, to monster-husband in marriage, to unconscious lover, who can be met only in the dark; and thence to regression to the role of mother's son, as indicated in the flight of Eros to Aphrodite, and finally to redeemer-god, as dramatized by the rescuing of Psyche. The stages of masculine-feminine polarity symbolize the stages of wholeness, within the psyche, between persons, and with the divine.

CHAPTER TWELVE

Stages of Animus Development

J UST AS THE ANIMA'S DEVELOPMENT initiates the development of the masculine personality, the animus in its stages of transformation connects the deeper feminine self to the female ego and initiates the development of the feminine personality. For the female ego, the masculine is experienced in interior forms as the animus and in external forms as the male, and each evokes the other. Sexual polarity in its literal and symbolic dimensions threads its way through all the lines of human existence, though most human beings are only half-consciously aware of its central importance in their lives.

Because little has been written about the stages of animus transformation—and most of what has been written has been by men—and because there is no encompassing mythological paradigm to draw upon as with the anima stages of man, I will discuss the way the female encloses the masculine in two ways. First, I will present a summary of Erich Neu-

mann's description of the four stages of feminine development in women, adding to this a description of the various
functions of the animus in relation to femininity drawn from
a variety of sources and clinical examples. Then I will use a
modern story, that of Dorothy of Oz, as a paradigm of a
young girl's successive encounters with the animus function.

THE FIRST STAGE

THE FIRST STAGE of feminine development is one of psychic
unity, a unity where there is no separation of the ego from
the unconscious; the individual is contained in the all-embracing, maternal, and protective power of the unconscious
on an intrapsychic level, and within the mother, the group,
and the clan on an extrapsychic level. The active living
quality of the psyche and the dynamic opposition to its
processes are held within what Neumann calls the maternal
"uroboros, the serpent forming a closed circle, the tail swal-
lower." [1] This first stage of feminine development corresponds to the uroboric and matriarchal phases discussed in
Chapter Three. This original, pre-ego containment stage is
the same for both sexes, but it is experienced very differently
by the two. For both sexes the original dependence of the
ego on the unconscious is experienced as a state of identity
with the mother who, "quite independently of her own
individuality, impresses the infant as the maternal uroboros
and the 'Great Mother.' " [2] For both sexes, the experience of
the opposing dynamisms of the psyche is first projected onto
the differences in sex, and it is thus that

> every archetypal opposition easily assumes a masculine-
> feminine character and the opposition of conscious and un-
> conscious is also experienced through this symbolism, the

1. Erich Neumann, "The Psychological Stages of Feminine Development," *Spring*, trans. and rev. Hildegard Nagel and Jane Pratt
(New York: The Analytical Psychology Club, 1959), p. 63.
2. *Ibid.*, p. 64.

masculine being identified with consciousness and the feminine with the unconscious. This . . . stems from the primary fact of the uroboric situation, that masculine consciousness is born from the maternal unconscious.[3]

For both sexes, the self as the center of the total psyche is experienced in immediate identity with the body. Thus it takes on the characteristics of the exterior physical sex.

For the boy, the experience of the opposing sexual elements occurs sooner than it does with girls, and it has immediate decisive effects upon him. He experiences his original identity with his mother as a relation of like to unlike, as a relation to a nonself, to an "other," an opposite, symbolized by all the obvious sexual differences. In order to be himself and to have himself to himself he must stand against his early identity with the nonself; he must free his ego and go his own way. His self-discovery takes place in opposition to the primary relationship with the mother, and this effects a greater isolation through its new emphasis upon objectivity and ego consciousness. He identifies his ego with consciousness because his self-discovery coincides with his freeing himself from his mother and from the pre-ego containment in the unconscious that she symbolizes. Not until much later, when his ego position is firmly established can he resume relationship to the unconscious. If he fails to free his ego, a typical Oedipal problem results where he experiences his masculinity as something that belongs to someone else—his mother—castrated as a result of maternal uroboric incest.

For the girl, self-discovery is contained in her early identification with her mother, because she feels strongly drawn as like to like. The experience of opposing forces projected onto and conveyed by the difference in sexes is exterior to this nascent relationship of mother and daughter and thus does not disrupt it. Hence there is less emphasis with a girl than there is with a boy in developing an ego position with which to oppose the unconscious that the mother symbol-

3. *Ibid.*, p. 65.

izes. Instead, a girl's ego development takes place not in opposition to but in relation to her unconscious. She feels dependent on it and turns toward unconscious processes, not away from them. The feminine ego is less consciously defined than the male's and often less firm. It stresses objectivity less and is therefore less clear. It is more subjective and as a result less estranged and less isolated from its own roots in the unconscious.

Although this ego development occurs in childhood, a woman can remain at this stage her whole life. The danger here is not castration but fixation. She can come to experience herself without ever leaving the possessive circle of the Great Mother archetype. She remains childish but not estranged from herself, enjoying the advantages of natural wholeness and completeness but not the qualities of an individual person. A culture often exerts pressure on a woman by holding up before her this kind of undifferentiated, natural femininity as a type of ideal womanhood. Any woman who seeks to develop beyond this stage may have to fight to free herself from such cultural pressures.

Identification and Differentiation

BECAUSE THE MOTHER-CHILD RELATIONSHIP is one of identification, that mode of relating is stronger in women than in men. In this original relationship a woman's experience of herself as feminine is the same for her as experiencing her mother as feminine. Her instinctive way of relating, therefore, is through identification, not through discrimination; it leads to tendencies to become overinvolved, overemotional, and to find and enmesh herself continually in the same situations.

The woman who lives at this stage of development is not unlike Toni Wolff's Mother type. She exists within the self-conserving matriarchal circle symbolized by the close mother-daughter relationship of the mythological deities

Demeter and Kore. Everything is self-evident and natural. A man is an outsider for her; she experiences him but never surrenders to him. He is seen only as a fixture of the household or a begetter of children. She has her own unconscious notions about the character of men but no individual relation to them. She loves the male as a child or as a boy, or reduces him to her tool or satrapy. In still more negative form, the male is felt as enemy or alien, arousing hostility and producing serious symptoms, such as frigidity. At this stage, the woman experiences her femininity unconsciously, as natural maternal instinct. Her animus does not perform its function of relating her to her deeper self but is entrapped in the archetype of the Great Mother, rushing in to fill her lack of personal response with collective standards, with general truths and dogmatic preconceptions to which the situation must conform. The capacities to discriminate and abstract, which the animus function normally stimulates, lie fallow or erupt in a primitive form. A woman fixated at this point issues opinions or insists on expressing general convictions which may be valid but are simply not relevant. As a result, she does a kind of emotional violence either to persons speaking or to persons addressed or to objective facts. The undeveloped condition of her powers of discimination has the negative effect of inducing her to greet both valuable and worthless ideas with the same enthusiasm. Occasionally, the effect of all this may be to cut away her prejudices and to permit her to discover values that a man might quickly dismiss.[4]

For a woman trying to free herself from this stage, the archetypal power of the feminine as Mother assumes terrifying proportions. The move to differentiation seems to activate the static and elemental aspect of the maternal in its most negative form. It becomes a strong regressive pull, an entrapping, devouring mother. An example of this is the

4. See Emma Jung, *Animus and Anima*, trans. Cary F. Baynes and Hildegard Nagel (New York: The Analytical Psychology Club, 1957), p. 15.

fantasy of a young woman possessed by a spider phobia, a frequent symbolization of the devouring mother. She suffered from feelings of being trapped. When encouraged to see if an image might emerge to explain what was trapping her, she saw herself in a large cage with black, furry bars. As she looked upwards, transfixed with fear, she saw that the bars were a giant spider's legs.

Efforts to combat this collective pull of the unconscious may contain elements of the very thing that is being fought. Group movements that urge women to form a sexual collective in order to free themselves from this undifferentiated collective state exemplify this paradox. Members of such groups urge other women to become independent of men while at the same time they are themselves tyrannized by animus judgments. They are still subjectively dependent on the masculine elements of their own personalities because they have not sufficiently developed or related to the animus function. Instead of becoming independent of the masculine, they grow more and more unconscious of the animus and project its tyranny onto all men. This does not help to combat discrimination against women.

THE SECOND STAGE

THE SECOND STAGE of feminine development, Neumann thinks, still is focused on the containing uroboros, but it is invaded by the paternal and hence dominated by the Great Father archetype. This stage of feminine development corresponds to the patriarchal stage discussed in Chapter Three. The masculine is experienced as an anonymous, transpersonal, and overpowering *numinosum*, completely other than the ego, thereby making the ego conscious of its own limits. The image of divinity now appears as a male figure and first emerges mythologically as "power groups of demonic masculine characters, such as the Cabiri, the Satyrs, and the Dactyle, whose multiplicity still betrays their anonymity and formless numinosity." [5] These are followed by phallic-chthonic gods which are still subordinate to the "Great Mother," such as Dionysus, Pan, or Wotan; or by personifications of nature such as clouds, rain, wind, or sun; or by animals such as the bull, the snake, or the goat, which are worshipped as gods of fruitfulness.

A woman experiences this invading masculine, carried by a man or by the animus, as a transpersonal ravishing penetrator who breaks into her consciousness, overpowers her, transports her outside herself, connects her to her own instinctual nature, and fundamentally changes her personality. She is no longer contained in her mother; she no longer identifies herself with her unconscious, no longer lives in the shadow of a superior feminine being. Now she knows the raptures and ecstasies of her own sexuality. Such an invasion may also be greeted with fear, as symbolized in the image of death, for the woman is now severed from safety as mother's daughter.

Such archetypal symbolism underlies the sexual disturbances of many women. They unconsciously feel themselves too small to receive the transpersonal phallus and see the male as dragon-monster or rapist, a Hades bearing Kore away to the underworld. If a woman can accept and surrender to her tremors of anxiety, those tremors can be transformed into the intoxicating pleasures of orgasm. A woman may then be liberated from the self-conserving containing phase and may enter an entirely new phase of self-surrender. Because she experiences the masculine as a numinous force, her orgiastic seizure has a spiritual as well as a physical aspect. She can, therefore, experience orgasm with intense spiritual excitement, for generally "she understands, symbolically speaking, not with the head but with the whole body, . . . her spiritual and corporeal processes are bound together in a way quite foreign to the average man." [6]

---

5. Neumann, "Psychological Stages of Feminine Development," p. 71.
6. *Ibid.*, p. 72.

An unexpected example of the transforming effects of the ravishing masculine was the experience of some women who had been brutally raped by the Russians when they entered Berlin in World War II.[7] Bourgeois housewives, whose relations with their husbands knew little sexual depth, reported experiencing exultation and orgasm for the first time at the hands of the Russians, feeling that they knew at last what it was to be a woman. The complete surrender into which they were forced upon threat of their lives and the fact that they were not responsible for what was happening to them allowed them to throw off their bourgeois respectability and give in totally to the anonymous power of their sexual instinct. This effected profound changes in their experience of themselves; they knew now the sexual power of their own depths, however degraded the actual incidents may also have made them feel.

Our mores and customs may support this second stage of development or hold a woman in it for too long a time. It is common to think that a woman's fulfillment can come only when she opens herself to a man. Cultural emphases on the ceremonies of defloration, on all the rituals of the wedding night, also illustrate this.

A young woman's dream shows the ecstasy a woman may feel in response to the invading male while still feeling contained in an uroboric state of being: "I was at some unnamed gas station with my mother and sister. A strange man came by and I was seized with an irresistible attraction to him. He threw me to the ground and kissed me, burrowing deep into my throat and penetrating me at the same time. It was so intense that I felt his tongue and penis meet inside me so that he formed a circle through my body. My ecstasy was so great I fainted." Here the maternal circle of mother, daughter, and sister was invaded by an anonymous man in the

---

7. See Anneliese Aumüller, "Jungian Psychology in Wartime Germany," *Spring* (New York: The Analytical Psychology Club, 1950), *passim*.

most ordinary situation, at a gas station. The man formed a paternal uroboros through the girl's body, reaching from her head, or spirit, to her sexual center. The intensity of the event was registered in her swooning; while unconscious—dreaming—she passed out, touching an even deeper level inside herself.

A woman who is fixated at this stage is not unlike Toni Wolff's Hetaira type in her negative aspect. She is the eternal daughter of a Spiritual Father, and, in its secondary personalization as the Oedipus complex, she is still emotionally attached to her actual father. A clear example of this bondage to the paternal uroboros is to be found in the dream of an attractive girl who sought therapy because she had repeatedly become engaged to men but could never go through with marriage. Analysis had made some dent in her beautiful but cold façade, when an opportunity came for her to work in Europe. To her, Europe was a land of promise, full of new men and new possibilities. But stopping therapy seemed inadvisable. Initially, she had had suicidal intentions that had subsided as she became engaged in the analytical process, but the conflicts that they expressed had not been resolved. She was adamant, however, even to the point of disregarding a warning dream that was unusually stark in its archetypal imagery: "I was a beautiful princess trying to escape from a king's castle. I had managed to get outside the castle, but then four horsemen came galloping after me. I was all in white and had on precious jewelry. They were in black armor and were riding black stallions. They scooped me up and took me back to the castle. The king did not want me so much as he wanted my jewels. I knew I would not get away again." Later, after the dreamer had gone to Europe, she sent a frantic letter requesting a referral to another analyst in Europe. She felt entrapped again. Suicidal depressions had returned and with them a series of unresolved relationships. The dream depicted her imprisonment by an impersonal masculine figure, the king, who did not care for her personality at all but only for the precious values she carried. She was a passive victim in the dream as she was in life.

This young woman's symptoms illustrate another aspect of fixation at the paternal stage. There was an hysterical quality about her and a complete lack of awareness of the seductive inducements her body was signaling while her mind was alert to repel invaders. It is clear again that when one moves from the matriarchal to the patriarchal stage, the initial self-conserving impulses oppose the new development and turn a negative face to the invading masculine. This is often the archetypal basis for quarrels between mother and daughter over how late to stay out or whom to date, etc.

If a woman remains fixed in the patriarchal phase, not only does that stage turn negative in tone, but the already negative qualities of the previous phase intensify. It is as if her natural, matriarchal bias turns against her. She feels unrooted in her own body, unconnected to the instinctive processes of her psyche. This is manifested in hysterical symptoms, where the woman's emotionality seems unattached and undigested and assumes an overly dramatic quality, characterized by a high-pitched voice, copious tears, light-headedness, or a sense of going too fast or of having too little insulation against the world. Sexual coldness, anesthesia to feeling, and even frigidity are frequent symptoms; they are usually combined with a desire to reach out and establish physical and emotional relationships, which, because they are so often unrecognized, or unrecognizable, produce a seductive, teasing quality.

In extreme cases, a woman's inability to assimilate or surrender to the masculine, either in an outer relationship or to the animus within herself, can effect such a severance from her own deeper femininity that she may feel dissociated to the point of borderline psychosis. She feels small, helpless, and weakly feminine in relation to a tremendous masculine being, which is seen alternately as an omniscient, all-powerful, and magical Prince Charming who will rescue her, or as a plotting persecutor out to crush her. This sense of small-

ness gives her whole bearing an infantile quality, regardless
of her age; she is girlish, with bows in her hair and wearing
childish expressions. This girlish comportment is encouraged
when the standards of fashion hold up childish styles as symbolizing an ideal femininity. A woman who is thus dissociated
from her adult femininity may even lose touch with such
concrete realities as eating, sleeping, doing laundry, etc., as
if her natural functioning in the previous mother phase had
turned against her, making it impossible for her to do even
the simplest domestic tasks.

A poignant illustration of this is a single woman of middle
age who suffered from delusional fantasies about her many
employers. With each new job, she projected all the positive
qualities of the numinous masculine onto her boss: he "knew"
her moods, her inner thoughts, her emotional needs, and in
all his dealings with her constantly demonstrated this "knowledge." For instance, the way he asked her to type a letter
communicated to her an as yet unexpressed love and a plan
to marry and rescue her from the rigors of making a living,
from despondent loneliness, and lack of incentive to make a
home for herself. He would marry her and give her a
reason to learn to cook and do laundry. She, in response,
would be effusive, adoring, frantic in her efforts to please
her boss. She had fantasies of an imminent proposal. As
time passed and he did not propose, the fantasies became
negative. Now he was using his secret knowledge of her to
torment her, arousing her feelings in order to frustrate her,
suppressing her, showing her no respect. Her helpless passive
femininity took on a victimized tone: she was ill and he was
taking advantage of her frailty; she was a poor woman at the
mercy of a badgering brute. He was denying her feelings and
making her frigid. Nightly fantasies now consisted of endless
ruminations over all the things he had done to her. She
became captious, sarcastic, defensive, and offensive to her
boss and inevitably evoked his most unpleasant responses.
She was unable to establish a relationship with him, let alone
with her own projected animus. The boss was not an indi-

vidual person, he was "men." Her animus function was completely dissociated. She found herself caught in such compulsive reasoning as this: "If it weren't for the boss's behavior—if he would only change—everything would be fine."

The Anima Woman

ESTHER HARDING's lucid description of the "anima woman" who can be "all things to all men" offers another example of a woman fixated at the second stage of development.[8] The "anima woman" has little individual personality or genuine personal feeling for others. Instead, she carries with her—and identifies with—the image of woman that men project onto her. She is extraordinarily attractive to men, who find in her a reflection of their own feelings. As a result, a man feels that this kind of woman really understands him, and that his true self emerges when he is with her. Dr. Harding sketches three stages of development for the anima woman. The first is typified by a maidenlike, innocent Ophelia personality that unconsciously pours itself into the mold of femininity that a man prefers. She directs her energies toward adapting to and pleasing a man. She is soft and yielding and seems full of love, but if one particular man is not available another will do just as well. She presents herself to a man not as a person but rather as an embodiment of his projected anima image. She unconsciously lives out her feminine instincts and catches men, but not with any real awareness of what she is doing. The second stage presents the egoistic type of anima woman who is more aware of her power over men and uses it to her own advantage—to cut a good appearance socially, to inflate her own ego, to get money, or to run a house. She calculates how much feeling to give a man and

8. See Esther Harding, *The Way of All Women* (London: Longmans, Green & Co., 1936), chap. I, *passim*.

keeps him unaware of the manipulated quality of her responses. The third stage brings still more consciousness. In it the anima woman tries to integrate the instinctive and egoistic attitudes of the first two stages. She does not want to abuse these gifts but wishes to use them in the service of genuine love and relationships.

There are also three dominant types of anima women, each fixed in her own stage and firmly resisting any kind of development. One is the childlike maiden, sweet and innocent, who has a difficult time facing old age. The second is the tempestuously emotional woman, who seems intense and passionate because she unconsciously lives out all her emotions and instincts; her outbursts usually appeal to men who are themselves overrestrained and overrational. The third is the cool, aloof, and distant woman, who is completely passive and indifferent to a man, expressing no wishes of her own. A man sees her symbolically as goddess or as albatross. These types are so much a part of our culture that they are even reflected in the female characters in contemporary films.

The anima woman is the result of a woman's passive identification with her animus.[9] The animus does not perform its function of connecting unconscious contents to a woman's ego, thus effecting a deeper relation of her ego to her feminine self. There is no ego position now. Where personal preferences and points of view should be expressed there is a vacuum instead; she expresses herself in vagueness, ambiguity, and ambivalence. Such a woman fails to relate consciously to her femininity, living it rather through her animus, which is projected onto a man. She only feels alive when she is with a man. A woman of this type once declared in analysis that she felt "invisible" except when she was with a man and that he gave her a "personality." In such circumstances the animus replaces the ego function. The man is

9. See Esther Harding, "The Anima and the Animus" (a paper read to The Analytical Psychology Club of New York, January 19, 1951, privately printed), p. 29.

annexed as so much personal property belonging to her. She feels herself dependent on the man, even feels herself his victim, but actually she is tyrannized by the animus within her, and unconsciously tyrannizes over the man, referring all his feelings and actions to her own needs. Culturally, this view is expressed by the often-heard directive that a man must be head of the house although the woman may remain "the real power behind the throne." This same ambivalence about woman's power is expressed in the discrimination against women in employment, in salary and promotion patterns based on the strong conviction that "real women are passive and dependent on men." This tyranny has its reverse tyranny in divorce laws that severely punish and impoverish men.

An example of the inner tyranny of the animus, with its lethal effect on the male, and woman's unconsciousness of it, is shown in the following dream. The dreamer felt herself the victim of her husband's compulsive drinking, which she continually forgave and "understood": "I was waiting for my husband when a gangster drove up in his car. He was mad at my husband for not paying off his debts. As my husband came up to us, the gangster shot him; I pretended not to see. My husband was not yet dead and the gangster told him that I had shot him. I said nothing for fear the gangster would shoot me. Then the gangster handed me the gun, saying, 'Here, finish him off.' " The dreamer would not take responsibility for her own aggressive reactions to her husband, which stem from legitimate causes. Disengaging herself left her, as well as her husband, a helpless victim; and the negative aggression worked itself out unconsciously.

What is demanded in order to avoid fixation at this second stage is a more active ego relation to the animus, so that the animus serves the ego rather than the other way round. If the animus tyrannizes over the ego and functions autonomously without relation to the rest of the psyche, it has negative effects. It is important to remember that the animus is an archetype and hence is made up of nonpersonal energy that must be concretized in personal experience. If the personal ego abdicates this responsibility, the instinctive archetypal behavioral and emotional patterns take over. In this way, this second stage remains uroboric; the ego is contained within the pattern of archetypal forces. Wholeness demands a conscious ego relation to the masculine. If prevalent cultural standards discourage this relationship by holding up the second stage of development as the definition of the ideal woman, this can be very difficult indeed, for then the ego must fight free of containment in an outer collectivity while still struggling to get free of inner containment.

THE THIRD STAGE

IN THE THIRD STAGE of feminine development, the masculine assumes an individual and personal form, represented archetypally by a hero who frees the daughter from bondage to her father and then establishes an equal relation with her. This stage corresponds to the integrative stage discussed in Chapter Three. The hero can be an outer man or an inner animus figure; and most often he is both, because women usually project masculine qualities of consciousness onto actual men. Thus either "a 'real' man and partner assumes the freeing role of consciousness and dissolves the old form of encompassment in the unconscious, or else it can be an 'inner' man, a power of consciousness in the woman herself, which accomplishes the freeing." [10] In either case, the feminine ego feels incapable of freeing itself under its own power from the paternal uroboros and thus establishing a more equal relationship with the masculine. The feminine ego feels dependent upon the masculine and in need of help from it. Outwardly, this is illustrated by a man, say a husband, helping a woman free herself from her original family circle. Inwardly, however, she remains dependent on her animus

10. Neumann, "Psychological Stages of Feminine Development," p. 77.

function, which acts as an enlivening impulse, stirring up new possibilities of life. As Jung says, "masculinity means knowing what one wants and doing what is necessary to achieve it." [11] The animus also brings archetypal contents to consciousness through a reasoning attitude that sees things from a more general perspective than does the ego, which is caught up emotionally in the middle of things.[12] The animus also appears as the capacity to initiate independent action, to focus on and to discriminate between what belongs to the unconscious and what belongs to the ego.

A woman at this stage, quite unlike the anima woman, is not identical with her unconscious feminine instincts. The animus helps her to find perspective in her unconscious materials and to relate to them directly, to focus upon them. A beautiful dream of a woman illustrates this animus function, which separates out from the unconscious something of great value to the ego and serves the ego in a loving way, rather than replacing it or tyrannizing over it:

> F and I were swimming in the water. I got out. He dove deeply and brought up from the depths a cure for an incurable disease. He then got out of the water and gave a short lecture to an audience on what he had discovered. He pointed to a lustrous golden circle of the zodiac, focusing on my sign, Capricorn, which was at the top. There were two pictures of the mountain goat, one very strong and primitive, the other delicate, not at all weak, and very beautiful. They both had fishtails. He described his discovery from the watery deeps by pointing to a chart of the heavens.

11. Jung, "Woman in Europe," *Civilization in Transition* (*CW*, X, 1964), p. 126.

12. See Elizabeth Howes, "The Nature and Function of the Animus" (a paper read to The Analytical Psychology Club, San Francisco, n.d., property of The Kristine Mann Library, The Analytical Psychology Club, New York); Mary Briner, "A Problem of Modern Women as Reflected in Dreams" (a talk given at the American Women's Club, Zurich, 1960, property of The Kristine Mann Library, The Analytical Psychology Club, New York); and Marie Louise von Franz, "The Animus," *Man and His Symbols*, ed. C. G. Jung (New York: Doubleday, 1964), pp. 191–92.

> Then he came over to me and kissed me long and lovingly,
> and said: "I love you deeply and will love you forever."

The dreamer and the animus were both in the unconscious
waters. The dreamer's ego differentiated itself—she gets out
of the water—and the animus then found a precious cure for
an incurable disease, to which the dreamer associated cancer.
This led her to think of her mother, who had had that
disease, and of her father, whose birth sign it was. Cancer to
the dreamer was life doubling back on itself, which she felt
perfectly described her mother's unused emotional energy,
which had become destructive, and her father's withdrawal
from feeling, which was the result of fear. She then reflected
on details of her own ensnarement in a family habit of never
freely expressing feeling, and she realized how destructive
this had been for her. The dream also linked a number of
opposites together: deep waters and high heavens, the goat
who scaled heights and at the same time had a fishtail with
which to swim in the depths, the primitive and the refined
goats, F as a man and herself as a woman. The dream touched
her deeply, and she experienced a tremendous sense of liberation upon waking. F was to her a man of unusual clarity,
stability, and objectivity who made her feel grounded and
also clarified her own point of view. The fact that he gave a
lecture in the dream made her feel he had brought to the
surface a truth that was valuable to many people. The fact
that he kissed her so lovingly afterward made her feel that
she, with his help, must apply this truth to her own personal
situation.

Patriarchal Marriage

OUTWARDLY, this third stage usually issues in marriage, the
particular type of marriage prevalent in Western culture,
which Neumann calls patriarchal and Jung calls medieval.[13]

13. See Neumann, "Psychological Stages of Feminine Development,"
p. 79. See also Jung, "Woman in Europe," p. 126.

The patriarchal form of marriage has been a collective way of dealing with the masculine-feminine polarity, the backbone of patriarchal culture until modern times when symptoms have appeared "of its weakening and clandestine disruption, 'marriage problems' ranging from unbearable moods to neurosis and adultery." [14] Defined roughly, and for Christians with the sanction of St. Paul, the patriarchal or medieval model of the couple sees the man symbolically as representing the heavens and the wife as representing the earth. As the man has allegiance to God, so the woman must have allegiance to the man.[15] This form of marriage corresponds archetypally to the relations of earth to heaven, of flesh to spirit, of man to God. The human relation to the divine is translated into a particular style of relation between the sexes.

This patriarchal type of dependence of a woman upon man and man upon woman establishes a symbiosis where each gives up his or her own natural psychological contrasexuality. The man identifies with all that is consciously masculine, with consciousness and the ego structure; the woman identifies with all that is consciously feminine, and in particular with the unconscious. Masculine and feminine are polarized. Masculine equals masculine and feminine equals feminine and

> the ideal demanded of both man and wife is that they should identify with this unequivocalness.
>
> This symbiotic structure forms the foundation of the family and of patriarchal culture, for it guarantees not only security and definiteness, but also a fruitful tension of the opposites between men and women.[16]

A man's unconscious femininity, in the form of the anima, is projected onto a woman, and a woman's unconscious masculinity, in the form of the animus, is projected onto man. As mentioned above, on closer examination it often

14. Jung, "Woman in Europe," p. 128.
15. See Neumann, "Psychological Stages of Feminine Development," p. 79; Eph. 3:21-24.
16. Neumann, "Psychological Stages of Feminine Development," p. 80.

turns out that while the outer form of the marriage is patriarchal (where the man is the head of the family), there is a
concealed inner matriarchal form (where the wife is the real
power).

This form of marriage and this division of roles have been
perpetuated in the education of children in Western culture.
A masculine woman or a feminine man, in spite of their
present frequency, are still anathema to those who hold traditional cultural values. Those who do not fit into the ideal
patriarchal-matriarchal pattern often become displaced or are
suppressed in our society, much like shadow elements in the
individual personality that are quelled because they oppose
the prevailing ego morality. These groups of displaced persons build up tensions in the collective unconscious that are
easily activated in times of political unrest. They often
generate a revolutionary atmosphere; because they feel displaced in the most intimate aspects of their lives—in their
sexual relations—they may try to achieve through a change
in society what they have been unable to secure in personal
transformation.

In modern times, there seems to be a shift in the archetypal constellations of marriage. This shift is indicated by
such cultural changes as the increasing legal ease of divorce,
the growing numbers of women's groups that protest the
patriarchal-matriarchal version of femininity, the increased
public appearance of homosexuality, the blurring of sexual
definition through unisexual clothes and hair styles among
the young, and the pressing need felt by many people to
develop themselves more fully, which is to say in terms of
their masculine *and* feminine characteristics. All of this
clearly implies that the God-man relationship is seeking a
new form of expression in a new form of relationship between the masculine and feminine. God is not to be conceived now in masculine terms alone; a human being is not
just one sex or the other; a relation to the divine is not asexual
and beyond sexuality. The past ideal in which man is seen as
master in the male-female relationship is no longer held by

women who live in the present. They want to love all of a man, his inferior sides, his feminine traits as well as his consciously developed masculinity. And women have been forced to develop some masculine traits themselves in order not to be left helpless in the modern world. If a man wants to meet a woman half way, he too "will be forced to develop his feminine side, to open his eyes to the psyche and to Eros. . . . unless he prefers to go trailing after her in a hopelessly boyish fashion. . . ."[17]

The patriarchal-matriarchal polarization of the sexes has demanded that each sex suppress contrasexual characteristics. This has encouraged, in my opinion, division among the sexes, which contributes to the atmospheres of war and the likelihood of an actual armed conflict. When a woman represses her masculine animus characteristics, she frequently falls victim to the unconscious tyranny of her animus, and then in turn tyrannizes the men in her life upon whom she projects the tyrannous animus. An animus-ridden woman turns hard and resentful. She withholds her warmth, her giving and forgiving. This undermines a man and makes him feel less than a man. Such an animus-ridden woman frequently will nag her husband and even berate him for "not being a man," which means, however, that he does not conform to her animus image of what a man should be. She harps on her husband's weak points and always sees herself as the stronger of the two, the more intelligent, etc. A man who is thus attacked may, in desperation to assert himself as a man and to shut the woman up, react violently—toward her, toward the children, or toward others. A man who becomes infected by such an animus-ridden atmosphere, loses touch with his own sense of proportion and will react in a less conscious, more primitive way. Furthermore, in the patriarchal-matriarchal polarization of the sexes, a man projects his anima emotionality, tenderness, and eros onto the woman. This makes him feel even more dependent on her and

17. Jung, "Woman in Europe," p. 125.

estranged from himself, because if she withdraws he is cut off from these aspects of himself. Thus his own direct access to the feminine principle of relatedness through his own anima fails to balance the aggression that his wife has aroused in him through her nagging. His aggression, then, gathers force and may easily be used to prove his maleness, which has been so fiercely attacked. Because what action he takes is largely in *reaction* to a sense of threat, what dominance he strives for will usually show itself as dominance *over* someone else. If too many men need to assert themselves at the expense of others, war becomes possible.

To see this connection between our own sexuality and relationships and the possibility of war and to acknowledge it openly may make it possible to repersonalize our world. We see, then, the effect of our personal relationships upon all men and upon the spiritual condition of mankind. The true war is love's war—to fight for love and to reconcile the opposites, not to fight to kill others and to obliterate their civilization.

In Jung's view, a woman's psyche that is regulated by the feminine principle can only find its realization in love. For the female, love and the spirit are intermixed. If deep relationship in love is denied her, her spiritual development and contribution to culture are stunted too. For her to have no access to her feelings and to become merely a comrade to a man has destructive effects upon her personality, upon the man's, and upon their relationship. Sexual passivity or even frigidity may occur as an unconscious defensive reaction to the mode of sexuality that keeps each in an exclusively male or exclusively female role that denies the fact of contrasexuality. The woman may develop an identification with what is defined as male sexuality, showing only an aggressive, urgent form of sexual behavior, or she may indulge in a primitive effort to bridge the separation of the sexes in the form of homosexuality.[18]

To be forced into a one-sided feminine existence, while

18. *Ibid.*, p. 119.

patriarchal culture carries the values of consciousness and ego development, leaves a woman unfulfilled in the central areas of her psychological life and makes her dependent on the man in both her own eyes and his. If a woman is fixated at this third stage of development, one negative result is that both sexes will see to it that the woman is confined to a "nothing but" femininity, to a secondary and inferior role that does not permit her to contribute anything to her culture: "women are accustomed to think of the masculine way as something in itself more valuable than the feminine way and superior to it. We believe a masculine objective attitude to be better in every case than a feminine and personal one." [19] Her confinement to the "merely personal" areas of home and family under the guardianship of a man justifies the male depreciation of the feminine and encourages her to feel that hers is a "natural" inferiority.[20] Personal subjective areas become trivial, as a result, and fail to contribute their larger values to our culture. We come to believe that objectivity, reasonableness, and a cool discernment are appropriate in all situations, and that such "masculine" objectivity is always preferable to being feminine, subjective, and personal.

Animus Tyranny

A WOMAN often falls prey to a tyrannizing animus that depreciates not only her ideas and objective interests but also her feelings, as nothing but feminine moonings or empty simulations of the masculine. Adler's "masculine protest" and Freud's "penis envy" are manifestations of such a depreciation of the feminine; the animus of a woman who is "nourished" by such a cultural background will scrutinize all her

19. Emma Jung, *Animus and Anima*, p. 22.
20. This conscious sense of inferiority is, of course, compensated for by an unconscious sense of superiority and power. Thus it is, for example, that women unconsciously express condescension toward men, thinking them to be "childish," "animals," etc.

motives and make negative comments on her every action. The animus will stifle initiative and work to create a growing sense of inferiority. The animus may also attack a woman's emotional life by telling her that her "love affair is a shallow business, bound to end soon because love affairs always do; or that she must not trust the man because men are always fickle . . . or that her children should be pushed out of the nest, or . . . that a home should be provided for them until they are ready to fly." [21] The animus may even echo the traditional patriarchal ideal that women ought only to be wives and mothers, haranguing a woman at every moment, especially when she is on her way to work. The hallmark of the negative animus is irrelevance. Instead of focusing on and emphasizing what is pertinent to a particular situation and to a woman's personal feelings, her animus will focus on all possible irrelevancies through generalization, bromide, banality, and collective judgment.

If a woman consents to being confined to the narrowest possible definition of the feminine role, that of bedmate, mother, and cook, she regresses to being the daughter to the patriarch, surrendering the values of matriarchal consciousness because they do not suit the opposing patriarchal values. She simply imitates patriarchal ideas rather than trying to develop them in her own way. Her attitudes, then, are really only a veneer concealing slothfulness and passivity. Thus she remains basically a daughter depending on her father-husband for whom patriarchal ideas are genuine. When he tries to converse with her, the vague and misinformed quality of her thinking confirms his worst fears about her shallowness. In extreme form, the male may exercise a sadistic tyranny in which he sees his wife as nothing but his property, with no rights of her own. In milder form, a man may become both father and mother. His values are primarily the patriarchal

21. Irene de Castillejo, "Animus: Friend or Foe" (property of The Kristine Mann Library, The Analytical Psychology Club of New York), p. 8.

ones, but following the patriarchal definition of the male role he is also his wife's protector and nourisher.[22]

In another variation of the patriarchal ideal a woman projects her animus onto a male fantasy ideal who is perfect in all physical, mental, and spiritual ways.[23] In such a case, a marriage becomes a humdrum functional contract, and the woman's real emotional life is conducted in fantasy. Her relationship to her husband may be one of compliant sexuality, while her intense passion is expressed in masturbation with her fantasy lover. This then produces the oft-cited narcissism of woman, where all libido is bound up with her own image and her interior fantasy adventures while outwardly she is indifferent to her mate. This is simply another kind of animus domination in which a woman's ego falls into identification with the contrasexual archetype and there is no feeling available to go out to anyone else: "the soul image, anima or animus, is not projected onto another; a person cannot 'fall in love,' because he is too identified with, too much in love with, his own other side." [24] An example of this is a woman patient who indulged in a fantasy relationship with a former boyfriend, even to the point of writing him letters during the first five years of her marriage, letters which fortunately she did not mail to him. Her dreams often centered around her husband's displeasure with her, and his telling her that she did not love him. Another woman often appeared in her dreams and instructed her in how to take an active interest in her husband. This type of compliant but absent wife drives husbands to despair or even to violence. They can find nothing to criticize in their wives' actions, but nevertheless they know that their wives are not really with them, let alone "for" them.

A woman fixated at this stage of development may also

22. See Neumann, "Psychological Stages of Feminine Development," p. 81.
23. See Harding, *Way of All Women*, pp. 41–43.
24. Vera von der Heydt, "On the Animus," *Guild of Pastoral Psychology*, no. 126 (July, 1964), p. 9.

project her animus onto some social cause, movement, or religion and become a fanatically aggressive partisan in its behalf. Personal relationship to her husband is reduced to almost nothing. She loses her spiritual initiative, projecting it onto some external group rather than using it for herself. Although the form is different, the animus is just as tyrannizing in this type of fixation as in the "nothing but" type of femininity cited above. The animus stands in front of the ego, shielding and confining it, not giving the ego enough room to develop, meeting every effort of ego initiative with criticism, alluring fantasy, or excessive dedication to someone else.

Another negative variation of fixation at this stage is the woman who feels bitterly disillusioned with the male. She feels that her man has freed her for relationship but has failed to relate to her himself. As a result she may regress to the first matriarchal phase in which the dominance of the Great Mother archetype is strengthened, especially in its aspect as devouring mother. The woman then sees her husband as her enemy and tyrannizes him in every possible way, making him responsible for her misery. The husband has not lived up to the collective image of the hero; he has failed to establish an individual relationship with her. In her disappointment, the wife harps endlessly on his failures. Mythologically, this may be represented by the story of Jason and Medea. Jason frees Medea from the dragon and the dominance of her father but then forsakes her, being "no match for her dangerous individuality and passion, which never could be housed in a patriarchal marriage." [25] Bitterly disillusioned, Medea regresses to the devouring mother and eats her children and flies away in a dragon chariot. This gruesome tale describes the archetypal basis of many marriage problems in which the mother has devastating effects upon her children because of lack of fulfillment with her husband. A woman's relation to

25. Hilde Binswanger, "Positive Aspects of the Animus," *Spring* (New York: The Analytical Psychology Club, 1963), p. 95.

her animus is then just as negative as it is with her husband, and it is the negative side of the animus that she expresses. She uses power instead of love; she isolates instead of bringing people together: she dominates instead of yielding and seeks prestige instead of relationship.

A woman may regress back to the matriarchal phase by attempting to force herself into the role of the "good wife." She usually, then, completely loses touch with her own masculine qualities. Virtue for her is to be faithful to traditional patriarchal standards, which in fact hinder her own individual development. She then sees all masculine elements as negative and as suppressing her. Curious symptoms may result. One instance is that of a woman who felt nauseated whenever planes flew overhead. They seemed to symbolize a hovering masculine element to which she was inadequately related and which frightened her.

Neumann comments that for a woman who tries to play the role of the good wife, the call of her own development may come in the form of breaking the marriage vows. Fidelity to a marriage that is loveless becomes cowardice, the result of her fears of doing something contrary to standards of respectability. Genuine faithfulness "now means doing the fatefully necessary thing, even when it does not correspond to the traditional canon, to a collective value. In this case loyalty to individuation, to one's own fate and one's own necessary development, is more meaningful than loyalty to a pre-individual attitude." [26] A woman who realizes that for her love and spirit are mixed together, and that only in their joint realization will she find her fulfillment, comes to another meaningful understanding: love is above and beyond the law; it fulfills the law—the law does not fulfill it. Her standards of respectability are revolted by such understanding. To follow love may mean, then, to follow her own individual way and to get in touch with what is disturbing and

26. Neumann, "Psychological Stages of Feminine Development," pp. 89–90.

anxious, to go the downward road into the undifferentiated layers of being, not allowing her so-called virtue to separate her from others or inwardly to estrange her from herself. Jung describes this situation poignantly:

> . . . love, her most personal, most prized possession, could bring her into conflict with history.
>
> . . . no sooner does she begin to deviate, however slightly, from a cultural trend that has dominated the past than she encounters the full weight of historical inertia, and this unexpected shock may injure her, perhaps fatally . . . if she submits to the law of love, she finds that she is not only in a highly disagreeable and dubious situation, . . . but actually caught between two universal forces—historical inertia, and the divine urge to create.
>
> . . . No one can make history who is not willing to risk everything for it, . . . to declare that his life is not a continuation of the past, but a new beginning.[27]

This kind of struggle to get free from patriarchal symbiosis and from collective models of respectability, in order to achieve individuality and authentic relationship, frequently underlies severe marriage problems and divorce. Nora, in Ibsen's *A Doll's House*, is an example. Neurosis itself is sometimes a result of the conflict of being unable to adapt to the collective idea of what a relationship should be and also being unable to sustain a new individual form of relationship.

The effects upon a woman of fixation at the previous stages of feminine development are very precise. In the first stage, she finds self-conservation—positively, by remaining in touch with herself, negatively by remaining fixed within the matriarchal unity. In the second stage, she finds self-surrender—positively as she yields to the invading, awakening masculine, negatively, as she dedicates herself eternally and childishly to the masculine at the expense of her own development. Now in this third stage, fixation means self-loss. In its positive form, it means she will lose her unconscious containment within the masculine by forming a conscious part-

27. Jung, "Woman in Europe," pp. 129–30.

nership of equals with the male. Negatively, she may lose the momentum of her own development by confining herself to the feminine pole of the masculine-feminine polarity, not ever going beyond the patriarchal definition of the feminine role.

THE FOURTH STAGE

THE FOURTH PHASE of feminine development is marked by stages of confrontation and individuation, by self-discovery, and by self-giving. This stage corresponds to the stage of individuation discussed in Chapter Three. The dominating archetype in this phase is the self. When this fourth phase of development occurs within a marriage relationship, the partners must give up their matriarchal-patriarchal symbiotic style of relating to each other and to their own sexuality or suffer the breakdown of their marriage. This phase of development requires the full participation of both partners. Many divorces occur because the urgent necessity of one partner to develop psychologically is misunderstood or not participated in by the other. The struggle to develop this phase both individually and in the marriage relationship seems to be characteristic of modern times. The psychology of the patriarchate is ending: the man is no longer purely masculine; nor is the woman purely feminine. The confrontation which is characteristic of this stage of development means that each person will discover the original contrasexual nature of his own psyche and of his partner's. The man must begin to relate to his unconscious feminine side, to his anima, as the woman must to her animus. The partners must build their own individual patterns rather than merely conforming to collective models.[28]

The experience of confrontation is not the same for both

28. *Ibid.*, p. 131. See also Jung, *Mysterium Coniunctionis* (*CW*, XIV, 1963), p. 180; and Neumann, "Psychological Stages of Feminine Development," p. 90.

sexes. A man's conscious identity is directly in accord with the values of patriarchal culture which stress consciousness and the head ego. To assimilate his feminine side remains a private affair for the man. It is initiated by his anima or by a woman and is worked out in personal relationships. A patriarchal culture does not demand this assimilation and even disapproves of a man having feminine sensibilities.[29]

A woman, however, from the time of childhood and all through her education, has had to develop both masculinity and femininity. This has been one of the opportunities our Western culture offers the female, but not without serious complications, for in her conscious development according to patriarchal values there has also been in her a self-estrangement from her instinctive femininity. The phase of confrontation for the woman, therefore, is not urged by the animus, as it is by the anima in the man, but by the self. The dominance of the self archetype urges her to individuation in order to come to herself and to develop her own uniqueness and wholeness. The self for the woman is, of course, feminine—and here is a salient point. This highest phase of confrontation and individuation in both sexes is initiated by the feminine: for the man, through the anima, which leads to the self; for the woman, through the feminine self, not through any contrasexual elements. The feminine, in this sense, is the completing element; it is the feminine which completes the individuation of *each* sex. The masculine initiates the emergence of consciousness from primary unconsciousness; the feminine initiates the completion of consciousness by re-establishing contact with the unconscious.

It is noteworthy that depth psychology, which deals with so many of the values and qualities of the feminine, such as irrationality, the unconscious, understanding through the heart, and understanding in a concrete, individual way, and which contributes so much as a result to the development of

29. See Neumann, "Psychological Stages of Feminine Development," p. 93.

feminine qualities in men and women, is one of the few professions which wholeheartedly welcomes women into its ranks, either as analysts or patients.

The Feminine Contribution to Culture

WOMEN AND THE FEMININE-AS-ANIMA may be the agents of this fourth stage because they are not so firmly identified with the patriarchal values as men are. A woman's heart ego stems from different roots than a man's. There is always something foreign in her identification of her ego with patriarchal consciousness. To challenge patriarchal values is, therefore, less threatening to her than it is to a man, whose identity is bound up with these values. In following her own development, she makes an incalculable contribution to her culture: she becomes an agent for a fundamental change in human relationship; she furthers a fuller development of her own unique being or the man's; she occasions as much as possible a greater consciousness of the significance of sexual polarity. Through these contributions a woman participates in what seems to be a new and still emerging archetypal constellation of relationship between the sexes and of man to God. Just as the patriarchal-matriarchal form of marriage, where the man is sovereign and the woman servant, is less and less applicable to our world and our experience, so too are symbolic articulations of man as representing heaven and woman as signifying earth, or of man as representing God and woman as his human servant. The rejection of God as a distant being occupying a special heaven is all but complete in our time. The need for quickening old symbols is expressed in every liturgical renewal. The groping for new forms to express modern religious experience is sounded in every kind of new music and depicted in every kind of new art and architecture. Feminine initiation of a new form of human relationship, either through the anima in man or through woman directly, in which each person is both sexes in one and the two become one by a full exchange of contrasexualities, implies the emergence of a new vision of God in the midst of human individuality and sexuality.

Because this is a still-emerging phenomenon, it is difficult to state it in highly explicit terms. Nonetheless, there are constant signs of its occurrence in the eloquent visions and dreams of both men and women. Here is one, the vision of a woman. Its first occurrence was short and more open to the ear than anything else. A vaguely formed female was stating: "You seek a new way, a feminine way, a new-sided God, not just the one side which is known, but with the new side which is unknown." A full-sized dream came six months later: "In it," the dreamer reported, "there stood a saintly man who insisted on staying away from heaven until all others could also find heaven. There was also a man who knew of the entrances into heaven. I speak to him and he says: 'This is THE AGE OF THE FEMININE. Those who choose the hard way to enter the kingdom of heaven make it possible for others to enter, for some people are so afraid that they only accept such a chance when it is put in their hands with full accompanying instructions. Therefore I assign you the hard way—the third way—of the feminine whore.'"

The dream gives a direct statement of the emergence of the feminine, both in the dreamer's personal life and in a new cultural era. Furthermore, it is the savant of the entrances to heaven who has spoken, which implies that the emerging feminine has spiritual significance. The dreamer associated the salvation and the health of the soul with "heaven." With the genuinely saintly man, whose way was not hers, she associated her own pseudo "saintliness," which was really only fear and led only to dishonesty. Her fear of breaking cultural taboos and her need always to be right and saintly had often led her to ignore a deeper need to be true to herself. By its description of a second way of dealing with heaven—the way of those who would deny themselves salvation unless they are sure it can be obtained by following altogether acceptable rules—the dream went on to expose further her safe, respectable behavior as motivated by fear. The hard third way is her own way to salvation, as well as her contribution to human redemption. By taking the hardest way, she frees the easier paths for others to take. In her associations, in analysis, this hard way referred to her recent feelings of being blessed by a full and total love, which also made her fearful, because it seemed out of the bounds of that narrow respectability to which she had for years tried to conform. Her committing herself to this love, which, though long hoped-for, came, like the expected savior, in an unexpected, unconventional, and even offensive form, is symbolized in the dream by "the feminine whore." The archetypal symbolism of the whore recalls the cult prostitutes who were dedicated, body and soul, to the goddess of love. Here, however, the dreamer not only felt the call of love but felt *called* to love by a particular man; she felt a commitment to transpersonal life through a *personal* relationship. The dream followed her own acts of acceptance and commitment and seemed a clear reply to days of serious self-doubt over whether following this love was right or merely selfish. The dream answered—this is your way, and it has more than personal significance; it signifies a new age in human development and a spiritual stature where devotion to love as transpersonal is effected through its incarnation in personal relationships.

Confrontation and self-discovery in this stage involve individuation and self-giving. True confrontation occurs only after each partner has recovered his own contrasexual unconscious nature. Each can then relate out of a whole nature to the wholeness of the other.[30] Jung describes this kind of relationship as the archetypal *quaternio*, where the male-female polarity is joined consciously as a meeting of two persons and unconsciously as a meeting of anima and animus.[31] The man then ceases to project his feminine anima onto the woman and takes up instead the task of becoming related to it himself.

30. *Ibid.*, p. 91.
31. See Jung, "Psychology of the Transference," *The Practice of Psychotherapy* (*CW*, XVI, 1954), pp. 207–8, 227.

He is no longer simply masculine, and thus he and his partner must relate to both his feminine and masculine sides. The same is true for the woman and her animus: a four-sided relationship must now be effected between the man and the woman, the anima and the animus. The complications this involves are manifold and demand the utmost mutual understanding. From the very beginning the partners must reckon with such differences in the two natures as the masculine finding relationship through differentiation and the feminine through identification. These different styles of relating are shown in the pleasure men get from conversation, where ego confronts ego, and consciousness confronts consciousness, in contrast to the pleasure women gain from just being with the other sex, in a wordless awareness of otherness and an unexpressed sense of spiritual union. The woman who wishes to be at one with herself must make peace with her animus, which so often makes irritating, separating remarks, in an effort to get the ego to be better focused and thus arrive at its own individual point of view. The man who may prefer to keep a safe distance must deal with his anima, which constantly presses for emotional involvement and relatedness.[32]

Individuation is not a private affair but is indissolubly bound up with both the relation to a partner and to society. Jung has often been criticized for neglecting the communal and social dimension. In fact, society is for him a constant and conscious element in the reciprocal exchanges of male and female. The development of a conscious relation to one's self and the pursuit of one's role as a unique and fulfilled human being in society is played out, between two persons, and includes all of their psyches, the conscious and the unconscious.[33]

32. Neumann, "Psychological Stages of Feminine Development," p. 92.
33. See Jung, "Marriage as a Psychological Relationship," *The Development of the Personality* (*CW*, XVII, 1954), pp. 192–93, 195, 198–99; "On the Nature of the Psyche," *The Structure and Dynamics of the Psyche* (*CW*, VIII, 1960), p. 226; and *Psychological Types*, trans.

Thus, although man and woman have their own patterns of development, the stages that have been outlined do not belong exclusively to one or the other. The masculine-feminine polarity and the interrelation of male and female partners reach through all the stages of the individuation process which stands at the end of conscious personal development.

> From the deepest to the highest level, from the containment in the unconscious to the re-winning of the Self in transformation, what is one's own will be experienced in the other. And always the "wholly Other" proves itself—as the masculine-feminine polarity of the individual's own inner opposition—to be the mysterious Numen by which the individual's development is sparked, and into which it flows when, finally, the "otherness" is overcome.[34]

The Positive Animus

THE WOMAN in this stage of confrontation and individuation develops a new relationship to her animus. She no longer experiences it as a projection onto her partner but is now actively and consciously related to it as an inward function of her own psyche. Her confrontation is not only with her partner but with the animus within her. Her individuation always involves the effective functioning of her animus as mediator of unconscious contents to her ego.

The animus is an archetype and thus, in Jungian terms, a foundation stone of the psychic structure, extending its functions far beyond the limits of consciousness. The ego, then, can integrate the effects and contents of the animus but cannot absorb the animus itself.[35] The animus remains autonomous and can only be related to, never incorporated. As an archetype, the animus is neither good nor bad in itself. If

H. Godwin Baynes (London: Kegan Paul, Trench, Trübner & Co., 1946), p. 562.
34. Neumann, "Psychological Stages of Feminine Development," p. 97.
35. See Jung, *Aion* (*CW*, IX, Part 2, 1959), p. 20.

the ego is inadequately related to the animus, a strong negative tone will be projected. Emma Jung describes four ways in which the animus connects woman to her own masculine side: as mediating power, expressed in acts of will and aggression; as deed, as shown in a woman's initiative and general capacity to act; as word, evinced in the separation of subject and object through rational discrimination and articulation; and as meaning, marked by a woman's spiritual aims and aspirations.[36]

Irene de Castillejo's formulation may be even more helpful. She thinks it is confusing to tell a woman "to connect with her masculine side." Instead, she says simply that the basic nature of woman is feminine and that the animus is an archetype in the feminine psyche with an impersonal, collective nature which presents many images in personal guises. The animus is not the source of knowledge or of innate gifts but rather a capacity to focus upon, shed light upon, and connect the contents of the unconscious to consciousness. A woman is herself in direct contact with her sources and resources, but often in a diffuse and vague way. She needs the animus to focus on things that she already knows innately, so that she herself can realize that she knows them. The animus does not give knowledge but permits a woman to gain it "by throwing his light on the page so that she can read the words. Whether or not she understands the words she reads will depend upon her education and her power to think . . . this is a question of type, not of Animus. The role of the Animus . . . is principally one of focusing and collecting." [37]

A woman will feel that her animus is positive if it focuses on clearly relevant material, appropriate to her own ego concerns and to the situation at hand. She will feel that her animus is negative when it focuses on irrelevant material, overwhelming her with mere clichés, dead slogans, and judgments, or distracting her with thoughts that may be generally

36. See Emma Jung, *Animus and Anima*, p. 3.
37. Castillejo, *Animus: Friend or Foe*, p. 11.

valid but are clearly not applicable to her at this particular point.

A woman must give her animus the necessary information. She must say to herself very clearly what she feels and what her values are. Castillejo describes the animus as a torch-bearer and

> an autonomous spirit whose sole concern is shedding light, focused light, light for its own sake. He has no feelings towards us, neither good nor ill, he has no feelings of any kind. Feeling is a human prerogative. He has no interest in us one way or another except . . . that he needs us for his very existence, for it is only in the human mind that he can dwell. He needs a human being to see the light he sheds . . . which helps her "focus" to see that is what she means or that is not what she means, or to get at the words which are beneath the surface of her mind so she can choose the ones she wants.[38]

A woman's ego must actively represent her beliefs and values and inform the animus of her feelings. Only in this way can she change her animus into a helper, letting it know the human feelings that need greater focus. A woman can tell whether or not what her animus brings her is appropriate. If she is deeply touched by an experience or has the feeling that things have fallen into place, then she can be fairly sure that what the animus tells her really does belong to her.

At this fourth stage of development, all previous phases are recapitulated inwardly. A woman must now be aware of how she is related to the masculine within her and be quite free of the primary maternal uroboros. Her own consciousness, as her "hero," must free her from eternal dedication to the paternal masculine, as given through some authority external to her, such as her father, brother, or husband. She must accept the masculine as it appears in her own feminine nature and become independent of patriarchal values and judgments that are foreign to her nature. At the same time

38. *Ibid.*, pp. 5–6.

she must return to the primary relationship of feminine ego with feminine self, but now in a more developed form.

She no longer has an undeveloped ego that is passively held in the unconscious like an infant in the orbit of her mother's being. Instead, she is a woman with a developed ego identity which actively relates to the feminine self. She feels inwardly renewed and creatively related to the whole of her psyche. She is on her way to becoming a complete person.

THE STORY OF DOROTHY OF OZ

THE STORY OF DOROTHY in *The Wizard of Oz* can be usefully interpreted, I think, as a paradigm of a young girl's series of encounters with the animus function and with her ego's integration of the contents that the animus brings to it.

The story begins with an altercation between Dorothy and a woman neighbor over Toto, Dorothy's dog. The neighbor threatens to have the sheriff take the dog away. Dorothy, saddened and fearful, longs for a place behind the moon, somewhere "over the rainbow," where there is no such trouble for her or anyone. A tornado suddenly blows up, and a flying window strikes Dorothy unconscious. Psychologically, Dorothy may be seen as the budding feminine ego, whose instinct, the dog, defies the containing matriarch, the neighbor. The matriarch-neighbor is negative and regressive, wanting to prevent the ego's differentiation, destroying its instinctive moves toward autonomy by an appeal to collective authority, the sheriff, who represents the law, which is generally right but at the same time is hostile to emerging individual consciousness. Like the eating of forbidden fruit, the ego's first step to consciousness is signaled by a breaking of rules. And, paradoxically, the negative mother (the neighbor) leads the fragile ego to take hold of its goals—to hold onto the dog— even more firmly, thus furthering the very ego development it opposes. Dorothy, the ego, indulges in wishing and mooning—seeking a place behind the moon—which stirs up the numinous power of the unconscious, the tornado, which represents an invasion of the transpersonal paternal uroboros. The windowpane that strikes Dorothy unconscious is an element that ordinarily furthers seeing and focusing, suggesting that rational head logic is of no use now. Instead, an active fantasy ensues. The whole event is introduced by a pet dog, which in reality often elicits a girl's first relation to her instincts, as she projects onto her pet her capacity to support and defend, to be loyal, to train and care for, to be a companion. An adolescent often has a more personal relation to a pet than to members of her family, whom she still thinks of in their collective roles of mother, sister, etc.

Dorothy wakes up in Munchkinland, a bona fide heroine now, having sailed there in her house, which has landed on and killed the wicked witch of the East, who was out riding the tornado on her broomstick. Dorothy had traveled to this fantasy land in the vehicle of her psyche, the place where she lives, her psychological space—her house. The trip was not self-motivated but was gathered from the storms of unconscious energy. Her dog, Toto, her instinctive energy, was with her. The wicked witch of the East, who was flying on her broomstick "to satisfy an itch," perhaps hints at masturbation, which often accompanies fantasy. The negative effect of masturbation is to produce a self-enclosed circle of the feminine personality, which is felt to be both the source and the object of gratification. In other words, the matriarchal self-conserving phase, though natural and pleasurable, retains self-control to the exclusion of relationship. The winds of the storm representing the invading paternal uroboros bring this to an end. The needs of the psychological living space kill it—the house lands on the witch. Liberation from this negative dominance is celebrated by the many as yet undeveloped and undifferentiated impulses and instincts represented by the Munchkins, who declare a holiday to celebrate their freedom from the bad witch.

The good witch of the North, Glinda, is responsible for introducing Dorothy to the Munchkins and comes to Dorothy's aid throughout the story. In the midst of the celebration, the wicked witch of the West, sister to the dead witch, flies in, enraged, and threatens Dorothy. Glinda advises Dorothy to get out of Oz country as soon as possible, which fully suits Dorothy, for she had wanted to return to her home in Kansas from the moment she arrived. Because Dorothy cannot go back the way she came, sailing through the skies in a house, she must somehow go forward in a new direction and with new means. Since she has no broomstick, she must walk. And she must go to see the Wizard of Oz, who can help her get home. "Where do I begin?" asks Dorothy, and Glinda answers, "At the beginning; follow the yellow brick road."

Glinda may be interpreted to represent the archetypal power of the positive transformative feminine. The third witch of the West, who is wicked, symbolizes another negative form of the regressive, devouring aspect of the maternal unconscious. A characteristic of bad witches is an ugly face which is out of proportion, with a long nose, hooked chin, etc. This disproportion symbolizes the negative effects of the feminine psyche when it is out of balance, the mind going one way, the heart another, the instincts still another. The presence of three witches and the allusion to a fourth, two good and two bad, suggest the totality of the feminine psyche and the four psychic functions.

Regression is not possible for Dorothy, who represents the ego. She cannot pretend that nothing has happened. She cannot be carried—sustained—any more by unconscious forces; nor does she have archetypal power—a broomstick; nor is continued masturbation—also represented by the broomstick —the solution. If she wants to get back to conscious human reality, Kansas, her ego must travel under its own power, on foot, and begin at the beginning, where she is fully present to herself. The yellow road is reminiscent of Castillejo's idea of the animus as light-giver, and the road's firm brick surface testifies to the firmness of the function that can take her where she wants to go.

On her journey to the Wizard of Oz, Dorothy and Toto have three successive encounters, with the straw man who wants a brain, with the tin woodman who wants a heart, and with the cowardly lion who wants courage. The four of them then journey to Oz together in order to obtain from the Wizard their deepest wishes. There are various skirmishes along the way with the wicked West witch, the most notable being the encounter with the danger of falling asleep under the spell of the poppy field, just before entering Emerald City. Finally, they reach the Wizard, who agrees to grant their wishes if they will bring him the broomstick of the West witch.

Psychologically, each figure may be seen to represent facets of the animus function which the feminine ego must integrate. The straw man lacks a brain; he cannot make up his mind about anything. This indicates insufficient development of the capacity to focus upon and reason about whatever issue is pertinent at the time to the ego. This state is seen in women when they are preoccupied with quests for "answers" to life's riddles. It is an attitude that masks another problem entirely—their ignorance of their own minds and indecisiveness about their own points of view. Instead of the animus focusing on this indecisiveness and the various viewpoints which need to be sorted out, it becomes contaminated with a kind of pseudo thinking, in the pursuit of hopelessly general and unanswerable questions. A pervasive sense of confusion ensues. Everything becomes hazy and hidden behind a smoke screen of pseudo issues. This is symbolized in the Oz story by the danger of the straw man being set on fire and creating a lot of smoke.

The tin man lacks a heart and needs lubricating oil to avoid becoming rigid and rusty. Similarly, if a woman does not inform the animus of her feelings, the animus functions autonomously and without relation to what she feels. This produces a rigid dogmatism in her that makes her seem to others, and feel to herself, hollow and cold, without emotional substance.

The lion lacks courage, has no nerve, cannot stand his ground; he deserts his position in the face of challenge. If the animus function is focused on material relevant to ego concerns and is at a more developed stage directed to the concerns of the self, a woman has the capacity to stand on her own authority and to insist on what is appropriate for her regardless of overwhelming opinions or pressures to the contrary. When this animus function is undeveloped, a woman, like the cowardly lion, will be unable to maintain a firm position and will run away when challenged.

Dorothy's concern is to find a home, a psychological residence, large enough to house these emergent functions. Emerald City symbolizes the precious goal, the place where all these wishes can become reality. Her journey there may be seen as a journey to an enlarged consciousness which will make actual these successive potentialities. This city is a small prototype of the greater city of the self, or the celestial city of salvation in religious literature. It is significant that just before entering the city the greatest danger occurs—of falling asleep in the poppy field. This may be said to represent the danger of becoming entrapped in the unconscious just when one is approaching the goal of retrieving what one wants to bring to consciousness—of being unable to integrate the unconscious into consciousness.

The Wizard prescribes the usual test before a wish is granted. This represents the testing of the ego's firmness of resolution to reach its goal, its willingness to sacrifice its securities and to face the largest dangers in order to win a more profound safety. In Jung's terms, it is a sacrifice of the limited ego supremacy to win relation to the self. The danger for the feminine ego is to confront and depotentiate the negative aspects of the feminine archetype in the form of the devouring mother. Dorothy must obtain the witch's broomstick, namely, the mobilizing power of the negative feminine. Again the dog becomes significant. The witch captures Toto —the ego's basic feminine instincts—and Dorothy is caught in trying to rescue the dog. Dorothy manages to free the dog, which then goes after her friends for help, because she herself is trapped. This may be interpreted to mean that the basic instinctive dynamisms, the natural energies of the psyche, bring to the ego's aid the various elements of decisiveness, heart, and courage upon which the animus has focused during the journey. For the sake of rescuing Dorothy (the ego) each of these nascent capacities achieves its end; for Dorothy, the lion will brave anything, the tin man is moved to concern and compassion, and the straw man now can decide what must be done.

The three friends do not immediately rescue Dorothy, however, but are trapped themselves by the witch, who promptly sets fire to the straw man. This suggests that all of these psychic functions must confront the negative feminine, which will start to destroy them, that is to say, cause them to regress into unconsciousness again. This is the supreme test and the supreme danger. Each of these functions must stand against the power of unconsciousness and become firmly differentiated. In the midst of these masculine functions, Dorothy, the feminine ego, is the one who must effect the necessary actions. This means that the ego is in fact supported by the animus, but to be free of the unconscious it must itself become the executive agent. Dorothy throws water on the smoking scarecrow and splashes the witch, who then melts away. The scarecrow function—the as yet undeveloped capacity to be decisive and clear—is the most vulnerable. If this function can be burned up, the struggles for heart and courage are easily lost. Instead of allowing the animus functions thus to regress to unconsciousness, the ego must liquidate the hostile power of the negative witch, implying that the psychic energy she personifies will return to the general stream of libido available for constructive uses.

Armed with the broomstick, the group returns to the Wizard. Dorothy discovers that he is a fraud, merely an ordinary man with an amplified voice surrounded by awesomely impressive smoke screens. In Emma Jung's schema, the Wizard would be the last animus function with which one comes to terms. The lion would represent power; the tin man, the deed, motivated by affective will; the straw man, the word, the capacity to differentiate and articulate the relation of subject and object; and the Wizard, meaning and spiritual significance. The ego defies the animus as meaning-giver; it dispels the illusory projection which puffs up an ordinary man into a bigger-than-life magician.

The unmasking brings the Wizard down to earth, and he gives Dorothy's companions their wishes, but in an unexpected way. He changes their attitudes toward themselves and the virtues they seek. To the straw man who wanted a brain, he gives a doctorate in "thinkology," saying universities are full of brainless people. To the lion who wanted courage, he gives a medal and a parade, saying it is parades that make heroes. To the tin man who wanted a heart, he gives a testimonial about how much he is loved by others. The Wizard thereby brings to effective life the animus function of focusing on meaning. The ultimate meaning of these virtues lies in one's having the right attitudes toward them, recognizing they are there all the time and need only to be developed. The various awards have a double meaning, caricaturing the projection of these virtues onto outer prestige symbols which are intrinsically meaningless, and symbolizing their inner reality by pointing to them through representations which are far less than the realities which they represent. This casts their inner reality into bold relief.

The Wizard says he can only get Dorothy out of fantasy, Oz, and back to reality, Kansas, by taking her there himself in a balloon which he does not know how to operate. The three animus functions are left in charge of the unconscious world. Dorothy agrees to set out on the balloon journey, but Toto goes off to chase a cat and, because she is running after the dog, Dorothy is left behind as the balloon takes off without her. If Dorothy had gone off in the balloon, the ego would have remained in the power of the wizardly animus, which is not equipped to function in reality, on the ground. Again, the dog, the connection to her own instinctive processes, is irresistibly drawn to the feminine, symbolized by the cat, the animal that has always been connected with the female deities, and thus the ego remains connected to her own earth. The animus, which focuses on spiritual contents, is where it belongs, sailing through the heavens, and the ego is firmly lodged in reality.

For all these happy endings, Dorothy is bereft, at the end of her resources, terribly sad to have to live the rest of her life in Oz. Again the tale points up the danger of being trapped in an unconscious fantasy world. Only when the ego has exhausted all of its resources does the self's power come to its aid. At this point, then, the good witch, Glinda, reappears and says that Dorothy has possessed the power to return to Kansas all along; it is simply a question of attitude. In other words, for the feminine ego, the obtainment of wholeness is in the last analysis quite within the power of the feminine self. The animus function goes through the necessary stages along the way, but the final coming to fulfillment is given by the feminine self to the feminine ego. The change of attitude represents self-acceptance; one sees that one's deepest desires are in one's own backyard. Dorothy then wakes up in her own bed, at home with her aunt and uncle and her friends around her. She awakens to a new appreciation of the value of what she has always in fact possessed. She opens her eyes with a new attitude and discovers a new preciousness in the old familiar reality.

Dorothy's young age, of course, points to the fact that this is only one in a lifetime of many transformations. The Dorothy tale reminds us that the great task of a woman is to bring herself to terms with her own animus, as well as to establish *rapprochement* with the men around her. This task stresses that the lifegiving sexual polarity, which unites consciousness and unconsciousness, demands at the same time a coming to "the other" after long venturesome probings to find just what otherness represents. Dorothy, like a woman's ego, discovers a central truth, that otherness is located both far inside herself and far outside herself. We are once again confronted with the mystery of the two sexes, both far apart from each other and contained within each other, and the mystery of the divine and the human, both far apart from each other and contained within each other.

PART IV

The Feminine and Christian Theology

Nevertheless, in the Lord woman is not independent of man nor man of woman.

1 Cor. 11:11

We are made for love: it is our first vocation.
Ralph Harper, *Human Love: Existential and Mystical*

Every soul that is truly in love is already, by that fact, committed to the adventure of God, an adventure of communication and union . . .
Suzanne Lilar, *Aspects of Love*

CHAPTER THIRTEEN

The Feminine, the Religious Function, and the Doctrine of Man

THEOLOGY, with its task of communicating the timeless contents of Christian faith to an ever-changing but time-bound human situation, can perhaps be understood as describing the history of love, in particular the ways men have been touched by and have responded to God's love. Psychoanalysis attempts to do the work of love by trying to remove the blocks that obstruct loving, to soften the bruises of rejected love, and to heal the deep wounds that are caused by lovelessness. For all its theories, its perversions, its arrogance, and its clumsiness, the intentions of psychoanalysis are always directed toward love: to seek its presence, to document its effects, to further its development, to prepare for its coming, to open our eyes to see its arrival, and to celebrate its fulfillment. Theology deals explicitly with the love between God and man with all its implications for the love of man for himself and for his fellow men. Psychology deals explicitly with love among men and implicitly with man's relation to the divine. The relationship between theology and depth psychology, therefore, is like the relationship of mystical love to existential love.

THE FEMININE AND THE RELIGIOUS FUNCTION

JUNG'S PSYCHOLOGY OF THE FEMININE formulates certain problem areas in the Christian tradition and leads to a re-examination of those areas from new points of view. One cannot say that the feminine is the answer to contemporary religious malaise, because such a simple-minded answer is offensive not only to one's sensibilities but also to one's sexuality. One *can* say that the recognition of the feminine as a mode of being, of perception, and of organization as the heart ego is vital to the psychology of being human and therefore central to our understanding of man's relation to God. Jung's understanding of the religious function of the psyche is not to be equated with the feminine, but clearly there is a close connection between the two.

The religious function of the psyche is an irreducible drive toward a relationship in which the personal self is linked to the transpersonal source of the power and meaning of being. This drive shows itself inwardly in the production of images which make perceptible the symbolic meaning of experience, through the images of God or through images to which the rest of the psyche relates as to a god. These images, which act as unifying centers in the psychic universe, reconcile opposing tendencies. The religious function seems to urge the fullest development of the individual personality, for the symbols it produces are characterized by their function of realizing and reconciling into a wholeness the polarities in which the psyche is structured. This same drive toward wholeness shows itself outwardly in the construction of beliefs, in dogmas, in theologies, and in liturgies.

Looked at psychologically, "God is a symbol of the overwhelming impulse of the soul to goodness and joy, and at the same time an expression of the supreme yearning of the soul for redemption." [1] Looked at theologically, there is in the psyche an image of God, or, more accurately, the form of such an image, and the desire for it as a means of unifying and centering the psyche and reconciling its opposing tendencies.

> The idea of God is an absolutely necessary psychological function of an irrational nature. . . . There is in the psyche some superior power, and if it is not consciously a god, it is the "belly," at least, in St. Paul's words. I therefore consider it wiser to acknowledge the idea of God consciously; for, if we do not, something else is made God, usually something quite inappropriate and stupid such as only an "enlightened" intellect could hatch forth. [2]

Jung and his followers give strong attention to the symbolic meaning of the feminine and its role in psychic functioning, for to them the feminine symbolizes a distinct modality of consciousness and spirit that belongs to both sexes. Its recognition and integration are necessary for individual growth through integration of one's contrasexual elements, for growth in human relationships to the point of individuation, and for growth in relation to God. Sexual polarity is the metaphor and the means of the soul's union with God.

A syllogism can be constructed to make clear the precise connection of the feminine and the psyche's religious function. The psyche is composed of various opposites, such as conscious-unconscious, reason-instinct, active-passive, etc.; the symbolism of the masculine-feminine polarity represents all of these polar opposites. [3] Growth to psychic wholeness, urged by the religious function, which produces images of God, must include the fulfillment and reconciliation of these

---

1. Josef Goldbrunner, *Individuation*, trans. Stanley Godman (New York: Pantheon, 1956), p. 166.

2. Jung, *Two Essays on Analytical Psychology* (CW, VII, 1953), p. 71.

3. See Jung, *Psychology and Alchemy* (CW, XII, 1967), pp. 36–37.

polarities. The feminine, therefore, is a factor which must be recognized as essential for the full exercise of the religious function. Thus, if the feminine is neglected, undervalued, or misconstrued, the result psychologically is a diminishing of one's growth toward wholeness, and the result theologically is that the *imago dei* does not achieve its full stature.

The masculine-feminine polarity is understood literally in terms of the physical expressions of sexuality. In its symbolic meanings the polarity of the sexes represents different qualities of ego consciousness, of spirit, and of union with the divine. Sexuality in its most concrete physical expression is directed to forming personal identity and to informing the exchanges of the sexes with an over-all sense of unity. Sexuality in its symbolic meaning deals with one's awareness of, and motion towards, union with an "other," be it a person, one's soul, another modality of consciousness, or another dimension of being.

The general question of the relation of mystical love—between God and man—and existential love—between man and woman—becomes accessible in a treatment of the feminine and its implications for Christian theology, because the feminine is part of the central sexual polarity which informs anything the psyche does or any relation it achieves. When one sees this, one cannot avoid concluding that the two loves are inseparable and that a fully developed human being is fully devoted to God. One sees, then, that the full expression of one's individuality is part of a full surrender to the divine. The full experience of human sexual love—in its literal and symbolic range of meanings—is the intimate experience of the Incarnate Word, where the created world becomes transparent, invisible significances become visible, and the intangible presence of God becomes tangible reality, illuminating the least detail of human life.

THE IMAGO DEI

THE CREATION OF MAN in the image of God, the *imago dei*, can be understood psychologically as the capacity to produce symbols that center and unify psychic opposites and depict man's yearning for direct experience of his relation to a source of being beyond himself. Theologically, the *imago dei* has been interpreted to mean the creation of man as a creature who has the capacity to relate to his Creator although this capacity has either been diminished or even lost as a result of the Fall. We read in Genesis that "God created man in His own image, in the image of God He created him, male and female He created them" (Gen. 1:27). This can be interpreted to mean, I think, that God's image is to be found in the polarity of male and female and that the primary concretization of the covenant between God and his creature is to be found in the relationship of man and woman. I emphasize this interpretation because it makes clear the essential importance of the feminine. If the feminine is neglected, in its contrasexual form within the masculine, or is misunderstood as a second-best category of human sexuality, then not only is the fullness of human being damaged but the relation of the human and the divine is damaged as well.

Support for this interpretation—that we find our understanding of the divine and our relation to God in the masculine-feminine relationship—can be gathered from Protestant, Catholic, and Russian Orthodox theologians. Karl Barth, for example, says that man's being is given as a creature in relation to God and that the primary sphere of relationship in which being is expressed is between man and woman. A person must be either a man or a woman and "in consequence he is equally necessarily and totally man *and* woman. He cannot wish to liberate himself from the differentiation and exist beyond his sexual determination as mere man. . . ." [4] Barth

4. Karl Barth, *The Doctrine of Creation: Church Dogmatics*, ed. G. W. Bromiley and T. F. Torrance (Edinburgh: T. & T Clark, 1961), III, pt. IV, 118.

approves of Schleiermacher's idea that in the meetings between a man and a woman "everything is to be divine and
human. . . . It must be God who is manifested in lovers.
Their embrace is really His embrace which they feel and
will in common." [5]

Nicholas Berdyaev emphasizes that man is not only a
creature who is necessarily in relation to the opposite sex,
but his individual being is also defined by sexual polarity.
Barth says of Berdyaev's views: "Man devoid of feminine
elements would be an abstraction divorced from the powers
of the cosmos. Woman without masculine elements could
not become a personality." [6] In contrast to this emphasis on
inner contrasexual polarity, Barth emphasizes a relational one.
Man and woman are directed to each other, "each being for
the other a horizon and focus, . . . a center and source. This
mutual orientation constitutes the being of each. It is always
in relationship to their opposite that man and woman are
what they are in themselves. . . ." [7] And I would add that
it is precisely because the opposite sex is so much an opposite, that relating to it captures the dynamism of relating to
the otherness of God. It is in this sense that lovers have celebrated the presence of God in each other, and that as a couple
they have been seen to embody the unity and differentiation
of divine being.

The Catholic theologian F. X. Arnold agrees: "It is in the
duality and unity of man and woman . . . that mankind is
most truly the image of the living God. . . . According to
Biblical doctrine, it is also in the polarity of man and woman
that mankind partakes of that likeness." [8] Arnold sees sexual
polarity as intrinsic not only to Creation but also to Redemption. He cites Paul's vision of the mysterious union of Christ
and the Church in the conjugal mystery of man and woman;

5. *Ibid.*, p. 122 n.
6. *Ibid.*, p. 159 n.
7. *Ibid.*, p. 163.
8. F. X. Arnold, *Woman and Man*, trans. Rosaleen Brennan (Edinburgh-London: Nelson, 1963), pp. 18–19.

he sees the bridal imagery of medieval mysticism as symbolic of Christ's relation to the soul and to mankind as a whole, as the Fathers were so fond of pointing out, ending with their depiction of the marriage feast, or the wedding of the Lamb, as metaphors for eternal life.[9] Woman plays a central role in man's relation to God according to this theology. Eve is "at once the symbol of the chosen bride and of all the failings of humanity. Then comes Mary, the second Eve, in whom God's espousal of mankind is fulfilled and in whom the archetype of a new humanity is revealed. And finally at the end of human history there will appear the woman of the Apocalypse. . . ."[10]

Vladimir Solovyev sees the relation between male and female as embodying the "mysterious Divine image" in which man was created; it "represents an essential analogy, though not identity, between the human relation and the Divine."[11] For Otto Piper, the Biblical record of the Creation shows "that the sexual differentiation of mankind and the destination of the sexes for mutuality form the foundation of human history. Hence there can be no human activity that is completely independent of the man-woman relationship."[12]

Jung's research into the religious function of the psyche provides clinical evidence for the centrality of the masculine-feminine polarity in the healing symbols and images of the divine that emerge from the unconscious. Such symbols are characterized by their reconciliation of psychic opposites in the literal male-female imagery of sexual intercourse or marriage, or in such mythological elements as the marriage of the sun and the moon, the union of the king and queen, the mixing of heaven and earth, light and darkness, or in mysterious combinations of number symbols such as three and four.

9. *Ibid.*, p. 20.
10. *Ibid.*, pp. 21–22.
11. Vladimir Solovyev, *The Meaning of Love*, trans. Jane Marshall (London: Geoffrey Bles, 1945), p. 56.
12. Otto A. Piper, *The Biblical View of Sex and Marriage* (New York: Scribner's, 1960), p. 55.

Sexual polarity and sexual unity are often found in symbols of the self, as if to suggest that male and female are transcended, paradoxically, only by their fullest affirmation and not at all through their abrogation or diminution.

As we have seen, Jung's conception of the anima and animus, personifying contrasexual elements in the psyche, emphasizes that becoming conscious of this inward sexual polarity promotes wholeness and motivates us to participate in something beyond ourselves which we experience as spirit. Sexual polarity is central for Jung to achieving union with ourselves or with another person; it is a principle expression of our inherent relation to God. This is one facet of the complex issue of the *imago dei* implied in Jung's thought, though often neglected, even by Jungians, because of insufficient understanding of the feminine.

THE FALL

IF THE ORIGINAL FORM of creation of the human, the *imago dei*, is contrasexual both individually and interpersonally, then one facet of the Fall of man from that original structure of grace must be a distortion of sexual polarity. An excellent way to look at this facet of sin, I think, is in terms of the contrast between sexual polarity and polarization, both between man and woman and within each sex, in the relations of ego and anima or animus.

Polarity and polarization can be understood as two ways that pairs of opposites may relate to each other. In polarity, the opposites are related to each other by mutual attraction; they are drawn to unite with each other without destroying the distinct individuality of each pole; on the contrary, the individuality of each is heightened and realized. In polarization, the opposites pull away from each other and conflict with each other. The two poles split apart and destroy the individuality of each other. The masculine-feminine polarity expresses a vital tension and attraction between two distinct sexual modes of being. It is as if there were between them a tonicity, an elasticity, an electric unity. Sexual polarization denotes the calcification of masculine and feminine modes of being into inflexible opposition and a decrease, if not a total disappearance, of circulation of their mutual energy.

In previous sections, I have given examples of the weakening and distortion of the ego's relation to the anima or animus because of polarization and all its negative effects. That debilitation of inward polarity into polarization often is the result of the ego falling into a partial or total state of identity with anima or animus. The signs of this destructive process are inflation or deflation, compulsion or projection.

Disorders for both sexes frequently stem from over- or undervaluation of the feminine, either gross submergence in it or cold detachment from it. The given polarity between the sexes is then out of joint because the two poles are not in true relation but have fallen into struggles of master and servant or sovereign and rebel, of mutual protest or of "masculine protest" and assertions of sexual "equality." The very need to draw on the word "equal" shows that polarity has fallen into polarization and that a struggle for power has developed. Instead of each person living his own distinct sexuality and blend of male and female psychic factors, each sex now clashes with the other and each exacerbates the negative expression of the other.

The Fall from sexual polarity to polarization of the sexes can be illustrated in many ways. In polarization, the different modes of perception and reaction of the two sexes produce feelings of separation and challenge. Each feels the other does not and cannot understand his point of view because he is so fundamentally different; each lives in a completely separate world. This produces an unquenchable longing and loneliness and a matching defensiveness; every time the two sexes come together they feel more separated. In polarity, on the other hand, the two sexes enjoy all their differences and feel them as opportunities to join and to disjoin with purpose, to come together bringing more and more of themselves. Everything, even the smallest detail in their lives is a joining, not a humdrum sameness but a uniting of differences.

In polarization, the uniqueness of the two and their differences become blurred in a gradual process of unconscious identification induced by physical and psychological proximity.[13] One reaction to this unconscious merging of identities is the feeling each has of taking the other for granted. Unfortunately, our marriage customs encourage this view, as shown in such all-too-familiar expressions as "the settled married years" or "marriage begins when the honeymoon is over." In polarization, one or both partners may assert a bristling, challenging independence or individuality as a means of preserving his uniqueness and keeping it from sinking into unconscious identification. In polarity a man and woman experience familiarity not as an obliteration of individuality but as a means of increasing their appetite and appreciation for mystery—the boundless mystery of sexual intimacy, the ever-new revelations of spirit in otherness. Polarity encourages the full uniqueness of each partner through the full enjoyment of the masculine and feminine modalities within each partner. Each becomes weak enough to need the other and strong enough to accept the other.

In polarization, a *quid pro quo* modality is established, varying in its expression from the most reasonable form of mutual responsibility to the most vulgar form of trading obligations. This kind of interaction is a consequence of what Suzanne Lilar calls "reasonable love," in contrast to "unreasonable love." Reasonable love has traditionally been considered the best basis for a marriage because it involves cooperation, respect, comradeship, compromise, and consideration—everything but real love. Reasonable love is the basis of the patriarchal-matriarchal form of marriage and is created more by the influence of cultural standards than by anything resembling passionate love. Lilar objects that

13. See Jung, "Marriage as a Psychological Relationship," *The Development of the Personality* (CW, XVII, 1954), pp. 189–92.

these edifying sentiments were usually masks for much less edifying motives: all too often, under the pretext of protecting the family against the dangers of love, the object was to protect the patrimony and guarantee the exercising of marital privileges. This policy was completed by institutions and by a morality that was strict toward the woman's moral lapses and indulgent toward the man's, and its result was to exclude love from the woman's destiny.[14]

The legal and moral subjugation of woman produces the *quid pro quo* contractual relationship: I will do for you if you will do for me; I will fulfill my obligations as wife, mother, and sexual partner if you will fulfill yours as breadwinner and father. If you fault your obligations then I am entitled to fault mine. All this is reasonable, but it is not love. The *quid pro quo* arrangement has devastating effects upon a couple's sexual life. Satisfaction of instinctual needs usurps the place of love. Self-gratification replaces self-giving. Gratifying the partner is a performance, done with the hope of ensuring fidelity or of proving one's own prowess. Frequently, a woman succumbs to a compliant sexuality in which she feels she must never exercise her own preferences lest her partner seek satisfaction elsewhere, or she withholds or grants sexual intercourse in exchange for her partner's fulfillment of his obligations to her. The couple may succumb to what has been called the tyranny of orgasm, where the presence or absence, frequency or infrequency of orgasm is interpreted in terms of a severe moralization. One, then, is or is not a good spouse, is or is not being a real woman, provides or does not provide an excuse for other relationships. The notion of conjugal duty desacralizes sex; it robs love of its spontaneity. One feels forced to love, the grimmest of contradictions in terms.

In polarity, sexuality gives varied expression to the love the two persons feel. Love spontaneously generates sexual meetings which are open to every kind of physical expres-

14. Suzanne Lilar, *Aspects of Love,* trans. Jonathan Griffin (New York: McGraw-Hill, 1965), p. 10.

sion, including or not including satisfaction, according to the tempo of the moment. Giving love replaces self-gratification and duty.

In polarization, there is a constant danger of two people relating to each other through the roles they play rather than from the heart. There is a maternal-paternal axis, comradeship, the relationship of housewife to breadwinner. Lilar describes the danger for a woman, and hence for a couple, in such an arrangement. The spirit is extinguished, and even if sexual pleasure is fully enjoyed, there is lacking the kind of encounter that gives sexual pleasure its purpose. What is lacking is that experience of grace in which the ecstasies of the flesh are no longer "distinct from that of the spirit, in which the path from one to the other is always open. . . . This is the commonplace pathos of the reasonable marriage: The woman brings to it her desire for the absolute, and is only required to run her house well." [15] Role-playing may become so automatic that it invades love itself. Love becomes something one "should" feel. The partners learn to expect its presence in themselves and in the other if certain known symptoms are present, or worse, both play the role of dropping role-playing and becoming "natural" and "spontaneous."

If a woman is forced to play a role, by herself, by her husband, or because of other pressures, she will often adopt either a maternal role, or its opposite, an antimaternal posture. Both of these roles lead to overidentification with her maternal instinct, the former in a compulsive endorsement of anything maternal, and the latter in a constant watchfulness to combat anything maternal. Her eagerness to satisfy the needs of others has not only collective approval but collective encouragement. Similarly, the image of woman as feeder, laundress, and nurse for her man is collectively endorsed, packaged, and advertised. The woman who does not

15. *Ibid.*, p. 26.

have these skills or concerns is considered less feminine. Overemphasis on a woman's maternal aspects may make her vulnerable to the danger of masochism.[16] Such a woman desires to give herself, to serve something beyond herself, but often ends up feeling like hired help, plundered of her deepest hopes of service and given over to a shallow domestic life. And everyone around her knows it, from her sighs of unexpressed misery, her tendency to suggest things always in terms of what is good for the other person, never for herself, and her constant concern for food—her meticulous care about what she serves, about how much she serves and when she serves it, and the obvious burden it is for her to prepare it day in and day out. This is a masochistic service with the sadistic corollary of making others feel guilty for being so much trouble, for not being considerate enough, for making her work so hard. This pejorative kind of service parodies true service. The main point of passionate commitment of oneself and of becoming totally one for the other is missed entirely. Outer service hides a hard, unyielding, impenetrable core.

In polarity there are no roles to play; there is only the relation of person to person. That is central; the rest is merely peripheral. When this center is maintained, all else falls into place and revolves around it. All else literally means "all else" —one's profession, relatives, colleagues, problems, children. All these other relations find their proper place within the central and centering love between the two persons. Life is lived from the inside out; there is no detachment from the other, and there is no gross identification. Two persons' identities are not reduced to a common denominator; rather, their uniqueness is augmented through union. Polarization, in contrast, means living from the outside in; one has a detached view in which one compares one's own situation to that of others, toting up who is better off in carefully arranged col-

16. See above, **Part III, Chapter Ten,** pp. 199–200.

umns and categories. One feels separated from one's own experience. One travels to and from experiences collecting
them like suitcase labels that show where one has been.

In polarization, aggression is often expressed over peripheral issues which are forced to serve as vehicles for the un-
spoken central issues. Thus the aggression is doomed to a
destructive outcome, for it is not directed toward the true
fight but perverted into false wars. The couple argues about
failures to fulfill obligations, dress or appearance, styles of
conversation or idiosyncratic habits of gesture or posture,
never quite getting at the central issue—that each withholds
himself from the other in some major way. In polarity, aggression is conscripted in the service of love and is directed
toward scouring away what is not love and uncovering the
true dignity of each partner: "love disengages, strips and
discovers: it separates what is worthy to be loved from what
is not." [17]

One is simply oneself alone in polarization; in polarity one
cannot be oneself, except in and out of the love one shares.
It is the difference between parceling out and being a part
of. In polarity, one's circumference is enlarged through a
loss of self in the other and the gaining of a greater self. This
greater self is not just one or the other, nor just the two together, nor just a fusion of the two, nor just the meeting of
a soul with God. The circumference encircles the two, the
fusion, and the relationship with God. Lilar gives the example of the painter Rubens' marriage to Hélène Fourment,
and contrasts this kind of "unreasonable" love with the "reasonable" type:

> He and she lived through an experience . . . of a fusion so
> complete that the couple they formed existed as a living,
> organic entity independent of them. What distinguishes un-
> reasonable love from the other kind is not that it leads more
> surely to success or happiness, but that in it the two people
> are mingled. This mingling is both a miracle and a mystery,

17. Lilar, *Aspects of Love*, p. 169.

and is essentially different from the non-sacred understanding between husband and wife who are friends. . . . Procreation apart, all that reasonable love holds in store is solitary successes—even when these are won by the two people side by side . . . Hélène . . . was a lens for him, through which he saw things lit with a supernatural glow.[18]

REDEMPTION

LOSS OF POLARITY, falling into polarization, is one aspect of sin. Polarity cannot be regained through human powers alone. Redemption is received, not willed. This is almost every patient's experience in analysis. Conscious reasoning, conscious willing, do not solve besetting problems; nor do they help simply to turn problems over to unconscious processes without the intervention of the ego. Solutions come from a mysterious mixture of conscious and unconscious processes, an interplay so hidden that even analysts are hard put to say what "cures" their patients. Theologically, the doctrine of sin symbolizes man's impotence to save himself and symbolizes as well his reliance on the "new being" manifest in Christ, as Tillich puts it, or the "Word" of God shown in Christ, as Barth explains it.

True sexual polarity exists in love, and love makes possible true polarity. Such a saving, renewing love is manifest in the figure of Christ. If it is correct to suggest that one effect of the Fall is the repression and devaluation of the feminine, and to say that sin is redeemed through God's love shown in Christ, then a logical inference is that one effect of that redeeming love is the recognition and recovery of the feminine in its particular participation in the exchanges of love.

The feminine modality of consciousness and spirit is particularly receptive to the quality of being that is revealed in Christ. Psychologically, the feminine quality of ego consciousness does not divorce itself from unconscious proc-

18. *Ibid.*, p. 34.

esses, but rather adjusts itself to them. Seen theologically, this ego quality does not assert itself against its Creator. Its understanding is a conceiving, a bringing forth, an affective participation in unconscious contents. This modality is surely part of the experience of being seized upon in the revelation of Christ. Knowledge for the feminine mode of understanding is individual transforming knowledge, not abstract theory. This is the saving truth which Jesus stressed, rather than any merely theoretical truth. The feminine mode of activity is one of acceptance and of opening, a kenosis like Christ's, an attentive desire to others, and a contemplation of them. The feminine encompasses the intrinsic defining modes of religious meditation. The feminine sense of time is always of the moment; it is not *chronos*, but *kairos*, the intersection of timeless truth in human history which is at the heart of Christianity. Spiritually, feminine consciousness seeks the redemption of the lowest things, following the spirit of such scriptural sayings as "the stone the builders rejected shall become the cornerstone," and sharing as much as possible Christ's identification with the least of his brethren, reaching out with him to the harlot, the sick, to the forlorn, the depressed, the alienated.

For the feminine spirit, there is an indissoluble bond between sensual and religious passion, between the abstract and the concrete, between eternity and history. This spirit is receptive to the power of Christ which redeems the smallest parts of life, making each one whole. True feminine wisdom is from the heart as well as the head; it seeks the holy in the lowly, finding where it can the sanctifying power of the Holy Spirit. In contrast to the frequent criticism that Christianity neglects the feminine, I would say instead that much of the texture and tonality of the message of Jesus and his means of communicating it through symbol, parable, and living what he preached are expressive of the feminine modality of consciousness and spirit. Perhaps this is one reason that women were so attracted to him; when everyone else had betrayed him, it was the women who remained at the foot of the Cross.

The feminine quality of the Gospels is not explicit, but it is there for us if we have eyes to see it. Jung's psychology helps open our eyes to this feminine presence because it focuses upon the nonrational dimension of felt experience, of affective participation, of mystery, and finds it in the logic of growth and the clarity of wholeness. By formulating a psychology of the feminine, Jung gives us a perspective from which to see how Christ's message redeems and makes use of feminine modes of being.

THE INCARNATION

THE RECOGNITION of the feminine style of consciousness in the revelation of Christ has the important result of re-establishing the sexual polarity, both within the masculine and feminine modes of individual consciousness and between the sexes. Once the value of the feminine pole has been recognized, the sense of the sexual polarity must be renewed, for once again there are two opposite poles. The redemption of the sexual polarity in the Incarnation implies that the experience of full sexual polarity is a central means of receiving and effecting the love revealed in Christ. Derrick Bailey writes, "it is in Christ that sex assumes its real significance, for in him alone can man and woman find the disciplined freedom which enables them to learn through their relational experiences something of the deeper meaning of their masculinity or femininity." [19]

The mysterious symbolism of the Virgin Birth can be better understood with the help of Jung's psychology of the feminine. The Annunciation to Mary by the angel, or mes-

19. Derrick Sherwin Bailey, *The Man-Woman Relation in Christian Thought* (London: Longmans, 1959), p. 289.

senger, of the Spirit, can be understood as paradigmatic of the woman's reception, conception, and transformation by a numinous content brought to her by her animus. Mary's pliant opening and consent is iconographic of the feminine response to such an event, an event that augments and makes explicit a woman's deepest feminine responses. This is not to say that that is all there is to the Annunciation or to attempt to psychologize it away. It is possible, however, through such psychological insight to participate again in the mystery of the Virgin Birth symbolism, for one sees there one's own experience translated into and enlarged by these grander dimensions.

Another example of how the experience of full sexual polarity is a means and signification of the Incarnation is to be found in the love between the sexes. Some may object that there is a large gap between human love and the love of God, insisting that they are of a different order, and that the love of God has ultimate meaning, whereas human love is only too finite. But where do we experience the ultimate except through the finite—through the limits of our finite understanding, our finite vision, our finite relationships? The two dimensions are not the same, but they are inextricably bound together. The divine makes itself known in the human, and the human is made known in the divine. That is the mystery of Incarnation. Love is a seamless garment, all of one piece, and the love between the sexes participates in the reality of love that Christ revealed, however fragmentarily and in however distorted a way. Insofar as human lovers fully accept their love and the dignity of both modes of being, masculine and feminine, and center their lives around the love which centers them, they are living in God. They know God in their love and they know their love in God. Juliette Drouet's words to Victor Hugo describe it superbly: "It is you that I adore in God and God that I adore in you." [20] The love with which the lover loves his beloved is the love given

20. As quoted in Lilar, *Aspects of Love*, p. 192.

him by God and the love with which he can love God. And the love with which the lover is loved by the beloved is the same. "We love Him because He first loved us." To love the beloved is to love God, and to love God is to love the beloved. It is an endless *circulatio* where the divine spirit of love becomes fleshified in human love, and the fleshly love becomes spirit in being offered back to God. One thinks of Hopkins' ringing words: "deliver it, early now, long before death / Give beauty back, beauty, beauty, beauty, back to God, beauty's self and beauty's giver." [21] St. John of the Cross, to describe the ecstasy of mystical contact with God, uses images drawn from the joys of love. When he is most personal and direct, he is most sensuous; thus he implies that the metaphors of sexual love are the best symbols for the deepest relation to God. "In the Song of Songs," writes Barry Ulanov, "the language of worship is the language of love, manifestly fleshly love. . . . Nothing better describes the mystery of hypostatic union which is instinct in the Incarnation." He concludes that "the Incarnation effects a double movement of the spirit, the divine inhabiting the human and the human seeking the corresponding enclosure in the divine." [22] The sexual mode of intense self-giving at all levels, without reservation, is the best means of expression for a constant opening to the penetrating love of God.

Sexual polarity not only incarnates God's love in Christ in the love of lovers—it goes further: it can also do the work of Christ or become a means through which Christ's work is done. True love redeems the beloved to his original dignity and wholeness; it raises him from the degradation of the Fall. This is the process of sanctification. Love endlessly unburies the beloved, scouring away his false poses and pretenses, casting out his illusions, seeking him as he is *au fond*,

---

21. See "The Leaden Echo and the Golden Echo," *Poems of Gerard Manley Hopkins* (London: Oxford University Press, 1948), pp. 53–54.

22. Barry Ulanov, "The Song of Songs: The Rhetoric of Love," in *The Bridge* ed. John M. Oesterreicher (New York: Pantheon, 1961), IV, 98, 105.

in truth. Love illuminates the beloved, revealing his likeness to God, his absolute worth, his royalty. Love cleanses the beloved, digging out his secret flatteries, faults, and flaws, separating what is worthy to be loved from what is not. Love shows the beloved in his original relation to the divine. With a passionate attentiveness and a pitiless lucidity, love sees sacredness incarnate in the personality of the beloved; love salutes the other's worth. Sanctifying by the certainty of its presence, love can elect lovers into love and consecrate the most trivial details of their relationship. Everything becomes meaningful because everything becomes a means by which lovers recognize their supernatural vocation.

Lovers participate in the mystery of the Trinity. Love is the certainty in which they have faith and with which they wait openly, in hope, for every new manifestation of the mixing of the human and the divine. Solovyev says that genuine love is impossible without acknowledgment of the unconditional significance of the other person, and that that is possible only through faith.[23] The mystery of the unconditioned Divine, the Father, seeing unconditional worth in the human, the son, and bestowing that worth in an act of self-giving love, the Spirit, is fully reflected in the mystery of unconditional love between lovers.

Solovyev also talks about sexual love as a means of incarnating God's love. The true meaning of love is to deliver the self from egoism. In his opinion, only sexual love does this fully. As speech is to the organization of human society and culture, so love is to the creation of true human individuality.[24] Love is not just a feeling but the reality that is realized through feeling. The feeling of falling in love just marks out the problem; the lover now has an idealized view of the beloved. The task of love is to make that idealization real, to uncover in the beloved the original image of God, and to distinguish it from both the beloved's self-illusions and the

23. See Solovyev, *Meaning of Love*, p. 59.
24. *Ibid.*, p. 35.

projected illusions of the lover. In concretizing and fleshify-
ing this image, love clearly performs the work of Incarnation.
Genuine love is possible, however, only in full masculine-
feminine polarity. The work of love is to re-establish sexual
polarity within each partner as well as between them, to turn
the polarization of the sexes into polarity:

> . . . the authentic man in the fulness of his ideal personality,
> obviously, cannot be merely male or merely female, but
> must be the supreme unity of both. To realize this unity or
> to create the true man, as a free unity of the male and female
> principles, preserving their formal individualization but
> having surmounted their material separateness and diver-
> gence, this is the *problem* proper and the nearest task of
> love.[25]

Thus we come full circle; man is seen to be created in the
image of God *as male and female.* One strong implication of
Jung's psychology of the feminine for the Christian doctrine
of man is to recognize the significance of the feminine in
the *imago dei.* This leads one to stress sexual polarity in man's
being—both within himself, as articulated in Jung's formulation of the feminine principle and the anima and animus,
and within the relationship of the two sexes. To interpret the Fall in these terms is to recognize that in it the
feminine is devalued and repressed as an inferior mode of
being, no longer in full polar relation with the masculine, but
seen only as tangential to the masculine or as a deficient version of it. Redemption begins with the Incarnation, which
brings with it a renewed valuation of the feminine modes
of being. Thus is initiated a restoration of the male-female
polarity within individuals and between the sexes, as central
channels of incarnation for God's love in Christ. The argument is circular—not to evade the truth, but because the
truth is of one piece: the Incarnation begins restoration of
the sexual polarity and the sexual polarity effects the Incarnation.

25. *Ibid.,* pp. 33–34.

Not only does the Incarnation mean a renewed recognition of the feminine; the feminine mode of being also encourages recognition of the Incarnation, for the feminine concept of love is expressive at many points of the quality of love revealed in Christ.

The feminine concept of love, in Lilar's words, is "unreasonable." It shuns the "reasonable" basis for marriage of comradeship, mutual respect, and obligation as much as it shuns erratic liaisons based on so-called sexual equality and freedom. A woman, or a man whose feminine side is strong, wants a mingling of the erotic and the conjugal, wants intense passion to be the basis of a permanent relationship which will provide time and space for gestation and maturing in which the spirit can become flesh and the flesh spirit. A woman wants love to be absolute and wants to assume the royal authority of love, where it is sovereign and all else is subservient to it. She wants to give herself to a man and experience in a particular relationship the infinite majesty of a divine reality. She wants that great paradox, the eternal reality of love in a temporal relationship, all the abstract powers of love concretized in her daily experience of the indissoluble bond of flesh and spirit. She rejects the polarizing of the sexes into obligatory roles or into antithetical modes of being and affirms instead their true polarity. Similarly she sees the love revealed in Christ as paradoxical and as concretizing the absolute in the singular, illuminating the eternal in the temporal and the sacred in the mundane as it recognizes and redeems male and female. To adopt the feminine concept of love is to approach and to increase one's readiness for the love revealed in Christ.

The Recovery of the Sacred

To UNDERSTAND the sexual polarity as a signification of union within oneself, with one's partner, and with God implies a "resacralization" of sexual love, I think. We need not a demythologizing but a remythologizing of our common experiences into the mysteries which they contain and of which Christian symbols speak. The sacrality of a couple's love is not the product of respect, of consideration, or of affection. Whether their union is sacred or profane is decided by the way they receive their sexuality: they must feel and know and resolve their sexual polarity.

If there is love without sexuality or sexuality without love, there is no sacrality. Sacrality is determined by sexuality-in-love. Lilar writes:

> Nothing is easier than to exhibit in sexuality the essential features of the sacred—its absolute otherness, its ambiguity, its ambivalence, its polarity, its twofold character of positivity and negativity. Here, unquestionably, we are in that zone of extremes which is also, as a Catholic assures us, a zone of communication, "because the sacred dissolves the determinations of individual beings and makes possible a fusion that is like a kind of liquid condition where there is no longer separate existence." [26]

Sacrality is opposed to the profane. The profane is the search for the safe, the secure, "for a balanced or just environment that permits living in fear and moderation without exceeding the limits of the allowable." [27] The various polarities of life are polarized when the opposing poles reciprocally neutralize each other. The profane is a preference for a state of relative calm and tranquillity, where stability seems guaranteed. The sacred is not the safe but the certain, not the guaranteed perpetuations of life but rather its consuming intensities. "The sacred is what gives life and takes it away, it is the source from which it flows, and the estuary in which it is lost." [28] The profane tries to preserve life and to protect its resources. The sacral offers life in an endless

---

26. Lilar, *Aspects of Love*, p. 158.
27. Roger Caillois, *Man and the Sacred*, trans. Meyer Barash (Glencoe, Ill.: The Free Press, 1959), p. 137.
28. *Ibid.*, p. 138.

oblation. Those who participate in sacral love live in life's fires, and know that they live there:

> The real lovers . . . need no argument to convince them that love sanctifies. They know it: in love everything is possible, everything is permitted, everything is sacred, provided that sexuality is adopted in all its mystery, its gravity, its totality.
>
> The first gift lavished by love is this sense of infallible certainty, this unequalled confidence, this ever ready rightness of choice—whether it concerns a gesture to be risked or some great decision taken . . . There is no better gauge of the greatness of a couple than its consciousness of its sacrality.[29]

This resacralization of sexual love indicates the proper function of aggression, which Christianity has often been criticized for neglecting. Aggression functions in the service of love. Aggression's first task is to further ego assertion in the full development of one's inner sexual polarity, in the relation of ego to anima or animus, and to differentiate one's sure identity in relation to the opposite sex. The ultimate purpose of such ego assertion is not to polarize but to give oneself to full sexual polarity. The second task of aggression is continually to assert the centrality of love and to cut away all that is not love. Here aggression is employed in the task of differentiating the central from the peripheral, casting out all that would relativize love. The parable of the fig tree is apt: Jesus was hungry and the fig tree was not in season, so he killed it. Love that is central and given *primary* importance by the lovers has no season but is regulated only by an endless self-giving and receiving. Anything which pretends to seasons is a masquerade of love and therefore to be destroyed. Aggression provides the strength to separate the authentic from the false and the pretentious and to celebrate the centrality of true love.

The recognition of the feminine, therefore, leads to cor-

29. Lilar, *Aspects of Love*, p. 158.

rections of those faults usually laid at the door of Christianity. Contrary to the criticism that Christianity severs the spirit and the flesh, the recognition of the feminine reveals that vital to Christ's love is the sexual polarity which affirms the union of flesh and spirit. Contrary to the criticism that Christianity devalues both ego and aggression, the full recognition of the feminine asserts the proper function of aggression, to serve love.

CHAPTER FOURTEEN

The Feminine and the Doctrines of God and Christ

R ELIGIOUS SYMBOLISM expresses the conscious and the unconscious mind, and the past, present, and future. For Jung, the religious symbol, as this book has stressed again and again, is a transformer of psychic energy. It frees psychic energies from the danger of regression to the past; it mediates unconscious energy to consciousness, thus deepening the meaning of the present; and it forms a bridge to the future by indicating the channels in which the energies will be employed. Religious symbols and doctrines unite the rational and the nonrational in the conscious and unconscious of the psyche. Thus, in addition to making elements known to consciousness and clarifying elements that we know with our reason, religious symbols contain elements we cannot know because they are still in the making. The religious symbol has the important function, then, of making perceptible and accessible to consciousness the power and meaning

314

of the ultimate realities to which it points and of objectifying the psyche's total conscious and unconscious relationship to those realities. Thus, if the symbol is insufficient, the realization and objectification of what the symbol points to, and of our unconscious responses to it, are hindered. The symbol, then, loses its validity. It fails to express the interpenetration of the subject and the object and therefore fails in its function as an organ of spiritual reality. When the feminine element is obscured in religious symbolism we can usually expect to find some hindrances to psychological development as well as a lessened degree of accessibility to our experience of ultimate reality.

THE EXCLUSION OF THE FEMININE

FAILURE TO INCLUDE enough of the feminine in religious symbols and doctrines has its most obvious debilitating effects upon females. Toni Wolff interprets the fact that more women than men are in analysis to mean that women are more estranged from their deeper natures than men and hence more neurotic, that women have a harder time becoming conscious of themselves and differentiating their egos from the unconscious. As I have argued in Part III, this is due in large part to the dominance in feminine psychology of the feminine principle, which favors relating through identification rather than through differentiation. But cultural repression of the feminine also makes differentiation of their own feminine natures difficult for women. Examples of cultural repression are to be found in the psychological theories that see women as deficient men, in the discrimination against women in business, and in those protest groups that seek to defend women by insisting that they are no different from men. Underlying this cultural repression is a fear of the feminine based on a fear of otherness. Wolff adds another salient point: The paucity of feminine symbol-

ism in the Godhead of Protestantism and Judaism contributes
to the estrangement of Protestant and Jewish women from
their deeper natures. Wolff writes:

> The image of God is the supreme symbol of the highest
> human attributes and of the most far-reaching ideas of the
> human spirit. How then can woman find herself if her own
> psychological principle and all its complexities are not
> objectified in a symbol, as in the case of man? The symbol
> takes effect in the human being by gradually unfolding its
> meaning. The relationship with the Deity keeps man in con-
> tinuous contact with all the conscious and unconscious
> contents which the Deity symbolically expresses.[1]

Feminine elements have disappeared from prominent places
in the Protestant churches since the Reformation. In its efforts to remove human mediators between God and man,
Protestantism has excluded concrete aspects of the feminine
from its few images and has destroyed spiritual aspects of
the feminine with the elimination of the veneration of the
mother of God. Tillich adds, "In this purge the female element in the symbolic expression of ultimate concern was
largely eliminated." [2]

Exclusion of the feminine principle from full representation in religious symbolism deeply affects our lives as individuals and as members of society. It is one way a man may
lose touch with his anima, which means for him a dissociation of conscious and unconscious processes and a split between his cognitive and conative faculties. Some form of
autonomous sexuality or rationality, operating out of relation to the total psyche, usually results from this split. For a
woman, the exclusion of the feminine is even more destructive; it results in her subjection to one of the forms of animus domination. The animus, instead of joining her deepest

1. Toni Wolff, "A Few Thoughts on the Individuation Process in
Women," *Spring* (New York: The Analytical Psychology Club, 1941),
p. 84.
2. Paul Tillich, *Systematic Theology*, 3 vols. (Chicago: University
of Chicago Press, 1951–63), III, p. 293.

feminine nature to her ego, suppresses her femininity by tyrannous devaluation, by power and ambitions, by constant assertion of a need to be right, by fractious competition with others and rigid defensiveness against them. For both sexes, loss of recognition of the feminine seriously diminishes the experience of the self. For a man, the feminine anima mediates awareness of his self to his ego; for the woman, the animus helps her ego focus on her feminine self.

The exclusion of feminine elements in religious symbolism has the effect collectively of suppressing the feminine modes of understanding, of acting, of spirit, and of the heightened sense of the moment. The diminution of the feminine modality leads to a general decrease in all symbolic modes of perception. Head ego dominates heart ego; and the sexes are polarized. The feminine is defined in terms of the masculine or is defended by denial of its own reality—over and over, both men and women insist that there is no real difference between the sexes. The psychology of the feminine becomes the psychology of its suppression. The feminine is characterized by sexual passivity (see Havelock Ellis), by sexuality *per se* to the exclusion of rational capacity (see Otto Weininger), by penis envy (see Freud), by social inferiority (see Adler), by cultural conditioning (see Karen Horney), by societal organization (see Margaret Mead).[3] Father Arnold describes the high price humanity has paid for its neglect of the feminine and its sometimes exclusive reliance on the male viewpoint:

> The historical catastrophes of our time can be traced back to the predominance of the active, self-reliant, male principle in our civilization and the corresponding atrophying of the feminine principle. . . .
>
> This world without women is more the world of adolescents than the world of men. It is in the last analysis a world of men on their own, . . . hardened by their own pride, no longer aware of sin or in need of grace. It is a

3. See Viola Klein, *The Feminine Character* (London: Kegan Paul, Trench, Trübner & Co., 1946), pp. 163–65.

world which has shaken off all transcendental ties . . .
without God.[4]

The effects on religion have also been devastating. Consciousness has been characterized in Western history as masculine, the unconscious as feminine. The predominant masculinity of religious symbols emphasizes the values of consciousness out of proportion. The values of consciousness have been so stressed and so assimilated in our time that inevitably religious symbols have lost their power for most people. They unfold no new, vital meanings. The newest religious symbol signifies only the death of the old—God is dead. Suppression of the feminine in religious symbolism brings with it the suppression of otherness within the Godhead and all symbolical representations of the unconscious. Thus religious symbolism dries up, cut off from unrealized contents that are prevented from emerging out of the unconscious into new conscious meaning. Suppression of the feminine in religious symbolism leads to suppression of the feminine in human life, which means suppression of the main appearance of otherness in our daily lives. There can be no polarity if there are not two poles. And equally, our lack of experience of sexual otherness all but negates our capacity to experience the otherness of the divine.

The general devaluation of the feminine has repercussions in the growing sense of urgency among women to reintroduce the feminine modalities into the cultural stream of consciousness. Jung links this cultural task to the lack of emphasis on human relationship in religion and looks to the feminine principle to remedy this condition.

THE VIRGIN MARY

JUNG UNDERSTANDS the Catholic dogma of the Assumption of Mary as theological recognition of the feminine in the

---

4. F. X. Arnold, *Woman and Man*, trans. Rosaleen Brennan (Edinburgh-London: Nelson, 1963), pp. 10–11.

Godhead and as a change in the psychic experience of the Godhead. The Trinity becomes a quaternity, as he sees it. Not only is a fresh accent put on the place of sexual polarity in the deity, but the concrete materiality of Mary also represents the possibility of human individuation.[5] Individuation is worked out through the successive reconciliations of opposites that are symbolized mainly in terms of the masculine-feminine polarity. In individuation, as in Mary's drama, the divine not only becomes incarnate but is consciously related to, just as Mary consciously related to the contrasexual numinous element within herself and in her relationship to Jesus.

Even though for most Protestants the life and Assumption of Mary are not vital religious symbols, she nonetheless represents for them as for many others the feminine in the Godhead. One recognizes with Tillich that it is unlikely "that Protestantism will ever reinstate the symbol of the Holy Virgin," because symbols cannot be re-established in their genuine power simply by an act of will or theological argument.[6] It is still possible and fruitful, however, with the help of Jung's psychology, to participate in the reality of the feminine which Mary mediates. For example, Jungians can see that Mary represents two modalities open to woman in the Middle Ages and not entirely outside modern woman's understanding or experience—Mother and Virgin. Furthermore, Mary is not a goddess but a human being, which means psychologically that some of the highest values in religion are to be found in the purest humanity.

There are many areas where the symbolism of Mary can be translated into a modern psychology of the feminine, opening our eyes to the depth of the religious symbol as well as to what it reveals about the feminine. There are striking parallels between Wolff's typology of the archetypal forms of the feminine and Mary's symbolic titles. Mary as Mother of God reveals a new depth of meaning in the

5. See Jung, "A Psychological Approach to the Trinity," *Psychology and Religion: West and East* (CW, XI, 1958), p. 171.
6. Tillich, *Systematic Theology*, III, p. 293.

Mother type, indicating how that modality is a means of participating concretely in a divine reality. Mary as Handmaiden to the Lord corresponds to the Hetaira type and shows how consent and submission can be ways of participating in divine reality without falling into the perversions of masochism. Mary achieves royalty through her servanthood. Mary as Virgin is like the Amazon type and symbolizes the way in which a complete ordering and opening of one's life to the divine may make one intact and chaste. Chastity is the rectitude of a life which puts central commitment totally at the center and which allows no perforations by merely peripheral or competing concerns. Mary as Queen of Heaven corresponds to the Medial Woman, illustrating the feminine capacity to be an intercessor as she mediates the human to the divine and the divine to the human. The feminine achieves its highest expression as vessel or grail in which human and divine achieve their just mixture.

> . . . the idealization of the lower nature exists together with that incipient realization of what is higher, and in this is the truth of the passion of love. Complete realization, the transformation of the individual feminine creature into the ray inseparable from its resplendent source "the eternal divine femininity, will be an actual, not merely subjective but also objective" reunion of the individual human being with God, the restoration in him of the living and immortal Divine image.[7]

Mary is just one of many expressions of the feminine in Christian symbolism and in the Bible that have not been sufficiently explored or made evident in Protestant tradition. There is Ruth, for example, who introduces new expression and experience of the feminine element into the Old Testament world, as has been handsomely demonstrated by H. Y.

7. Vladimir Solovyev, *The Meaning of Love*, trans. Jane Marshall (London: Geoffrey Bles, 1945), p. 62.

Kluger.[8] There are the ancestresses of Jesus, all perhaps of questionable nature from the viewpoint of collective morality but all, too, of singular importance for our understanding of the Christ figure. There are the Marys who were the friends, the family, and the faithful of Christ, the only ones to remain with him to the end of the Crucifixion and the first to see him after the Resurrection. There is the mysterious apocalyptic woman who appears at the end of time "clothed with the sun, with the moon under her feet" (Rev. 12:1); she recalls the moon symbolism of the feminine and the saying of Baal Shan, "When the moon shall shine as bright as the sun, the Messiah will come." All of these are figures to be examined and explored in order to make explicit the implicit feminine elements in Christian symbolism. For this purpose Jung's psychology of the feminine is an essential aid.

THE CRUCIFIXION AND THE RESURRECTION

ANOTHER APPROACH to making explicit feminine elements in Christian symbolism is the correlation of the suffering of the Crucifixion and triumph of the Resurrection to the painful and redemptive aspects of love between a man and a woman. There are many parallels between the Cross and our own lives as lovers in the necessary rougheings that come as we attempt to adjust the polarization of the sexes into polarity. The Cross reconciles us, too, to the unavoidable suffering involved in a love that is not simply a passing event or an accident, but to which we are preordained when we ourselves elect the life of love.

8. See H. Yechezkel Kluger, "Ruth: A Contribution to the Development of the Feminine in the Old Testament," *Spring* (New York: The Analytical Psychology Club, 1957), pp. 56–57. See also Rivkah Schärf Kluger, "Women in the Old Testament" (unpublished manuscript, property of The Kristine Mann Library, The Analytical Psychology Club of New York, 1958).

By our seeing the parallels between the sufferings of the Crucifixion and those of human love, suffering is redeemed from becoming mere misery, and we spare ourselves as a result much unnecessary suffering. The symbols of the Crucifixion and the Resurrection are then remythologized, by personal experience of what they represent. The little dyings and risings up of love in the human sphere achieve their proper perspective and majesty by their participation in the Passion, in which God lets happen the triumph of love and endures the death of the isolated life. A lover's consent to the destruction of his egoism and of the supremacy of his individual ego consciousness, both in his relations with others and with the divine, is a participation in Christ's consent to the Cross. It accepts, in Jung's terms, the conflict of ego and self and, in theological terms, the conflict of man's will and God's. Now the "other" represents all others, and all dimensions of existence are felt. Sexual love is enlarged to a new religious significance. Solovyev writes:

> If the root of false existence consists in impenetrability, i.e. in the mutual exclusion of creatures by each other, then true existence is to live in another, as in oneself, or to find in another the positive and unconditional completion of one's own being. The foundation and type of this true existence remains and always will remain sexual or conjugal love. . . . the single "other" is at the same time all, so on its side, the social *all*, . . . ought to manifest itself for each of them as a genuine unity, as the other living being which would complete him in a new and wider sphere. . . .
>
> Such an extension of the relation of intimate union over spheres of collective and universal being, enhances the individuality itself, communicating to it unity and fulness of vital content, and thereby elevates and makes immortal the fundamental individual form of love.[9]

To be conscious of the parallels between the sufferings of the Cross and those of love is to be open to transfiguration, where one shares with all religions the drive toward apotheo-

9. Solovyev, *Meaning of Love*, pp. 77–79.

sis, the urge to become one with God and fully to accept Christ's words, "You shall be like gods" (John 10:34) and be "fellow heirs with him" (Rom. 8:17). Much of philosophical theology claims that man is afraid of nonbeing, of the nothingness of life. The fear is just the opposite, I think. Man is afraid of an avalanche of being—there is so much there and so much of it is accessible to him. The most effective defense against this abundance is to focus on the threat of nonbeing and to avoid all the being suddenly made available. Man feels too small for being; he fears it will tear him apart. Love is the only thing that enables him to stand up to being, to withstand its abundance, to grow large enough to receive it.

The effort to make explicit with the help of Jung the feminine elements in Christian symbolism, then, reveals not only new dimensions of the Godhead and of feminine psychology but also new parallels between the sufferings and the triumph of the Crucifixion and Resurrection as they deal with the separations and reconciliations we encounter in moving from sexual polarization to full polarity.

CHAPTER FIFTEEN

The Feminine and
the Doctrine of Spirit

Sanctification is a process by which one is made holy and is received into the community of *sancti*—those who are blessed or, as Paul Tillich describes them, those who have been grasped by the power of new being manifest in Christ. The spirit as a "dimension of life unites the power and meaning of being in unity." [1] To sanctify, then, is to make the spirit efficacious in someone, so that a person feels not only the vitality of being but also its purpose. To experience this power has the effect of gathering one up into a unity, a wholeness, however temporary. All of one's self is claimed—body, mind, conscious, unconscious. One is suddenly aware of the specialness of being a person, a unique person, who in being made whole knows the presence of the holy, and who in responding to the holy knows that he has become whole.

1. Paul Tillich, *Systematic Theology,* 3 vols. (Chicago: Chicago University Press, 1951–63), II, 179–80.

Sanctification is a process that assumes many forms. The feminine is one element in that process. A connection between the feminine and the Holy Spirit is hinted at in the symbol of the dove, which traditionally represents the Holy Spirit in Christianity and is associated with Aphrodite, the goddess of love in Greek mythology. Iconographically, the dove is a messenger of the goddess and of the Holy Spirit. The messenger is properly feminine because what it does is to expose dark mystery to the light of the world, just as the feminine modality lifts the material of the unconscious into the light of consciousness. A deeper connection is found in the need for a feminine modality of understanding in the response to the mysterious presence of the divine.

OTHERNESS

FOR THE FEMININE STYLE of ego consciousness, as we have seen, understanding comes through the process of turning toward and opening to what is to be understood, whether it is another person, an idea, or an image from the unconscious. The ego does not condemn or condone these contents; it simply sees what is to be seen, looks at the contents, and meditates upon them in a thoughtful circumambulation, which is in itself a form of religious exercise. In such meditation, the ego accepts the materials to be meditated upon as an "other" without sentimentality or evasion, and without any ambition to change what it finds into something that might advance the ego's strength and purposes. In turning to this other—whether it be the outer world of events and people or the interior world of daydream and revery—the ego gives up its interests to the other. Merely to observe passively and to try to maintain the safe distance of a spectator is not enough.[2] The ego makes an active response to the

2. For discussion of the ways the ego can become actively involved with unconscious contents, see James Hillman, *Insearch* (London: Hodder & Stoughton, 1967), pp. 102–10.

other that it beholds and turns a passing fancy into an inward drama, transforming the materials of daydream into the materials of the imagination—Jung's "active imagination"—and thus into serious religious meditation.

When the ego relates to its contents in this imaginative way, it begins the process by which a self becomes possible. Conscious participation is needed for the development of a self; it must be constructed out of the reconciliation of various psychic polarities. There can be no consciousness of polarity where there is no recognition of otherness. Otherness is a *sine qua non* of the achievement of a self. One must be able to see and even to gaze upon otherness and upon an "other" if one is to have any genuine and direct knowledge of polarity. Polarity is otherness. For example, between people it is the meeting of two distinct persons, each recognizing and responding with feeling to the other. Polarization results from the fear of otherness, from attempts to suppress it, flee from it, or to hide it beneath a false veneer of sameness. The making of a self is not possible until there is full recognition of otherness. And that self must include both male and female elements. Everything in the development of one's self demands that one heed the unconscious, the contents of which impress themselves on consciousness as an "other." If the message of these unconscious contents is a particularly urgent one for the ego to hear, it usually will appear in terms of sexual imagery. Sexual language, attracting the ego's attention, arousing and luring it, is one of the best ways the unconscious has to engage the ego in conversation. The greater the ego's isolation, the more urgent will be the sexual imagery. Very often such imagery will disappear from dreams or fantasies once the ego's attention has been secured.

Outwardly, the fact and presence of otherness may also come through sexual polarity. The recovery of full recognition of the feminine is crucial, because upon it rests the possibility of that experience of otherness without which achievement of a self is impossible. Sexual polarity has a natural place in religious life, for in any relation between the sexes one feels otherness as an unmistakable presence like the presence of the spirit. In being drawn into a true relationship with each other, a man and woman find themselves called into relation with the unknown. The life of a couple offers daily opportunities to live the union of opposites and to perform the task of transforming love, as Solovyev sees it, from mere feeling to a state of being. Direct contact with the feminine and acceptance of it are necessary for the life of a couple to become a means of sanctification. Without such acceptance polarization is inevitable. A man will feel himself estranged from his own inner femininity and will usually try to compensate for his loss with exaggerated attachments to women—to his mother, or to his wife's maternal qualities, to his daughter, to his sister, or to women outside his marriage. A woman will lose her playfulness, her softness, and her strength and will become cold and hard. If both partners develop the feminine qualities within themselves and with each other, a couple can achieve openness and receptivity to the constantly growing presence that the encounters of polarity offer them. Familiarity will then not breed contempt but awe; the sense of self that develops then brings with it that sense of spirit which always complements a fully lived human sexuality. To have a sense of self is to have a sense of the spirit, of that "other" whose presence is conveyed to us in the exchanges of otherness between a man and a woman which we call love. In this way the feminine opens us to continuing revelations of the spirit.

THE SPIRIT AND THE FEMININE

ALL THE VARIOUS MEANINGS of "spirit" are relevant here and each can be correlated with an aspect of the feminine. Feminine sensitivity gives our lives a defining vitality by its openness to the mood of the moment and by its many responses to the alternations of fantasy and fact. Openness to this vigorous tonality of life opens us to spirit as "the breath of life," as the *ruach* or *hayyim* that animates God's creatures (Gen. 6:17, 7:15). The feminine as anima brings unconscious contents to consciousness. As a modality of perception it makes us aware of nonrational, intangible reality. This in turn opens us to the meaning of spirit as "the medium of consciousness" (Isa. 30:12; Job 9:18). The feminine principle of relatedness which always involves emotions opens us to receive spirit as "the seat of the emotions" (I Kings 21:5; Prov. 15:13). Cultivation of the feminine style of affective, personal knowing opens us to experience spirit as "intelligence and will" (Ezech. 20:32; Job 20:3). Development of the feminine modality of understanding through pondering and waiting until something takes shape and offers guidance in a concrete way makes us receptive to the brooding, creative activity of spirit, which imparts not only comfort but also the capacity to do great things. (See the "Wonderful Counselor" verses, Isa. 9:6.) Finally, cultivation of the feminine turning toward still developing possibilities in the unconscious may open us to spirit as the central source of life (John 4:24; I Cor. 3:16).[3]

The Completing Function

The feminine above all has a completing function. It opens up areas in which the spirit makes us holy by making us whole. In contrast to the goals of the masculine style of consciousness—goals of intellectual perfection, clear focus, and specialization—the feminine style of consciousness moves toward completeness. The feminine style of spirit is to make progress on a downward-going road, into the dark, into the roots of earth, into the unconscious. It is a style that does not exclude in order to purify, as does the masculine, but instead embraces all elements in order to redeem.[4]

3. Hasting's *Dictionary of the Bible*, s.v. "Spirit."
4. See Jung, "Answer to Job," *Psychology and Religion: West and East (CW, XI, 1958), p. 395. Here Jung stresses the complementarity

The feminine impulse to reach out to all and to look upon all equally, to hold onto materials and to meditate upon them, initiates great changes in a couple's life, whether the impulse comes from the woman, from the man's anima, or from both. A woman and the feminine anima seek a more complete life that may embrace the dark areas of the personality, which may be thought by some inferior and therefore excluded from consciousness. A woman wants to enlarge consciousness to include the whole person, and in this, Jung writes, she "gives expression to one of the cultural tendencies of our time: the urge to live a completer life, a longing for meaning and fulfilment, a growing disgust with senseless one-sidedness, with unconscious instinctuality and blind contingency." [5] This urge to completeness brings with it not self-consciousness but consciousness of the self, of all of the self, of its contrasexual qualities and its less developed aspects. The feminine turns toward and opens to what is actually there in the other, not to what one would like to be there, not to a fantasy, but to what is real. Jung describes this striving for reality:

> Is it not an old truth that woman loves the weaknesses of the strong man more than his strength, . . . Her love wants the whole man—not mere masculinity as such but also its negation. . . . A man who is loved in this way cannot escape his inferior side, for he can only respond to the reality of her love with his own reality. [6]

Love of this sort, Jung adds, not only binds the couple together but reaches out to bind the couple to humanity. In loving the other, we love all others. The reality a woman seeks, Jung says,

---

of the aims of the masculine and feminine, and the importance of both. I have emphasized the feminine because that has been neglected and misunderstood.

5. Jung, "Woman in Europe," *Civilization in Transition* (*CW*, X, 1964), p. 130.

6. *Ibid.*, p. 127.

is no fair semblance, but a faithful reflection of that eternal human nature which links together all humanity, a reflection of the heights and depths of human life which are common to us all. . . . Here I strip off the distinctiveness of my own personality, social or otherwise, and reach down to the problems of the present day, . . . Here I can no longer deny them; I feel and know myself to be one of many, and what moves the many moves me.[7]

When the two sexes reach out to assimilate each other fully —the dark as well as the light sides—they contribute greatly to the solution of our central human problems. Jung writes, "In its truest meaning for life and society it is an overcoming of personal isolation and selfish reserve in order to take an active part in the solution of present-day problems."[8] What looked like passive feminine submission or masochistic rumination when seen from the patriarchal point of view, becomes, when seen in the light of Jung's symbolic approach, an active acceptance and transformation of darkness and inferiorities common to all human beings. The feminine mode of response elicits from us a kind of participation that changes our own self and the selves of others. In this sense the feminine is a true channel of sanctification.

ATTENTION

THE FEMININE STYLE of response, of ego consciousness, may be likened to the religious virtue of "attention."[9] To give attention to a person, to an idea, or to an unconscious content is to leave one's self open to be penetrated by the other to whom one is attending. The "other" enters one and fills one's interior space. One's own thought and viewpoint are laid aside but are still within reach when needed. The ego's atti-

7. *Ibid.*
8. *Ibid.*, pp. 127–28.
9. See Simone Weil, *Waiting for God*, trans. Emma Crawford (New York: Capricorn Books, 1951), p. 105.

tude now is to attend to the other—whether it is another person or an unconscious content—in the sense of waiting upon it, listening to it, watching over it, giving heed to it, letting emerge what will emerge. The ego then enters what Buytendijk calls the feminine world—*le monde de souci,* the world of caring—and attends to the self and to the other the way a woman attends to the man she loves, attentive to him and to their mutual love, allowing it ample time and space in which to mature.[10] Enormous amounts of a woman's energy flow toward the man she loves and into him; she inspects him with care and concentration; she really knows his body, his moods, his thoughts, even his unvoiced yearnings.

The subtleties of the ego's feminine style of attention reflect all the four archetypes of the feminine. Like the Mother, the ego waits upon and protects what is still in need of development; like the Hetaira, the ego gives heed to, cares for, and promotes what is personal and individual in the other; like the Amazon, the ego accepts what emerges from the other as an objective goal; like the Medium, the ego listens to and articulates what emerges from the unconscious world.

In a woman's attention to the man she loves and attendance upon him, and his upon her when his feminine side is developed, each becomes the other's intercessor, the other's point of contact and supplication with the inner world. Between the inner darkness of a man's personality and the light of his masculine ego consciousness, a woman or an anima figure intercedes and translates darkness into light; the literal truth of consciousness becomes focused in the symbolic truth of the penumbral world. The feminine style of ego consciousness that attends to intuitions, imaginings, and feelings is now capable of interceding for a woman between her unarticulated hopes and longings and the declarative opinions of her animus, softening those opinions and bending them so that they apply to her personal situation. This intercessory

10. F. J. J. Buytendijk, *La Femme,* texte français d'Alphonse de Waelhens and René Micha (Bruges: Desclée de Brouwer, 1954), p. 9.

quality of the feminine spirit is symbolized by Sophia—the spirit of wisdom—interceding on behalf of mankind with the vigorous demands of Yahweh, and by Mary, the human member of the Godhead.[11]

The feminine style of ego consciousness takes the inner world seriously and allows itself to be carried along by a bidding fantasy or dream. The feminine attitude accepts what is, without sentimentality and without power-motivated ambition. Clarity of vision is to see what is, not what one would like to find, not what one wishes were there. Clarity of action is to accept what is, not endorsing or condoning or appropriating or even changing what is. One does not identify with or detach oneself from the other; one simply accepts who and what the other is. To accept the other fully into one's consciousness and to accept one's own response to the other fully is the feminine mode of activity. This is not passivity but, on the contrary, the most energetic inward action of which the soul is capable. It is the response of presence to presence.

CONTEMPLATION

IN ITS HIGHEST DEVELOPMENT, this feminine style of attention becomes a kind of contemplation; a dwelling upon the other that stirs deep changes of personality within both the contemplator and the contemplated. The feminine attitude to the other is a constant redemptive move to expose the darkness of mystery, to bring it into the open light, not to remove it. This is the way one makes contact with one's dark side, not trying to explain it away in ego-centered rational discourse, like a woman with an overbalanced animus or a man who is fearful of his anima and is worried because he does not understand his dark side. Feminine openness to the unconscious is openness to the unknown. Openness to the un-

11. See Jung, "Answer to Job," pp. 388–90, 397.

known, to the mystery, is what religion is really about, and this mystery is what sexuality is really about too.

Feminine attention to the inner world is a response that treats it as if it were outer reality, to deal with inner darkness as if it were outer light. The dark is light enough. Inner life, then, is no longer just subjective and ephemeral. It achieves the intensity of sanctification in the exchanges between the "I" and the unknown, between the "I" and the other. Our life becomes symbolic, transparent, and revelatory of exchanges with the divine. We live an inner history as well as an outer one. Giving attention is transformed into being present, giving ourselves. Seeing the other becomes a contemplation of the other which helps to transform him into a revealing presence. The meaning of our life takes on shape and direction as its purpose is illuminated. God becomes an intimate acquaintance, not a distant stranger or an outmoded concept that our consciousness has long left behind. We are reborn, resurrected, into a world of presences—human, unconscious, divine. We know something now of the abundant life, where each contemplation of mystery opens to a further contemplation, where each encounter with one we love reveals and illuminates a new darkness. Love is enlarged into loving; a feeling becomes an action; an action becomes a way of being; and a way of being becomes a point of ceaseless intercession between this world and the other world. It is in these ways that the feminine style of attention remythologizes the life of the soul.

Nourishment of the soul, in the past, was guided by religion. But now, as Jung comments, "religion leads back to the Middle Ages, back to that soul-destroying unrelatedness from which came all the fearful barbarities of war." [12] Religion itself is in need of what the feminine strives for: "Too much soul is reserved for God, too little for man. But God himself cannot flourish if man's soul is starved. The feminine psyche responds to this hunger, for it is the function of Eros

12. Jung, "Woman in Europe," p. 132.

to unite what Logos has sundered. The woman of today is faced with a tremendous cultural task—perhaps it will be the dawn of a new era." [13]

The feminine spirit with its urge to completeness and its acceptance of inner realities brings together the divergent worlds, disciplines, and methods of depth psychology and of religion in the service of human interiority. One of Jung's most valuable contributions was to open this world of interiority to clinical procedures. He offered data gathered from his observation of his patients and of himself. He offered a variety of approaches to the darkness within us, and his followers have continued to record their experience, like Jung, both in psychoanalytical terms and in terms of the spiritual life. What we are dealing with here is not merely a speculative possibility of an approach to human interiority but a daily clinical reality. That is why all those who seek to know more about the feminine and to call forth what it symbolizes in the world of the dark human interior are so much in the debt of Jung and the Jungian tradition.

With these thoughts, we end where we began, in the mutual reaching out of psychology and theology to love. To understand this depends upon our cultivation of the feminine. With it, we reach out to become whole, to become wholly revealed, to become wholly what we are meant to be, men and women, each complete in sexuality and contrasexuality. We are nowhere more revealed than in our loving as full human beings. In being fully open to love, we are open to God.

13. *Ibid.*, pp. 132–33.

APPENDIX

A Note on Eros
and Logos

O NE MUST RECOGNIZE, as Jung himself does, that the categories of eros and logos are not fixed and precise, and that at certain points they generate confusion. It is useful, therefore, to examine at what points the problems arise. The first area of confusion is that which Esther Harding tries to clarify: the association of eros, as representing the principle of psychic relatedness, with Eros, the symbolic personification of love. The reader may think that psychic relatedness means love and therefore that love is the principle that determines not only the feminine mode of being but also all females. Jung writes that love is the special determinant of the feminine person: "The woman is increasingly aware that love alone can give her full stature, just as man begins to discern that spirit alone can endow life with its highest meaning." [1] The reader is left with the impression that woman's

1. Jung, "Woman in Europe," *Contributions to Analytical Psychology*, trans. H. G. and Cary F. Baynes (London: Routledge & Kegan Paul, 1928), p. 185.

being is determined by a kind of love which excludes spirit
and ideas and which is dominated by feelings and personal
relationship. This may lead one to equate the feminine with
feelings, with subjective interests, and with nature as contrasted to spirit. Irene de Castillejo, a Spanish analyst, objects:

> To be told, as she often is told, that man represents the
> spirit and she the earth is one of those disconcerting things
> women try hard to believe, knowing all the time they are
> not true . . . she is not merely blind nature and life force.
> She has a spiritual nature of her own which has little to do
> with the masculine.[2]

Another serious problem arises from the inevitable association of eros as psychic relatedness with Eros the masculine
god of love. If the feminine principle is linked mythologically with a male god, then one is almost bound to conclude
that the determining principle of the feminine is masculine.
Jung never says this, and in fact tries to dissociate the feminine principle from the male god, but in his theory of the
animus he gives the reader the general impression that the
animus is the spiritual element in a woman and at the same
time her masculine side. Castillejo is again helpful by saying
that a woman's spirit is clearly feminine, not masculine, and
that the animus is not woman's spirit but rather is her capacity to focus and to clarify.[3]

Another problem arises from Jung's association of the
feminine principle of psychic relatedness with feeling and
from his tendency to confine woman's feeling to the more
subjective world of persons and values and to reserve for
man a relatedness to ideas and objective goals: "It is a
woman's outstanding characteristic that she can do everything for the love of a man. But those women who can
achieve something important for the love of a *thing* are

2. Irene de Castillejo, "Animus: Friend or Foe," (property of The
Kristine Mann Library, The Analytical Psychology Club of New
York), p. 5.
3. See *ibid.*, p. 13.

most exceptional, because this does not really agree with their nature. Love for a thing is a man's prerogative." [4]

All this implies that woman's primary modality is feeling —or, in Jung's typology, that woman is clearly the feeling type. This is confusing for the woman for whom feeling may be her inferior function, and for whom its opposite, thinking, may be her superior function. Furthermore, it is an inaccurate use of terms. Women have no more monopoly of the feeling function than men have of the thinking function, a polarization which Jung seems to imply in his association of logos with the masculine essence. For both sexes the functions of thinking and feeling are colored by the tonalities of their own particular sexuality. In other words, when a woman thinks or feels, she does so as a woman; with the full employment of all her functions, she may complete herself as a woman.

To associate the feminine exclusively with eros (relatedness and value reached through feeling) and to associate the masculine exclusively with logos (spirit and truth reached through objectivity) is to introduce a split in the sensibilities of woman. As a result of such a dichotomy a woman comes to connect her spiritual and ideational tendencies with masculinity and to see these tendencies as essentially foreign to her feminine being. The self-questioning of many intellectual women illustrates this. They doubt their own femininity; they are unsure whether their drive for a profession or a career threatens their femininity or exposes uncertainty about its value. This split or confusion is often what is behind a woman's worry that she cannot both marry and have a career. If she is too intelligent or forceful she fears that she will threaten men. She is puzzled about the relation of her mental powers and her spiritual drive to her maternal impulses and to her desire to surrender to her feelings toward a man and to a man himself. She gropes to ground

4. Jung, "Woman in Europe," *Civilization in Transition* (*CW*, X, 1964), p. 118.

herself in her own feminine being, to develop a sense of feminine spirituality and feminine "logos." To call this opening to her feminine depths "masculine" is more than confusing; it is destructive.

Jung is sensitive to the problem of the split of feeling from thinking but merely intensifies it with his definition of the feminine principle. He leaves us with a duality rather than a differentiation of two aspects of one whole.

> I use Eros and Logos merely as conceptual aids to describe the fact that woman's consciousness is characterized more by the connective quality of Eros than by the discrimination and cognition associated with Logos. In men, Eros, the function of relationship, is usually less developed than Logos. In women . . . Eros is an expression of their true nature, while their Logos is often only a regrettable accident.[5]

Jungians recognize, however, that the feminine principle informs both sexes. The woman's ego is guided by the eros principle, while her animus is related to the logos principle. The man's anima is related to eros, while his ego is ruled by logos.

Jung understands the exceptions to this description as evidence of the contrasexuality of human beings. Jung describes the unconscious dynamics of this estrangement from one's own nature:

> I have, . . . tried to equate the masculine consciousness with the concept of Logos and the feminine with that of Eros. By Logos I meant discrimination, judgement, insight, and by Eros I meant the capacity to relate. . . .
>
> As we can hardly ever make a psychological proposition without immediately having to reverse it, instances to the contrary leap to the eye at once: men who care nothing for discrimination, judgement, and insight, and women who display an almost excessively masculine proficiency in this respect. . . . They demonstrate, to my mind, the common occurrence of a psychically predominant contrasexuality.

5. Jung, *Aion* (*CW*, IX, Part 2, 1959), p. 14.

> Wherever this exists we find a forcible intrusion of the un-
> conscious, a corresponding exclusion of the consciousness
> specific to either sex, predominance of the shadow and of
> contrasexuality, and to a certain extent even the presence of
> symptoms of possession (such as compulsions, phobias, ob-
> sessions, automatisms, exaggerated effects, etc.).[6]

Another confusion may develop in the exploration of the
concept of "relatedness." Jung points out that he does not
want to define eros too exactly, for he sees that its definition
as relatedness is ambiguous.[7] On the one hand, relatedness
is the urge to connect, to get involved with concrete people
and feelings rather than with ideas and things, but, as E. C.
Whitmont points out, it is an urge "to get involved for the
sake of personal subjective emotional union, rather than for
the sake of any meaning or awareness of oneself or the
partner." On the other hand, this kind of relatedness must
not be confused with the usual meaning of the word relatedness, which Whitmont describes as "a consciously em-
pathic I-Thou *Begegnung* that is, a meeting, confrontation
or encounter . . . a 'recognition,' a relationship of mutual
creative involvement and understanding, of distance as well
as nearness." [8] It is difficult for women to hear that their
basic principle is relatedness, as if it were simply a "given,"
when they know from their own experience that they have
as much difficulty in building relationships as men do. Added
to their task of learning how to develop a relationship is the
worry that their need to learn how is proof of estrangement
from their essential femininity. This worry can grow into a
pervasive self-doubt, with every effort to improve relationship seen as proof of its lack. Furthermore, most women
know that their impulse to be in the midst of things emotionally is not necessarily equivalent to developing a relationship with another person.

6. Jung, *Mysterium Coniunctionis* (*CW*, XIV, 1963), pp. 179–80.
7. Jung, *Aion*, p. 14.
8. Edward C. Whitmont, *The Symbolic Quest* (New York: C. G.
Jung Foundation, 1969), pp. 174–75.

The association of eros with relatedness and love also generates a confusion about the nature of love in relation to truth. Here Jung's dualities—of logos as spirit and meaning and of eros as love and relatedness—are unfortunate. Harding tries to solve the problem by saying that eros is relatedness both in the sense of being connected with subjective emotion or love and in the sense of being connected to the spiritual meaning of nonpersonal value:

> The Eros is a spiritual or psychological principle, or, in the older term, it is a divinity. To be related to this principle means to be oriented to that which transcends personal aims and ambitions, it means gaining a relation to a non-personal value, just as to become related to Logos means acquiring a relation to non-personal truth. Either means, in fact, to be redeemed from a personal or ego orientation and from the desire for personal power and to give one's allegiance to that which is beyond the personal. It is this that is the religious attitude.[9]

Two dualities are implied: on the one hand, the relation to value through eros and the relation to truth through logos, and on the other, the transcending of personal drives and ideas in order to become related to the nonpersonal dimension. These dualities, it seems to me, are questionable. The way in which they are posed implies that we reach love through one modality, eros, and truth through another, logos, and that, in order to reach the transpersonal, the personal is not elevated but abrogated altogether. In fact, love and truth are not so easily separated; they are constantly to be found within each other. What is love is also truth for those who love, and what is truth is also love, and the transpersonal is invariably reached, connected to, and made incarnate by precisely the personal demands and desires of love. The personal dimension is not broken as a result but rather purified and fulfilled.

9. Harding, *Woman's Mysteries* (London: Longmans, Green & Co., 1935), p. 223.

Esther Harding makes the salient point that ego demands cannot be substituted for the demands of the self.

> Relatedness, the law of Eros, demands that one's own desires shall not be taken as absolute but shall be adapted to the needs and desires of the other person and to the requirements of the situation. This means that one cannot remain in a fixed or taken attitude but must be flexible.[10]

For some, there may be something misleading about putting it this way, however, for it seems to imply that serving higher nonpersonal powers excludes rather than completes the person. This is a theme in ascetical Christian tradition, too —that self-will must be broken if the will of God is to be served, just as in Catholic tradition a monk may take a vow of obedience to the abbot of his monastery or in Protestant tradition the devout are asked to annihilate the self in them and to replace it with Christ. In contradistinction to this set of doctrines, whether psychological or theological, I would say that the celebration of the love-which-is-truth is a means of growth into an abundant selfhood, where personal aims and ambitions are redeemed through their completion in loving persons, in one's work, or in any part of one's life. God is found and loved in the human person, and the fulfillment of the human person is found and loved in God. True love is a *circulatio* of personal to Personal, where each personal attachment is uplifted and lifted up in an unending circulation of the small to the large and of the large to the small. The largeness of God is found in the smallness of each personal detail, which makes each smallness into a largeness.

10. *Ibid.*, p. 143.

Index

Abortion, 199–200
Adler, Alfred, 21, 207, 262, 317
Aggression, 72, 199, 261, 302, 312;
  masculine, 233–34, 237
Alchemy, 63, 74–75
Analogy: of being, 105 n, 106;
  method of, 21–22, 131
Analysis: and Christian tradition,
  9–12; and reinterpretation of
  faith, 11, 73; and religion, 111–
  27 passim
Anima, 110, 155; as archetype,
  37–39, 274; as complex, 38; as
  contrasexual element, 13, 38;
  development of, 212–40 passim;
  differentiation of, 215, 217, 221,
  233, 240; function, 35–36, 232,
  269, 317; images, 37; as pattern
  of behavior, 37–38; as pattern
  of emotion, 38; problems, 39;
  projection, 39, 221–22; woman,
  252–53, 256
Animus, 110, 155, 306; of Amazon
  type, 207; as archetype, 31, 41–
  42, 274; as complex, 32, 50; as
  contrasexual element, 13, 41;
  development of, 217, 241–85
  passim; function, 35–36, 41, 45,
  245, 254, 256, 275, 280–84; 317;
  of Hetaira type, 204–5; images,
  41; of Medial type, 210; of
  Mother type, 202; as pattern of
  behavior, 41; as pattern of
  emotion, 41; as positive, 274–77;
  problems, 43, 50–51, 245, 250;
  tyranny, 246, 254, 260, 262–68,
  317
Aquinas, St. Thomas, 148
Archetype, 29, 31, 46–50; and

complex, 28–29, 49; of Great
  Father, 61–62, 69, 203, 246, 249;
  of Great Mother, 30, 61, 68, 72,
  169, 190, 198, 231, 242, 244–45,
  247, 265; and objective psyche,
  35, 46, 48, 51, 67, 142; occurrence of, 52–53, 55–56, 58; and
  religious images, 119, 123; of
  self, 32, 62, 122; of transforming journey, 55; of Wise
  Woman, 208. See also Self;
  Symbols, and archetypes; Virgin, archetype
Arnold, F. X., 294, 317
Attention, 173–74, 330–33
Autistic thinking, 131, 170

Bailey, Derrick, 305
Barth, Karl, 293–94, 303
Berdyaev, Nicholas, 294
Binswanger, Hilde, 156
Blake, William, 128
Buytendijk, F. J. J., 148, 331

Cassirer, Ernst, 92–94, 127, 143
Castillejo, Irene de, 275–76, 279,
  336
Christ, 7, 107–8, 113–14, 129, 182,
  294; cross of, 220, 305; and
  feminine, 303–5, 314–23; figure
  and psychology, 66, 108, 120–
  22; and self-denial, 11, 340–41;
  as source of meaning, 7. See
  also Self, and the Christ figure
Christian: faith, 5, 7–8, 73, 129,
  289; tradition, 9, 135, 290
Christianity, 107–8, 110–11, 113,
  116–17, 213; and aggression, 11,
  72–73, 312–13; and feminine, 14,

343

172; and sexuality, 11, 72–73, 102
Complex, 28–29, 30–32, 224; mother, 28–29
Consciousness: and ego, 27; as masculine, 18, 242–43, 258. *See also* Feminine, consciousness; Matriarchal, consciousness
Contemplation, 332–34
Contrasexuality, 268–69, 338; elements of, 38, 41, 212, 290, 293–94; and *imago dei*, 290–97; importance of, 155, 162–63; and wholeness, 141, 157, 213, 334
Culture, 146, 258–59, 262, 269; and feminine, 165–67, 207, 210, 244, 255, 270, 315, 329–30. *See also* Patriarchal, culture

Descartes, 91
Deutsch, Helene, 150
Devil, 33, 135
Directed thinking, 132
Divorce, 259, 267–68
Dogma, 90–91, 104, 123, 318
Dreams, 10, 22, 24, 36, 49, 76, 87–88, 142; daydreams (fantasy), 23, 58, 246, 264–65, 278, 283; examples of, 11, 34, 39–40, 52–53, 55–56, 63, 74, 100, 134–35, 144, 161, 180, 220, 226, 230, 236, 248–49, 254, 256, 271; interpretation of, 53–54, 63–64, 99–102, 181, 220, 257, 271–72
Dry, Avis, 118

Ecstasy, 159, 300
Edinger, Edward F., 66, 70
Ego, 12, 32, 66–67; as center of consciousness, 27; as complex, 30–31; differentiation of, 60, 69; female, 241, 243–44, 255, 264, 281–84, 326, 330–31; head ego, 170, 269; heart ego, 169, 270; identity, 29, 73, 222, 292, 301; inflation, 39, 44; masculine, 217–18, 225, 238–39, 243–44; and objective psyche, 71–72; passiv-

ity, 68; and self, 62, 72. *See also* Feminine, and ego
Ellis, Havelock, 317
Empirical approach, 17, 20, 25, 46, 89, 121, 125–27
Erikson, Erik, 151–52
Eros: figure of, 212–40 *passim*, 335–36; principle of, 154–56, 167, 333–41. *See also* Masculine, eros

Fairbairn, Ronald, 6
Faith, 115–16, 308. *See also* Christian, faith
Fall, the, 293, 296–302, 307, 309
Fordham, Michael, 66
Feminine: biological approach to, 140–41, 148–52; as category of being, 3, 86, 133, 154, 290; consciousness, 14, 168–82 *passim*, 291, 304–5, 328, 331–32; cultural approach to, 140–41, 145, 152–54, 166; and ego, 169–72, 175–77, 177–79, 183–84, 304, 325–26, 328; and God, 134–35, 157, 174, 271, 290, 292, 295, 303, 315–16, 319, 332–33; in men, 31, 212; and music, 172, 177; as neglected, 13, 86, 109, 118, 135–36, 315–18; psychology of, 139–40, 142, 305, 315, 317, 321; recovery of, 70, 109, 134, 303, 309–10, 312, 326; and religious function, 290, 292, 295; and religious life, 136, 304–5, 318; and religious symbols, 315–18, 320–21; and spirit, 183–90, 304–5, 324–25, 327–28, 331, 334; symbolic approach to, 140–42, 146, 154–57, 167; and theology, 15, 292, 335; wisdom, 190–91, 304. *See also* Christ, and feminine; Culture, and feminine; Matriarchal, consciousness; Principle, feminine; Type(s)
Freud, 6, 13, 19, 22, 54 n, 86, 98, 167; and feminine, 140, 149–51; and masochism, 181; and penis envy, 140, 149, 207, 262, 317

God, 5, 10, 58, 94–95, 104, 109; death-of-God, 10, 128, 318; images of, 12, 87–88, 126, 290–91; and sexuality, 214, 259, 270, 291–92, 294, 296. *See also* Feminine, and God; Love, and God; Projection, onto God

Harding, Esther, 182, 223, 252–53, 335, 341
History: and consciousness, 169; inner, 57
Holy Spirit. *See* Spirit, Holy
Hopkins, Gerard Manley, 307
Horney, Karen, 140, 152–54, 317
Hume, David, 90

Identification, 29 n, 201; with anima, 222–23; with animus, 253, 264; and female, 244–45, 315
Identity: female, 199, 203, 206, 209; masculine, 230; sexual, 163; state of, 29, 72; state of, with anima, 39; state of, with animus, 43. *See also* Ego, identity
Imagination: active, 24, 59–60, 326; and drawing pictures, 24, 59, 73; recovery of, 131–33
Imago dei, 292–96, 309
Incarnation, the, 292, 305–10
Individuation, 23, 71, 74–75, 89, 165, 266, 273–74, 319
Interpretation: analytic-reductive, 22–23, 30; synthetic-constructive, 22–23, 30, 50–51, 99, 100. *See also* Objective, level of interpretation; Subjective, level of interpretation

John of the Cross, St., 307
Jung, Emma, 275, 282

Kant, Immanuel, 91–92, 94
Kluger, H. Y., 320–21

Lévy-Bruhl, H., 67
Libido, 26–27, 114, 119–20, 164
Lilar, Suzanne, 298, 300, 302, 311

Logos, 155, 166, 334–41. *See also* Principle, masculine
Love, 333–34; and the Cross, 321–22; and depth psychology, 4, 289, 335; and female, 261, 299–300, 302; and God, 289–90, 302, 306, 334, 341; reasonable, 298–310; and theology, 4, 289; unreasonable, 298, 310
Luther, 105

Mandala, 65
Marriage, 165, 201, 204, 206, 257, 264, 267–68, 298
Mary, 178, 184, 188–90, 295, 305–6, 318–21, 332
Masculine, 41–42, 134, 146, 156, 246, 266–69; ego, 217, 238; eros, 218, 221–22, 225, 237–39; style of consciousness, 328; in woman, 41, 275. *See also* Ego, head ego; Principle, masculine
Masculinity, 212, 255–56
Masculine-feminine polarity: as central 136, 146, 166; and the Fall, 297–302; and the Incarnation, 309; and patriarchal culture, 258, 268; between and in persons, 232, 272, 274; symbolism of, 13, 27, 63, 86, 120, 144, 147, 291–92, 295; and wholeness, 133, 164, 240
Masochism, 150–53, 181–82, 199, 301, 330
Matriarchal: consciousness, 168–69, 179, 181–82; stage, 68, 72–73, 242, 266, 278
Mead, Margaret, 140, 317
Menstruation, 175–76, 183
Moon, 175, 180–81, 183, 185, 277; goddess, 178
Moreno, Mario, 156, 195, 205
Mother. *See* Archetype, of Great Mother; Complex, mother; Type(s), mother
Mystery, 36, 89, 105, 120, 128, 135, 214, 305–6, 325, 333
Myth, 49, 57–58, 124–25, 128

Mythical dimension, 92, 94
Mythologem, 56–58, 125

Neumann, Erich: and animus, 241–42, 246, 266; and Eros and Psyche, 215, 228, 231, 233; and feminine, 168–70, 178–79, 190–92; and stages of psychological development, 66–68
Neurosis, 11, 47, 87, 112, 258, 267
Niebuhr, H. R., 128
Numinous, 119, 186; content, 306; dimension, 69; experience of, 88, 90; and feminine, 187–89; image of, 89; and masculine, 246–47, 251

Objective, 76, 92, 122; level of interpretation, 99. See also Psyche, as objective
Oedipus complex, 54, 219, 243, 249
Other, 18, 185, 191, 198, 203, 243, 322; and anima, 36; and feminine, 18, 185, 191, 325–27, 330–33
Otherness, 19, 37, 238; and contrasexuality, 212–13; and feminine, 19, 318, 325–27; and prejudice, 175; and sexuality, 147, 175, 229
Otto, Rudolf, 89

Passivity: ego, 68, 73, 277; feminine, 150–51, 168, 251, 253, 261, 263, 330, 332; of men, 219; sexual, 261. See also Identification
Patriarchal: consciousness, 168, 174, 187, 330; culture, 258–59, 262; marriage, 258–59, 300; stage, 69, 72, 246, 249–50; values, 263–64, 266, 270
Persona, 32–33, 200
Piper, Otto, 295
Polarity(ies): psychic, 13, 15, 27, 46, 60, 69, 143, 146, 232, 290, 326; psychic, and religious function, 85–86. See also Sexual, polarity

Principle, feminine, 38, 154–55, 157, 165, 315–16, 328, 336; as elementary, 157–58; as transformative, 157, 159–60, 279
Principle, masculine, 146, 155
Projection, 127; of anima, 39, 222, 258, 272; of animus, 44–45, 258, 265, 274; and complex, 30, 34; onto God, 93, 104
Psyche: development of, 66, 68–70; as objective, 12, 18–19, 35, 46, 58, 71, 82, 122, 142–44, 213; spiritual activity of, 52, 122; story of, 215–40
Psychological functions, 78–81, 194. See also Types, psychological
Psychology: analytical, 82, 111–14; depth, 4, 167, 173, 335; and theology, 4, 7–9, 123–26
Psychosis, 34, 47, 56, 250

Reason, 115, 116 n, 117
Relatedness, 155, 328, 336
Relationship, 156, 268–69, 274–76, 293; to animus, 45, 274–77
Religious: experience, 15, 72, 85, 87–89, 104, 121, 270; function, 12, 14–15, 85–88, 90, 94, 113, 290–91, 292, 295
Remythologizing, 128–31, 133, 311, 333

Sacred, 310–12
Sanctification, 324–25, 327
Schleiermacher, Friedrich, 294
Self: archetype of, 20, 32, 62–63, 268; and the Christ figure, 65, 121–22; construction of, 143; and ego, 32; and feminine, 269; and religion, 214
Sexuality: feminine, 185–86, 188, 247–49, 299, 304; and religious life, 214, 304; spiritual function of, 14, 144, 147
Sexual: difference, 144–47, 175, 243, 317; instinct of, 72, 199, 204, 206–7; polarity and Christ, 303, 305; polarity and the Fall,

296–302; polarity and the Incarnation, 305–10; polarity in
and between persons, 214, 229,
238–41; polarity and its recovery, 134; polarity and religious
life, 326; polarity and the sacred, 310–12; polarity and its
significance, 13, 270, 284, 292,
296, 323; polarity and its symbolism, 36–38, 69, 86, 291; polarity and wholeness, 45; polarization, 232, 258, 260, 309, 323,
326–27; polarization and the
Fall, 297–302
Shadow, 33–34, 129, 204
Solovyev, Vladimir, 295, 308–9,
322, 327
Sophia, 189–91, 208, 332
Soul, 121, 122, 133, 213, 333
Spirit, 261, 298, 300; Holy, 68,
121, 184–85, 304, 306, 308, 324–
28
Spiritual: impoverishment, 105,
107, 114; life, 103; transformation, 182–84
Subjective, 76, 92, 122; level of
interpretation, 99–100
Symbol(s), 5–6, 15, 94, 96–99,
117, 120–23; and archetypes, 46,
98, 105–6; Christian, 6–9, 107–8;
and depth psychology, 5–6, 8;
as language of the psyche, 21,
142–43; loss of meaning of, 91;
reconciling, 12, 85–86, 100, 290–
91; religious, 14, 90, 119–21,
314; and sign, 114; and theology, 5–6, 8, 96–110 *passim*
Symbolic: approach, 17, 20–25,
58–59, 118; forms, 92–94; meaning of, 12–13, 112–13. *See also*

Feminine, symbolic approach
to
Synchronicity, 75
Theology, 4–8, 13, 95, 111, 289;
and depth psychology, 4, 7–9,
123–26. *See also* Feminine, and
theology; Symbol, and theology
Tillich, Paul, 5–6, 8, 116 n, 128,
324; and Christ, 108, 303; and
feminine 109, 319; and symbols,
96–97, 103, 105
Trinity, 101, 109, 117, 135, 308,
319
Type(s): Amazon, 194–95, 205–7,
209–10, 320, 331; Hetaira, 194–
95, 203–5, 209–10, 249, 320, 331;
Medial, 194–95, 208–11, 320,
331; Mother, 194–95, 198–99,
201–2, 209–10, 244, 319–20, 331;
psychological, 76–81

Ulanov, Barry, 307
Uroboros, 67; maternal, 242, 276;
paternal, 246, 249, 278

Virgin: archetype, 205–6, 319–20;
birth, 117, 305–6; Mary, 98–99,
103, 318–21. *See also* Mary

Weininger, Otto, 148, 317
White, Victor, 126
Whitmont, E. C., 38, 339
Wholeness, 57, 65, 82, 255; and
contrasexuality, 141, 157, 163–
64; and psychic polarities, 13,
15; and religious function, 85–
87, 290–91; stages of, 143, 240
Wolff, Toni, 194–95, 244, 249, 315
Women's liberation, 140, 145, 166,
174